King of the Jews

King of the
Jews

Nick Tosches

ecco

An Imprint of HarperCollinsPublishers

HarperCollins books may be purchased for educational, business, or sales promotional use. For information, please write: Special Markets Department, HarperCollins Publishers Inc., 10 East 53rd Street, New York, NY 10022.

FIRST EDITION

Designed by rlf design

Library of Congress Cataloging-in-Publication Data

Tosches, Nick
    King of the Jews/Nick Tosches.—1st ed.
        p.   cm.
    ISBN 0-06-621118-2 (hardcover)
        1. Murder—New York (State)—New York—Case studies.   2. Gambling—New York (State)—New York—Case studies.   3. Gambling and crime—New York (State)—New York—Case studies.   4. Rothstein, Arnold, 1882–1928.   I. Title.

HV6534.N5T67   2005
364.152'3'097471—dc22   2004057534

05 06 07 08 09 WBC/RRD 10 9 8 7 6 5 4 3 2 1

To my favorite opiated blonde

What the hell do I care?

—LEGS DIAMOND, 1931

Contents

Old Nick's Bible Studies

ONCE UPON A TIME, when New York City lived and breathed, there was a man marked for death, like us all.

His name was Arnold Rothstein, and he himself was the only God he worshipped, and he was a great and sinful man.

I am not here to make elegy for that city that lived and breathed and am not here to make praise-song of this man. What's dead is dead. I am here—like him, like us all—to make a buck. So let the tale begin, for I feel again an itch to buy my wearied, fleeting freedom from this lost and fallen place.

As Louie the Lump is believed to have said on his Bellevue deathbed: We speak here of gambling and gods.

D AMNED AS THEY have been by every lie or wisdom that has borne
the name of religion, the dice are older than them all. From the Indus Valley, long before there was a Rig-Veda to scripture against them—
"Play not with dice"—or, indeed, before there was any written language
to make scripture at all, the bones tumbled onward while civilizations
were born, destroyed, and forgotten. Writing in a pagan Rome that outlawed them, Terence laid the blunt and enduring metaphor to the unbeat-
able racket of being: "Life is a throw of the dice."

More than a century later, in 49 B.C., after his conquest of Gaul, Julius
Caesar decided to return to Italy in open defiance of Pompey. It was a de-
cision that would lead to civil war, Caesar's rise to dictatorship, and, on
March 15, 44 B.C., his assassination. In Ravenna, before crossing the Rubicon, the red-stone stream that marked the boundary between Cisalpine
Gaul and Italy, he is said to have declared his willful embrace of fate with
the words *iacta alea est:* "The die is cast."

And here we pause, first to piss, then to ponder. The pissing done, the
pondering begins.

At the outset of any great work of history, of which this is one (or so it
is now intended to be, an intention subject to change at any moment), it is
good not only to piss, but also to raise and bear the wisdom that has been
given us: "A lie repeated often enough becomes the truth." This is the profound underground fissure upon which all history precariously rests.
These words—"A lie repeated often enough becomes the truth"—have
been commonly attributed to Hermann Goering or, less commonly, to
Joseph Stalin. These attributions attest the words, for there is no evidence
that either of these gentlemen ever said any such thing.

Iacta alea est. The die is cast. The enduring belief that Caesar uttered
these words before crossing the Rubicon has its source in *The Lives of the
Twelve Caesars,* written by the Roman historian Suetonius in the early sec-

ond century, more than a hundred and fifty years after Caesar's death. These now legendary words, we long have been told, were Caesar's own Latining of a phrase from his favorite Greek playwright, Menander, who likely wrote in the fourth century B.C. (Menander's many plays are lost to us or have survived only in fragments. Terence's line about life being a throw of the dice is very probably from Menander, as Terence's *Adelphoe* was based on Menander's *Adelphoi*.) But the Greek historians Plutarch, writing late in the first century, and Appian, writing early in the second century, both have Caesar speaking the phrase in its original Greek: *Aner-riphthô kubos*. Caesar was a learned man of impeccable literacy. If he were to have rendered this Greek phrase—which translates as "Let the die be cast," not "The die is cast"—into his own native Latin, his words would have been *Iacta alea esto* rather than *Iacta alea est*. This alteration may have been a flourish of forceful effect on the part of Caesar or of Suetonius, or it may merely have been a scribal mistake in the manuscript of Suetonius that became our text. Plutarch alone tells us that the words, whether derived from Menander or not, were an old and familiar saying, little more than a "common phrase." Caesar himself, in *The Civil Wars,* wrote in detail of this decisive moment. He made no mention of speaking any such words.

T. S. Eliot, writing in 1919, observed that "Shakespeare acquired more essential history from Plutarch than most men could from the whole British Museum."

History: the harvesting of those lies that repeated often enough become the truth.

Shakespeare's *Julius Caesar,* written near the end of the sixteenth century, drew heavily from the first English translation of Plutarch, by Sir Thomas North. In North's translation of 1579, as in the original Greek of Plutarch, Caesar dies without words:

> For it was agreed among them that every man should give him a wound, because all their parts should be in this murther: and then Brutus himself gave him one wound about his privities. Men report also, that Caesar did still defend himself against the rest, running every way with his body: but when he saw Brutus with his sword drawn in his

hand, then he pulled his gown over his head, and made no more resis-
tance, and was driven either casually or purposedly, by the counsel of
the conspirators, against the base whereupon Pompey's image stood,
which ran all of a gore-blood till he was slain. Thus it seemed that the
image took just revenge of Pompey's enemy, being thrown down on the
ground at his feet, and yielding up the ghost there, for the number of
wounds he had upon him. For it is reported, that he had three and
twenty wounds upon his body: and divers of the conspirators did hurt
themselves, striking one body with so many blows.

For Shakespeare, such silence, no matter how powerful, would not do. He knew Latin and Greek, and it was in Suetonius, who had not yet been Englished, that he found a death scene with dying words. In Suetonius, upon seeing that Brutus, Caesar's own adopted son, was among his attackers, Caesar said: *"Kai su, teknon"*—a Greek vocative—"And thou, my son." Thence the never said but immortal last words of Caesar as first conjured in Latin by Shakespeare: *"Et tu, Brute."*

As Shakespeare's play opens but a month before Caesar's death, there is no crossing of the Rubicon. But Shakespeare already had used that bit in *Richard III:* "I have set my life upon a cast, / And I will stand the hazard of the Dye."

What Plutarch describes as having been little more than a "common phrase" in the first century B.C.—"The die is cast"—may likely already have been little more than a common phrase two millennia before, as the Indus Valley dice rolled into Mesopotamia and beyond. And today, after the long passage of another two millennia and more, the phrase is still common in the streets and high places of the Western world, from the Italian *Il dado è tratto* to the French equivalent *Les jeux sont faits,* used as a casino gaming call and as a literary metaphor by Sartre and Gide, to the German *Die Würfel sind gefallen,* to the endlessly familiar English.

Neither the Greek *kuboi* nor the Latin *aleae* was the only word for dice in those tongues. There were the Greek *astragaloi* and the Latin *tali.* The primary use of both *astragalos* and *talus,* still a part of our anatomical vocabulary (the former as *astragalus*), was to denote the anklebone. But another usage specifically denoted dice manufactured from the knucklebones of slaughtered sheep. Herodotus, writing in the fifth century B.C., used both Greek terms when discussing dice. Plautus, writing in the second century B.C., used both Latin terms. The bones. Chaucer damned them in the fourteenth century: "This fruyt of the bicched bones two, / fforswerying, Ire, falsnesse, Homycide." (As for the descriptive "bicched," *The Oxford English Dictionary* tells us that it "appears rather early to be certainly referable to BITCH in an opprobrious sense, from which moreover the formation is not easily explained." The odd word appears again only in the Towneley Mystery Plays of the following century, in which "byched bones" occurs twice.) Jonathan Swift in 1724 spoke of making the "bones rattle"—two verbs and less than two centuries away from "Shake, Rattle and Roll," the song about shaking, rattling, and rolling them bitchèd bones that Al Bernard recorded in 1919, a quarter of a century before that same phrase and title heralded the age of rock 'n' roll.

—❦—

N OVEMBER 25, 1928. From Lieutenant Francis A. Steinkamp, commanding officer, Ninth Precinct, to chief medical examiner. Subject: Case Number 6293, Arnold Rothstein.

At 10:45 P.M., November 4, 1928, Arnold Rothstein, 912
Fifth Avenue, 46 years, was shot, Room 349, Park Central
Hotel, 200 West 56th Street.

Apparently had been engaged in card game with others
in Room 349 on third floor of the Park Central Hotel, when
an unknown man shot him and threw revolver out of the
window to street. Body found lying near stairs in employees entrance to hotel, by Lawrence Fallon of 3164 34th
Street, Astoria, employed as house detective for hotel.

Was attended by Dr. McGovern of City Hospital and removed to Polyclinic Hospital suffering from gunshot wound
to abdomen.

Officer: William S. Davis, 2943, Ninth Precinct.

IN MY DEATH I am she of whom I permit you not to hear: she who knew that all breath is given us by the gods and to them must be returned. In my death, I breathe sweet air and sky of thunder.

For with powdered myrrh and wine I did make upon her the sign of my soul, and then did open her from breast to belly, and did abide within her, and with her blood I made the sign of my soul upon myself.

Be still and you will hear them: the names of the six powers of death, who bring forth every soul from every flesh.

I am resurrected, and in my resurrection know: He twice born is he twice killed.

Blessed is he who beholds this. Blessed is he whose soul is pure. Blessed is he who loves goodness. Blessed is he who despises wrong. Blessed is he who enters his way beneath the earth.

T HE BIBLE TELLS US many things. It tells us that in Egypt of old, a man called Amram, a second-generation Levite, married his aunt. Her name was Jochebed. It is written in the book of Exodus: "Amram took him Jochebed his father's sister to wife and she bore him Aaron and Moses."

Thus the King James Bible, one of the great prose works of the English language, published in London at a time (1611) when Jews were still prohibited from living in England. They had been expelled by King Edward I in 1290 and would be allowed to return under Oliver Cromwell in 1656.

This passage, which names Amram and Jochebed for the first time, comes four chapters after the tale of the birth of Moses, in which Moses, being born during a period of pharaonic edict decreeing that the midwives of the land were to kill every newborn Hebrew male, was spared by stealth, set adrift on the river in a little makeshift barque of bulrushes by his unnamed mother, and found and later adopted by Pharaoh's daughter.

The Bible is the work of wise-men and madmen, seers and poets, givers and thieves of power and beauty, vendors and victims of shame and of guilt, fabulists and mythographers, makers of lists more tiresome than Homer's *Catalogue of Ships,* seekers of miracle and splendor, seekers of bread and gruel, scholars of a past that never was, and prophets after the fact.

Much was made in the latter part of the twentieth century of a "postmodern literature," a "new writing" that turned away from realism and linear forms of narrative. But, as the Bible tells us, "The thing that hath been, it is that which shall be; and that which is done is that which shall be done: and there is no new thing under the sun." From its earliest words, written by an unknown hand, in the hill country of the kingdom of Judah or in the kingdom of Israel to the north, at an unknown time in the early tenth century B.C., the Bible threw all linear narrative and reality to the howling desert winds.

We are told in the first verse of Genesis that on the first day of Creation God said, "Let there be light"; and there was light. "And God saw that the light was good; and God separated the light from the darkness. God called the light Day, and the darkness he called Night." Later in the same verse, we are told of the fourth day of Creation, when God said, "Let there be lights in the dome of the sky to separate the day from the night"; and it was so. "God made the two great lights—the greater light to rule the day and the lesser light to rule the night—and the stars. God set them in the dome of the sky to give light upon the earth, to rule over the day and over the night, and to separate the light from the darkness."

And those who know Hebrew can read what has been kept from the world by every translation of the Bible since the earliest Greek versions of the Old Testament, the Septuagint, of the third century B.C.

It is not God who creates the world, but rather the gods. The Hebrew plural *elohim* appears many times in the archaic texts of Genesis before the gods, without notice, suddenly become God.

"God's name changes from **אלהים** [*elohim*] in Gen. 1:1–2:3 to **אלהים יהוה** [*yahweh elohim*] (predominantly) in 2:4–3:24, and then varies between **יהוה** [*yahweh*] and **אלהים** [*elohim*] in the rest of the text. Many interpreters, including Philo [ca. 20 B.C.–A.D. 50], the classical rabbis [ca. A.D. 70–1200], and modern critical scholars [ca. 1895–present], have tried to make sense of these changes in divine name, with differing degrees of success." Thus one modern scholar, Ronald S. Hendel, writing near the end of the twentieth century, in *The Text of Genesis 1–11*.

At the time that Genesis was composed, the cults of both kingdoms of the divided Hebrew monarchy, Israel and Judah, were of many gods, of whom the storm-god Yahweh came to be revered above the rest: El, the primeval lord of creation, whence all *elohim;* Asherah, consort of El and mother of the gods; Baal, the eldest of the storm-gods, son of El; Anath, blood-ravening goddess of war and love, daughter of El, sister and consort of Baal; Molech, to whom young sons and daughters were sent through the fire of child sacrifice; and the lesser gods beneath them.

The truth is simple. The origins of Genesis predated monotheism. Later, when monotheism took root, the literal meaning of *elohim,* the gods, had to be explained away. So it was, after some centuries, that the rabbi-sages explicated that *elohim* was a name for the one true God in all His manifold greatness. This, they said, was confirmed by the form of the verb that *elohim* governed—*bara,* "created"—which was inflected in the singular. As the verb must agree with the subject in number, *elohim* referred therefore, de facto and *de fide,* not to gods, but to the Almighty alone.

But *bara* is also the primitive root, the radix, the charged nucleus of all its descendant forms. The word is found in the Old Testament always with God, or the gods, as its subject; and the word is always the same. The creation of Adam and Eve: "And God said, Let us make man in our image, after our likeness. [. . .] So God created man in his own image, in the image of God created he him." Here again the word translated as God is in the plural, *elohim,* in the original. The first-person plural phrases "let us make" and "in our image" are, however, also in plural in the original. *Bara* remains the same. As there were no verbal tenses in the old Semitic scripts, this word held past, present, and future within it. (The Bible was first construed with tenses in the Greek of the Septuagint. Masoretic rabbis of the next millennium changed the old Hebrew texts by, among other interpretative alterations, adding to verbs certain characters that they assigned to indicate certain tenses.)

In Isaiah, the Lord is "about to create," is "creating," and "will create." In the phrase of the Qumran text of Isaiah known as the Isaiah Scroll, Yahweh describes himself as "making good and creating evil." Everywhere, *bara.* Most notably, it transcends verbs. Nouns such as "creation" and "Creator" are *bara.* The primitive root, the radix, the charged nucleus: *bara.*

Judeo-Christian apologists have reached far to explain God's elocutions in the first-person plural, as in: "Let us make man in our image." The "royal pronoun" has been proposed—the "we" of kings and queens—as has been the "plural of deliberation," as in the "let's see now" of the solitary, muttering cogitator. It happens that the royal "we" did not develop until the third century A.D., when Diocletian used it; and in fact, when Diocletian did use it, he did so to include in his pronouncements the fellow emperors who formed with him the imperial tetrarchy that he had instituted. Only later was it used by sole sovereigns. As for the "plural of deliberation," it is a grammatical sophistication along the order of the Latin "deliberative subjunctive." It is unknown in the primitive syntax of biblical Hebrew, and it is not encountered in the Old Testament.

I use the term "biblical Hebrew" for convenience. It should be understood that this term does not denote a standard language. Throughout the centuries of the composition of the Old Testament, the Hebrew language was a mongrel language, ever inchoate, ever in flux.

From the eighth-century Vespasian Psalter to Shakespeare, a period of not quite nine hundred years—less a span than that of the composition of the Old Testament—we find the word "gods" written first in Old English, as *godas, godo,* and *godu,* then in Middle English as *godes, godds,* and *goddes,* and coming to *gods* in Early Modern English. The name of the language itself, in less of a span, went through *Engliscum, Engliscra, englische, englissce, Engleis, Inglis, Englysshe,* and *Inglish* before emerging as *English,* which appears in the dedication of the King James Bible of 1611.

In the same time, from Old English to Early Modern English, changes in the grammar, syntax, word meanings, and the forms of characters and scripts of the language changed so multifariously that a reader living in the latter period would find it a daunting task to comprehend what had been written in the former. Old words vanished, new words came mysteriously and abundantly from sources that were far-flung, invested with definitions based on misunderstanding and understanding alike.

So much vaster were the changes undergone by the Hebrew language in the course of the more than nine hundred years in which the books of the Bible were written and rewritten. Linguists speak of Judeo-Arabic, Judeo-Aramaic, Judeo-Greek, Judeo-Persian, Judeo-Syriac, each with its own subset of little-known palimpsest dialects. From the paleo-Hebrew script of Judah to the profound Persian and Aramaic influences of the sixth and fifth centuries B.C. and the Hellenistic influences that came in the wake of the conquests of Alexander the Great in the fourth century B.C., the language of the Bible, whose first words were written in a script derived from Bronze Age Canaanite and whose last words were written in a script derived from Aramaic, is a polyglot sea far beyond containment by the term "biblical Hebrew" or any other term. The Hebrew language was never "Hebrew" to the authors of the Bible. The word *ibri*—Hebrew—

referred to a race. The language of that race was *yehudit*—Judahite—whence the word "Jew." It is a word origin that can be heard most clearly in the German *Jude*.

Assyria, in the north land of Babylonia, gained its independence at the end of the fourteenth century B.C. By the dawn of the next millennium, Assyria dominated Babylonia. This domination lasted for about four hundred years. Then, in 612 B.C., Babylon took the Assyrian capital of Nineveh and regained dominion of Mesopotamia. The Assyrian kingdom continued to exist as a subservient power under Babylonian sovereignty. Outside of Babylonia, however, the new Assyrian king, Nebuchadnezzar, sought to expand an empire that no longer existed.

During his forty-three-year reign, which began in 605 B.C., King Nebuchadnezzar pursued his will throughout the Near East. His armies besieged Egypt, Arabia, and the city-state of Damascus in Aram, which the Greeks would call Syria.

The kingdoms of Israel and Judah had been held in vassalage by Assyria since the eighth century. Hoshea, the last king of Israel, had entered into alliance with Egypt to plot a rebellion against Assyrian rule. Ahaz, the king of Judah, did not join the anti-Assyrian coalition. In a desperate attempt to save himself and Jerusalem, he had turned to forbidden gods and old rituals. Restoring child sacrifice, he made his own son "pass through the fire." The Assyrians laid waste to Samaria in the north and later the temple and palace of Jerusalem in the south.

In the reign of Nebuchadnezzar, the upper classes of Judah were expatriated to Babylonia. This marked the beginning of what came to be known as the Babylonian exile or Babylonian captivity, a period traditionally ascribed to the years 586 through 538 B.C.

Nebuchadnezzar died midway through this period, in 562 B.C. And it was in this period that the Aramaic language supplanted the Akkadian language, of which Assyrian was a dialect, as the common language of Babylonia. Akkadian survived for a time as a language of literature and learning, but Aramaic would be a principal language of international communication throughout the Near East for more than a thousand years to come.

The Jews flourished in Babylonia, the legendary birthplace of the great patriarch Abraham. Many of them found prosperity in this pagan land whose culture had been revered since long before Abraham was conceived.

Cyrus II conquered Babylonia in the autumn of 539 B.C. With this conquest all of the Near East, save Egypt, was now under the rule of the Persian Empire, the most powerful and grandest empire that the world had ever known. The Jews were given liberty to leave Babylonia at will. A good number of them seem to have stayed.

In the early fourth century B.C., Alexander the Great took all of Persia's empire and more than Persia had ever dreamt. From the Nile to the Indus, from Athens to the Arabian Sea: The empire of Alexander made the empire of Persia seem a paltry thing. Babylonia, like rest of Alexander's vast conquerings, became a part of the Hellenistic world. It was in Babylonia, in the spring of 323 B.C., that Alexander died, just shy of thirty-three.

Another Persian kingdom, Parthia, under Mithridates I, seized Babylonia in the mid–second century B.C. Parthian culture was a rich amalgam of Persian, Hellenistic, and Semitic influences. They worshipped Ahura Mazda, the ancient Persian deity who had become the ruling god of the Zoroastrian religion. But they worshipped Babylonian gods, Greek gods, and Hindu gods as well. At its height, the Parthian Empire held large populations of Jews and Buddhists alike.

Parthian Babylonia extended to the eastern bank of the Euphrates. The land west of the Euphrates was held by the Roman Empire under Augustus. In A.D. 98–117, under Trajan, and again in A.D. 193–211, under Septimus Severus, all of Babylonia fell to Roman occupation. The major Jewish settlements were on the east bank of the river.

Mesopotamia—the Greeks and the Romans still called it so; the Persians called it Khvarvaran; other names would come—was now only a place. Its time was ended. The majesty of its autochthonic vital forces, the magic and power of five thousand years, was dead.

In the early third century A.D., the Parthians of Persia fell in turn to the Sassanids of Persia. With conflict the Persians held at bay the imperial Roman forces that occupied the Syrian land to the northwest. The most feared and famed of these forces was XII Fulminata. This legion had been called upon by Titus, son of and successor to Vespasian, in the siege of Jerusalem in the spring of A.D. 70. The war in Jerusalem had led to the second destruction of the temple in the summer of that year. The temple had been looted before it had been burned, and all throughout the empire and beyond had seen the denarii minted from the silver of that looting. These coins bore the words IUDEA CAPTA ("Judea Defeated").

If the Jews had it bad under the pagan emperors, they had it no better under the Christian emperors, whose succession began with Constantine in the early fourth century.

And what was this thing that had happened, this thing called Christianity?

Z OE BECKLEY HAD SPUNK. She was a young woman making her way in the racket of journalism at a time when it was a boys' club. It is she who gives us the only portrait from life for which Rothstein ever sat. It is a portrait in miniature, and, like court portraits of old, which painted away the scars of smallpox and of plague, it is a portrait in which the subject guides the painter's hand. Alexander VI, the most infamous of the Borgia popes, has Pinturicchio place him in the presence of the redeeming Christ in a fresco in the papal chambers. And Beckley was no Pinturicchio. She was the fictionalist of "Treat Your Stenographer with Respect." But her serving little portrait is telling of the way in which Rothstein desired to be seen.

She must have captivated him, if only for a moment, in the New York autumn of 1927. A glimpse of silken stocking, a young and innocent suffragette smile. Her spunk. And he surely enchanted her. The piece was published in the *Brooklyn Daily Eagle* of Sunday, November 27, 1927. The title was "Dubs Who Can't Get Rich Call Him Crooked, but It's Brains, Says Rothstein."

Now and then there flashes in the world of business, finance, sport, art or theatricals a colorful figure which comes we know not whence or how.

But because it exerts enormous influence and kicks up a dust generally, and because it works in its own manner, upsetting precedent and succeeding by unguessable ways and means, we regard it with suspicion and call it hard names. Or we give it high admiration—and call it "a character."

Stream of Visitors Daily.

Such a personage is Arnold Rothstein, who can make or break a racetrack, a gambling house, a stock deal, a real estate development, or a newspaper (almost). He used to be called America's greatest gambler, but he says he has left that phase of his career behind. Ask any fairly informed person who Arnold Rothstein is and the answer will vary from "Oh, he's a crook" to "Gee—he's a wow!" A sportsman, a promoter of big deals, a multi-millionaire, a sentimentalist, a hardboiled egg, a whale of a good fellow and a power to reckon with.

There has not been a big prize-fight, a gold rush, a Wall Street flurry, a great horserace or a real estate boom in years that Rothstein hasn't had a hand in somehow. A torrent of men pour through his offices from early morn till dewy eve, and after. Thick-set men with sharp eyes, stubby boots and derbies-at-an-angle. Wiry, dapper little men in a nervous hurry. Large persons with booming voices, expensive cigars and plenty of leisure to wait for Arnold if he's engaged. Arnold is always engaged, always busy with this endless torrent of callers who want God-knows-what of him. Pretty much everything, is our guess.

Friendship a Religion.

Mr. Rothstein probably has more friends than anyone in the United States. The reason he has is that he knows how to be a friend. It seems to be his religion. But don't double cross him or he will roll up the sleeves of his white silk shirt and get right after you. And when he's finished the ambulance will be coming for you, clang-a-lang-a-lang.

Enough bad things have been said of Arnold Rothstein to fill a book. Good things, too, and they'd fill another probably bigger book. He has no illusions about himself whatsoever or the world's opinion.

"Know why you hear so much bad about me?" he queries amiably after you have crashed your way into his office at 45 W. 57th st., Manhattan, having waited hours in vain and tried to keep innumerable appointments made by his hard-pressed secretary.

"No," we answer, like Brother Bones. "Why do we hear bad about you?"

A MAN NAMED YESHUA was said to have lived in the early years of the first century. There have been many messiahs among the Jews. The earliest of them are said to have flourished before the man named Yeshua. They are known to us only as Judas, the son of one Hezekiah; Simon of Peraea; Anthronges the shepherd; and Judas the Galilean. Many flourished after the man named Yeshua, beginning with Theudas and then a man known only as the Egyptian. Manaheim, the son of Judas the Galilean, followed; then John of Gischala; Simon bar Giora; Jonathan the weaver. These and others appeared in the course of the first century. More were to come. The last of them was Shabbetai Zevi of Smyrna.

This self-proclaimed messiah was a rabbi who was compelled to violate the Torah through "strange acts" that were considered to be "holy sins"— deeds of personal renewal or, in Jewish mysticism, of cosmic retribution, known in Hebrew as *tikkun*. In his fortieth year, Shabbetai converted to Islam. This apostasy was understood by his followers as the most supreme of holy sins, the consummation of *tikkun*. Then Shabbetai renounced his conversion. The death of Shabbetai did little to diminish his cult, which came to number more than a hundred thousand followers at its height.

Shabbetai was born in 1626. He was ordained as a rabbi at the age of eighteen. He died in Berat, Albania, on September 17, 1676. By the nineteenth century, Shabbeteanism had spread throughout Europe and the Middle East. The Hebrew scholar Gershom Scholem (1897–1982) devoted a study to Shabbetai and the Shabbeteans, *Sabbatai Sevi: The Mystical Messiah, 1626–1676*, published first in Hebrew in 1957, then in English, in the Bollingen Series of Harvard University Press, in 1973. In this thousand-page book, Scholem expresses a belief that some Shabbeteans—Eastern Europeans such as Joseph Wehte and Aron Chovin—were instrumental to the rise of the Jewish Enlightenment and Reform movement in the nineteenth century.

Why has the Greek epithet *christos*—"anointed"—been applied to Yeshua alone?

"That Jews at the time of Jesus expected the coming of the messiah has been a central axiom of biblical studies." These are the words of Richard A. Horsley, chairman and distinguished professor of religious studies at the University of Massachusetts in Boston. "Recent critical analyses of Palestinian Jewish literature of late Second Temple times have indicated that there is little basis for that generalization." These show "that 'messianic' expectations were relatively unimportant in the literature of the time."

The most messianic of biblical texts is the second book of Baruch. Like the first book of Baruch, it has been removed from the Bible as we know it. The first book is present in two of the oldest and most authoritative copies of the Bible that have survived: the fourth-century Codex Vaticanus, now in the Vatican (Biblioteca Apostolica Vaticana, Ms. Vat. gr. 1209), and the fifth-century Codex Alexandrinus, now in the British Library (Royal Mss. 1 D.v–viii). The second book of Baruch survives primarily in a sixth-century manuscript now in the Ambrosian Library of Milan (Biblioteca Ambrosiana Ms. B.21 Inf. fols. 257ª).

Dr. Horsley, in the context of his previously quoted words, cites a work by Marinus de Jonge, emeritus professor of New Testament and early Christian literature at the University of Leiden: "The Use of the Word 'Anointed' in the Time of Jesus," from *Novum Testamentum: An International Quarterly for New Testament and Related Studies* (1966). In the words of Professor de Jonge, from which I have taken the liberty of omitting references to chapter and verse:

"*2 Baruch* was composed in the years following the destruction of the second temple in A.D. 70. It has the expression 'My Anointed,' 'my servant, the Anointed One,' and 'the Anointed One.' In all cases a royal figure is meant who reigns for a limited period, introducing a time of complete bliss and incorruptibility. It is said that 'my servant, the Anointed One,' will reign after wars and disasters on earth. The holy land will have peace; of the nations, only those that have not subjected Israel will be spared. Peace, joy, harmony, and health will abound. Also, 'For that marks the end of what is corruptible and the beginning of what is incorruptible.' "

King Herod Agrippa, the grandson of the Jewish king Herod the Great—who had his son Aristobulus, Herod Agrippa's father, executed—ruled for a limited period, from 37 to 44. He was the last to unite the Jewish territories, and has sometimes been considered a messianic figure. Of him it was said in Acts: "On an appointed day Herod put on his royal robes, took his seat on the platform, and delivered a public address to them. The people kept shouting, 'The voice of a god, and not of a mortal!' And immediately, because he had not given the glory to God, an angel of the Lord struck him down, and"—an especially nasty inversion of natural order—"he was eaten by worms and died." According to a non-Christian account, he departed this world less dramatically and more privately in the seventh year of his reign and the fifty-fourth year of his life.

No. A time of complete bliss, when peace, joy, harmony, and health will abound. What messiah, what savior, has brought us this deliverance? Not the man called Yeshua any more than the holy sinner named Shabbetai. Why is it that the followers of Yeshua alone have come to be known by the Renaissance epithet of "Christian," believers in the Anointed One? Are we not all the anointed messiahs, the saviors or ruinators of our own souls?

The first-century Gospel of Thomas survives as Codex II, tractate 2, of the Coptic papyrus texts known as the Nag Hammadi library. This Gospel, so mysterious and so beautiful, more powerful than any verse in the New Testament canon, has been suppressed by the church, for in it the church of the soul is the one true church. The inspired translation of these lines is by Elaine Pagels, from her book *The Gnostic Gospels*:

> *If you bring forth what is within you,*
> *what you bring forth will save you.*
> *If you do not bring forth what is within you,*
> *what you do not bring forth will destroy you.*

Outside of the New Testament, there is no convincing evidence that this Yeshua existed any more than the figure known only as the Egyptian. No mention of him appears in documents, official or otherwise, of his day. The sole corroboration of his existence lies in *The Jewish Antiquities* of Josephus, the first-century politician, soldier, and historian who was born in the year 37. As the year of the Crucifixion has been reckoned to be 30, 33, 35, or 36, Yeshua would have been a vivid memory to Romans and Jews alike in the years when Josephus wrote; and he would have been made especially vivid to Josephus.

Joseph ben Mattahias was born in Jerusalem, the most important city of Yeshua's short-lived messianic career. He spent the first twenty-six years of his life there, amid family, friends, a cityful of men and women who clearly would have remembered or been told tales of Yeshua's presence there. He moved to Rome in 64 and two years later served as the general of the Jewish forces in Galilee, where Yeshua was said to have worked miracles. He returned to Rome, where he was granted full citizenship and took the Latinized name of Josephus Flavius. In Rome he wrote his autobiography and his histories, and he lived out his years, which are believed to have ended with the century.

The major edition of the complete works of Josephus in the original Greek is that of Benedikt Niese. Its seven volumes of texts, notes, and commentary were published in Berlin in the years 1885–1895. In all the work of Josephus, there is one sentence that has grown so momentous to Christianity that it bears a title: the Testimonium Flavinium. It states that during the procuratorship of Pontius Pilate, "there lived a man named Jesus, a wise man, if indeed one might call him a man."

This, in a massive work by a verbose man who should have had—would have had—far more to say on the subject: inevitably more, in light of the circumstances—Jerusalem, Galilee, Rome—of his own full and learned life. This was, and is, all.

A bigger problem presents itself. The oldest surviving manuscripts of Josephus are from the eleventh century, and all of the early manuscripts were the work of Christian scribes. The Testimonium Flavinium was almost certainly the invented insertion of one such scribe who is lost and unknown to us. In fact, it was inserted in the wrong place. It falls between accounts of two unrelated events that took place in the year 19.

The charge that Jesus never existed was put forth in the second century by a devout Christian author, who expressed the charge in the words of an unconverted Jew. It is to be found in a work known to us as the *Dialogue with the Greek Jew Trypho,* by Justin Martyr, who met his martyrdom in Rome in 165, at the late age of sixty-five.

A specter, said to be known in his life to thousands but apparently remembered or remarked upon by none except his apostles, whom apparently no one remembered or remarked upon, either. Could they have conjured a legend to draw others away from wrathful Yahweh and embrace a God of love, compassion, and human understanding? Could that legend have been given a name, Yeshua—a late form of the Hebrew word *yehoshua,* meaning "Yahweh hath saved"—to ease the transition from Old to New? Could it be that he was said to have had a public life so brief— barely three years—to deflect the lack of any documentary notice of him? Legends have been made toward far less noble and meaningful ends. Worse tales have been told.

There is no concern in the Gospels for the year of the Crucifixion. No year is mentioned. But there is much concern for the time of year. In every Gospel, it is stated to have been the Passover season, thus suggesting the inevitable analogy with the sacrificial paschal lamb of sacred tradition.

And it is the Crucifixion that is the crux. The death of a common criminal, but a death nonetheless. And that is the great lesson of Christianity. They love you when you're dead.

This profound human insight has been ever true, and true it always will be.

They could not have foreseen the ultimate outcome. Their one true defense can be said to have been placed by them in the mouth of their Jesus. The Gospel of Luke: "Forgive them, for they know not what they do."

—◦✦◦—

S UZY WAS SITTING across from Jesus at Shannon's kitchen table. He was bearded, dark skinned, and very attractive. He was wearing one of those things around his neck, one of those things like preachers wear. Suzy was very attracted to him. He asked her if she wanted to fuck, and she said, "Absolutely." The went into the bedroom, where Suzy saw that Jesus wore a ring at the base of his cock. The ring had a dragon on it. Jesus made Suzy very hot. That's all she could remember.

—o✣✣o—

N OVEMBER 6, 1928. From House Surgeon Physician Alex F.
O'Hare, MD, Polyclinic Hospital, 335–361 West Fiftieth Street, to
chief medical examiner. Statement and particulars of the death of Arnold
Rothstein.

Residence: 912 Fifth Avenue.

Age: 46 years.

Color: White.

Occupation: Real estate and insurance.

Single, Married, or Widowed: Married.

Place of Birth: U.S.A.

Father's Name: Abraham E. Rothstein.

Father's Birthplace: U.S.A.

Mother's Name: Esther Rothschild.

Mother's Birthplace: U.S.A.

How long in United States: Life.

How long in New York City: Life.

Admitted: 4th day of November 1928 at 11:15 o'clock P.M.

By: Ambulance by police.

From: 55th Street and Seventh Avenue by police.

Examined by: Dr. Edward L. Kellog, MD.

Suffering from the following symptoms: Gunshot wound of
    abdomen. Conscious. Bullet entered lower right
    quadrant to outer side rectus muscle.

Injuries said to have been received: No accurate history
    was obtained to answer this section accurately.

Name, date, place, character, and results of any
    operation performed: Resection ileo-caecal junction.

Entero-colostomy. Suture of bladder. Suture of rectum.
Appendectomy.
Death took place on: 6th day of November 1928 at 10:15
o'clock A.M.
The immediate cause of death being: Gunshot wound of
abdomen. Peritonitis.

D URING THE MISHNAIC and Talmudic periods, the population of Babylonian Jews may have approached two million. This population was a sizable part of the region's inhabitants. Great Judaic universities flourished, and the Babylonian Talmud was compiled.

It was the Egyptian-born rabbi Saadia ben Joseph al-Fayumi of the early tenth century A.D. who first referred to the language of his religion as Hebrew. He was known as Saadia Gaon, a title bestowed upon him in his exalted position as head of the Jewish academy of Sura, one of the five great centers of Judaic learning in Mesopotamia. Baghdad, the Babylonian center of Jewish commerce founded in the eighth century A.D. at the crossroads of international trade routes pioneered by Jews a thousand years before, became under his leadership the highest seat of Jewish learning. Saadia wrote in Arabic and used the word "Hebrew" in its Arabic form. Centuries later, this new appellation was taken up from the Arabic by Jews who began to write Hebrew grammars in their own language. Then, some centuries after that, Izzy Pinckowitz started Hebrew National, and there were all those hot dogs.

I TRIED TO GO uptown, but the subway didn't go there. It went some-place I didn't know. And then I was lost.

I want one of those things you put in your pocket to keep the ink from getting on your shirt. One of those plastic things. You know what I mean. I never thought much about them. But now I need one. La plume de ma tante est sur la table.

The view of the river is nice. But sometimes, when the sun is strong in the clear winter sky, it is very depressing. When I was little I liked the light. But now I do not like the light. The light is very depressing. But sometimes there is no light, and that is good. Une belle vue. You can't step in the same river twice. But you can. I try to tell them but they don't want to listen.

And you can walk as far in a room as you can in a wilderness. And they bring you food. Jello too. Manna in the wilderness. It's true. And now I have one of those things to keep my shirt clean. And I can move the hands of the clock to make it be any time I want.

Labors to force a linguistic concord between God and the gods were such in the nineteenth century that *The Oxford English Dictionary* gave a circumspect definition to the jargon of this anomaly: "*Plural of excellence or majesty, plural intensive,* terms applied in Hebrew Grammar to a plural noun used as the name of a single person; the typical example being *elohim,* literally gods, deities, used as the name of (the one) God."

The greatest pedigree that could be found for any of these expressions of "Hebrew Grammar" was an 1837 notation from *The Elements of Syriac Grammar* by George Phillips stating that "a plural of excellence the Syrians have not." Also cited was an instance of "the plural of majesty," referring, of course, to *elohim,* from a posthumous edition of *Gesenius's Hebrew and Chaldee Lexicon to the Old Testament Scriptures,* by Friedrich Heinrich Wilhelm Gesenius (1786–1842). The oldest Hebrew grammars, written in Arabic by rabbi scholars of the eleventh century A.D., made no mention of these exalted terms or the reputed plural construction they came to designate many centuries later. The plural of excellence, which the Syrians had not, was also not had by any others, except perhaps the tribes of disingenuous latter-day exegetes.

The grasping after reeds is unnecessary. The Bible clearly indicates that God never speaks in the first-person plural. It is the gods, *elohim,* who do. Even if we were to accept the fanciful arguments for pronouns of royalty or pronouns of deliberation, pronouns of excellence or pronouns of majesty, they would be swept away from us by the devastating and lovely words of the third chapter of Genesis: "And the Lord God said, Behold, the man is become as one of us, to know good and evil: and now, lest he put forth his hand, and take also of the tree of life, and eat, and live for ever." Here it is Yahweh by name who is Lord God: *yahweh elohim* in the Hebrew. It is Yahweh, lord of the gods, who speaks.

Whom is he addressing, if not the other gods over whom he now seems to be rising?

Later, in the book of Deuteronomy, a unique phrase of rhythmic chanting meter: *Yahweh elohim yahweh echad.* The King James translation has it as "The Lord our God is one." The literal translation is The Lord, the gods, the Lord, one.

I CAN FEEL IT coming. That nurse. The white one. The one with the pretty legs. Nobody wants to be close to me anymore. But what about what I want? Things are not always what I want them to be, and they can't always be the way *they* want them to be, either.

They say that rape is a crime of violence that has nothing to do with sex. That's not true. I'm a nice man, and if I could have my way, I would live with her in a cottage and we would be happy. But I can't have my way, and this is the closest I can get to it. And it's not a crime, anyway. Nothing is.

If a man find a damsel that is a virgin, and lay hold on her, and lie with her, then the man that lay with her shall give unto the damsel's father fifty shekels of silver.

A man shall not take his father's wife, nor discover his father's skirt.

Go down, Moses, go down.

Z OE BECKLEY, the young journalist, must have captivated him. And he surely enchanted her. The piece in the *Brooklyn Daily Eagle* continued.

Most Persons Are Dubs.

"Because the majority of the human race are dubs and dumbbells and have rotten judgment and no brains, and if you have a few brains and have learned how to do things and size up people and situations, and dope out methods for yourself, they jump to the conclusion you're crooked. You can't make so much money, they figure, and be anything but crooked. If I had time I could tell you how to make money in any line you want, and make it straight.

"A crook is a fool. A liar is a fool. I never saw one yet that didn't hang himself if you gave him rope enough. To be a thief is an admission you lack brains. A thief always has contempt for himself. Every man wants to be honest, to live clean, tell the truth and keep his promises. But it takes brains, personality and opinions. I'll back my opinion to win every time."

Rothstein uses the word "opinion" as meaning "ability to estimate," and sometimes as though it meant "intuition."

Keen Analyzer.

It doesn't take him two minutes to size you up for exactly what you are and aren't—to catalogue you for success and worldly possessions, intelligence, education and experience. In short, to form an "opinion." And he is 99 and 44-100 right.

He wants to like you and have you like him, but if you don't, he's too busy to care. He doesn't give a rat for publicity, one way or the other, but if you call him a horsethief or a pickpocket, he will take time to find out why you do it, what you mean by it, where you got your "facts"—and you will either recant and apologize or find you have lost your job.

You gather by this time that Arnold Rothstein is a person to reckon with. He is. And like most men of his type, he has a most amazing emotional side to his nature, a nature that is sentimental, sympathetic, generous, kind and affectionate—the sort of affection that makes him speak of his beloved old father with dropped voice and misted eyes.

Started as Office Boy.

"My father now—there's a man!" says Arnold. "Man of character and heart. A philanthropist. A smart man. A great man. A good man. He is my ideal. Why don't you talk to him if you want a real story?"

It was as office boy in his father's cotton goods business that Arnold started. But he wanted bigger thrills than he got out of cambric and dotted swiss. He drifted to the pool rooms. To this day his speech is peppered with such phrases as "When I played pool for a living," "When I lived by my wits," "When I was a professional gambler," etc., etc.

"I wasn't fifteen before I learned my own limitations," he tells you. "I never played with a man I wasn't sure I could beat. I knew how to size 'em up. I still do. That's all there is to making money."

"What is worth while besides money?"

"Doing things for people," was the quick retort—"for your friends. I'd lie and steal and hang for a friend. What else is life for?

"Gee—if a man honors you by calling you friend, you have to go through hell for him. He'd go through for you if he was your friend. I've never yet been double-crossed by a person I trusted. Even if someone you trust forfeits your respect you can still see good in him, still help him. In other words, you can refuse to forfeit his respect. Until he lies or betrays you and then—"

Mr. Rothstein continued the sentence with a quick clenching motion of his extremely good-looking hands.

"Funny," he added contemplatively, "about truth. Plain truth is always the safe thing, for most people won't believe it. Funny about that. They'll fall for lies and bunk—and laugh at truth. Don't recognize it! Funny.

"I had a run-in once with August Belmont, who thought I was crooked and kept me out of the racetrack clubhouses. I was making money then by hundred-thousands. I explained just how I did it, told him he couldn't run his racetracks without me.

Wouldn't Believe Truth.

"He wouldn't believe I was straight. I had to tell him how dishonest I thought he was in order to make him listen. We ended by explaining to each other why we weren't dishonest. Told the truth and got things clear. And back I went to the clubhouses!

"Again, in the Fuller-McGee bucketshop ruckus, they had me on the stand asking a million questions, trying to hook some crookedness on me and make things out different than they were. Because I told the simple truth they wouldn't believe. In the end they will. People can't believe you are telling the truth; I suppose they don't expect it. Yet they know there are two million fools to one brainy man and that if you've got brains you can make money."

Rothstein is commonly supposed to carry a wad of a hundred thousand dollars with him wherever he goes. He says that's one of the stories that got around when he was making inconceivable sums on the races and it won't die.

He used to have gambling houses in Saratoga, Long Beach and New York and says he was "never gypped once by employees," although every other such owner knows he has to figure huge losses through overpayment to "friends," the "fixing" of games, etc., which was a regular part of the overhead.

Has Wide Interests.

Rothstein has quit the gambling game entirely now and has only five or six businesses to keep him occupied—an interest in a racetrack, a real estate development on Long Island, a golf club, a brokerage firm, an insurance office and a few promotion interests in manufacturing, traction, power and what not, outside of which he has nothing to do but worry over how to spend his income.

The racetrack was the Havre de Grace track, in Maryland. The real estate development, in Woodmere, Long Island, was the site of his Cedar Point Golf Club. His brokerage firm was the Warranty Brokerage Corporation.

He insists he has "no education" but speaks gently and in the good English of a collegian. He is an affable man of fair, smooth skin, brown eyes and hair and ready smile. He is well-groomed and shapely, looks 35 and says he is 45, was born in New York City and married at 23, lives in a huge, magnificent apartment on 5th ave., quite in contrast to his almost shabby offices in 57th st.

He is a blend of hardness and softness, naivete and sophistication, shrewdness and conservatism. He has conventional ideas about women and how they should be protected if "good" and dealt with if "bad"; wastes no words or effort on diplomatic guff. He is fearless, frank and unpretentious.

Criticism bothers him not at all, he is indifferent to publicity, not even keeping a scrapbook or loose clipping about himself, although reams have been written. He hates bunk, love beauty, appreciates the service that is done for him, and is not above listening to advice.

"My code of life is absolutely simple," says Arnold Rothstein. "Help a friend, be a friend, use your brains and fear nothing. Happiness? Hm!" He shrugged and grimaced. "I haven't a material wish ungratified. That isn't happiness. What is? Being a good scout, keeping busy and helping people."

August Belmont is cast here by Rothstein in a somewhat softer light. This is because he had gone on to the *schöner Berg* of the gods on December 10, 1924. His own father, Abe the Just, was still around. He turned seventy-two that November. Maybe Arnold's words were a sort of birthday gift. Thanks to the old man's unwitting help—through him the needle-trade union men had sought Arnold's help in resolving the strike of 1926—the garment industry was now a growing and highly lucrative part of the labor racket overseen by Arnold's associates Louis "Lepke" Buchalter and Jacob "Gurrah" Shapiro. Meanwhile, old Abraham had become one of the pillars of the Jewish Center, which he had helped to found, on strong Orthodox principles, with Rabbi Mordecai Kaplan (1881–1983), in early 1918. The account of Abraham Rothstein's role in the development of the Jewish Center, and of his intractable orthodoxy, that is given by Jeffrey S. Gurock in *A Modern Heretic and a Traditional Community: Mordecai M. Kaplan, Orthodoxy, and American Judaism* (1996) is the most revealing representation of him that we are likely to have.

Arnold Rothstein was at the height of his wealth and power in the fall of 1928. John F. Hylan (1868–1936), who had served as mayor of New York from 1918 to 1925, was a Tammany man. That was good, but in his second term Hylan had shown increasing signs of living up to his nickname of Honest John. He had decided to run for a third term but was defeated in the primary by Senator James J. Walker (1881–1946).

Walker, the most celebrated not only of Tammany mayors, but of all New York mayors, was born at 110 Leroy Street in Greenwich Village, the son of an Irish immigrant and a local Village girl. He wrote songs, and one of them, "Will You Love Me in December as You Did in May?," had some popularity and was recorded several times, in 1906. They called him Beau James and the Night Mayor of New York. He was married to a former singer, Janet Allen, but it was his mistress, the young British showgirl Betty Compton (1907–1944), nineteen when he took up with her, whom the city knew. He was a man of the speakeasies, the old neighborhood ways, and the Great White Way. He smoked, drank, lived well, showed up at the mayor's office as he saw fit. The heart of the city was his.

Arnold Rothstein thrived in his association with Judge George W. Olvany, who took over as the Tammany boss in 1924. In the late summer of 1925, after Tammany had abandoned Mayor Hylan for Walker, the incumbent warned publicly of "the wide-open town which Judge Olvany and the Tammany designee for mayor will give you if they are successful on primary day." Mayor Hylan said that Jimmy Walker was guilty of a vice that "I am ashamed to mention." He spoke of "the big gambler" who was the true dictator of Tammany. Speaking publicly on the evening of August 27, Hylan stated the identity of "the big gambler," which most already knew: Arnold Rothstein.

When Jimmy Walker won the election that fall, New York entered its greatest time as a city. It was wilder by far than "the wide-open town" that Hylan had warned against. It was a city where you could get whatever you wanted, whenever you wanted it. There was no night, no day: only the light of the sun and the light of the electric lamps and the lush darkness, the endless rushing midnight, the true soul of the place, that imbued even the blazing dawn, where sun and electricity became for one still instant the charged haze that was the single heartbeat of rest—taken upright at a bar or a gambling table, or abed in luxuriance of silk and faintly perfumed breath—that preceded the waking fiery breath of a dragon-dream and city that were one.

It would last less than three years, until the stock market crash of October 1929. The nighttime rhapsody of the Jazz Age would give way then to "Brother, Can You Spare a Dime?" But that brief span, from 1926 to 1929, was a time-seizing time of life and freedom that would reverberate, though ever more faintly, through the spirit of New York in the fifty and more years to come. Then there came a time—no one in old New York, no one, would have believed it—when you could not find a firecracker, let alone an opium den, in Chinatown; a time when you could not find sin in Times Square, save for the mortal sin of mediocrity; a time when you could not find an ashtray in a bar; a time when real life and real freedom, replaced by lip service to them, became the vice that New York, like the vast dying nothingness of America itself, was ashamed to mention.

But the shadows took Arnold Rothstein before the party ended. As he sat in his office like a preacher that day, telling Zoe Beckley of the simple ways of virtue, he had less than a year left to live.

My Jesus Hits Like
the Atom Bomb

*E**lohim* IS A NOUN of multitude. Like the myriad hosts of heaven found elsewhere in the Bible, as in Nehemiah, where Ezra tells the Lord: "The host of heaven worships you." Like the flock of God, as in the First Epistle of Peter: "Feed the flock of God which is among you." Like the vast legion of demons, as in the Gospel of Mark: "Legion is name to me, for we are many"; or a military legion in ancient Rome, as in George Rawlinson of Oxford's *Manual of Ancient History:* "The legion was light, elastic, adapted to every variety of circumstance." Like the pantheon, in its sense of an "assemblage of all the gods" or "the deities of a people collectively," as found in a definition of monotheistic religions that states that such faiths possess "all the attributes of Olympian religions, except that the pantheon of gods is subsumed under a single eternal, omniscient, omnipotent, and omnipresent being." Like the assembly of gods itself.

E. Theodore Mullen Jr., author of *The Assembly of the Gods: The Divine Council in Canaanite and Early Hebrew Literature:* "Common to the mythopoeic world of the Ancient Near East was the idea of a council or assembly of the gods that met to determine the fates of the cosmos. Depictions of such divine gatherings are found in the religious and mythological literatures of Mesopotamia, Ugarit, Phoenicia, and Israel."

The Semitic people of Ugarit dwelled near the Mediterranean coast of Syria from Neolithic times to the late second millennium B.C. They called this synod of the gods *phr'ilm,* or *phr'elm.* The gods were *ilm,* or *elm.* The Ugaritic language, an important influence on the development of Hebrew, began to insert a medial *h*-sound into its plural forms, and the gods began to be called *ilhim* or *elhim.*

There were no vowels in ancient Semitic writing systems. The numinous sigh, the primal *ah* with which every language begins, is heard in the names of the first letter of every alphabet. It is the *ah* of the Hebrew *aleph.* But unlike the Arabic *alif,* which also represents the sound of the sigh, the

Hebrew *aleph* represents a sound more similar to that of the ancient Semitic ☐, the *hheth* or *kheth* of the Phoenicians. The Semitic letter represents a guttural spirant, a fast choking of the sigh, a closing of the throat in midbreath, the *spiritus asper* of classical Greek grammar, the *ayn* of the Arabic alphabet. It is a sound that occurs in the West, but not in its languages. It is certainly not the initial sound of the Hebrew word that is traditionally rendered as *elohim*.

In non-Semitic tongues, this oldest element of human speech and sound-symbols—the sacred mark of the precipient, borning *ah*—was often invested with a sense of great power. In Sanskrit, it was the Word that existed before existence. Among certain Buddhist sects of Japan, it denoted the essence of all things or the incomprehensible void.

The Gospel of John: "In the beginning was the Word, and the Word was with God, and the Word was God." The book of Revelation: "I am Alpha and Omega, the first and the last."

The tilted symbol of the first letter of the Phoenician alphabet was set upright by the Greeks in the late ninth century B.C. to form their *alpha,* which the Romans took in turn, altering other Greek letters as the Greeks had altered the other Phoenician symbols. The Greek and Roman alphabets added what the Phoenician alphabet lacked: the opening, in its *aleph,* of the universal sigh, and other vowels as well. From Latin, the Romance tongues took the sigh with which their alphabets began. The non-Romance tongues of Germany and England began their languages and alphabets with the sigh as well. During what is called the Great Vowel Shift, the effects of which changed English pronunciation forever by the time of Shakespeare's birth, the values of long vowels and short vowels were transposed and the sigh became the anxious, clipped, repressive sound that is the first letter of the English alphabet as it is known today. So it was that the British colonies in America gave rise to the first nation whose language and literature were not born of the sigh.

In the case of Hebrew, vowel markings were formulated and added by the Masoretic rabbinate between the fifth and seventh centuries A.D., hundreds of years after the language was extinct as a vernacular, surviving only liturgically.

Like other Semitic languages, Hebrew had given way to Aramaic, which became the international vernacular and literary language through-out the Near East from the eighth century B.C. to the eighth century A.D. Only in the sixth century B.C., under the early Persian Empire, did the Hebrew alphabet evolve into the character forms familiar to later rabbis and scholars. The book of Esther, from the second century B.C., reveals Persian and Aramaic literary elements that are richer by far than its moribund Hebrew.

Esther's name derives from that of the Babylonian goddess Ishtar; and the book of Esther reveals that the Hebrew feast of Purim derives from the pagan Babylonian new year festival called *pûru,* an Akkadian word meaning "lot" or "die": in the Hebrew plural of *purim,* "lots" or "dice." Adar, the month of Purim, derives from the Babylonian month of Addaru.

Ishtar was the Akkadian name of the Sumerian goddess Inanna, who came to incorporate the powers of a Sumerian goddess of unbridled passion and fertility, a Semitic goddess of war, and a goddess of the planet Venus, the morning and evening star. "I am Inanna of the dawn," she says in *Inanna's Descent to the Underworld,* the Sumerian mytho-poem that may have predated the second millennium B.C. and foreshadowed all the mythic and literary descents to come—Theseus, Heracles, Odysseus, Orpheus, Virgil, Dante.

First and above all, she was the Divine Whore of Babylon.

The Sumerians, from whose soul she emerged, were not like other people. I defer to Jean Bottéro, emeritus director of Assyriology at the École Pratique des Hautes Études, Paris, and the author of much profound and learned work on ancient Mesopotamia.

Jean Bottéro tells us that the mysterious people whom we call Sumerians arrived in the land between the two rivers, the Tigris and the Euphrates, the territory of modern-day Iraq, in the early fourth century B.C., either from the east or from the southeast, along the Iranian coast on the Persian Gulf. Their ultimate origin is unknown. Their language was like no other. "In contrast to the Semites, who always maintained contact with their relatives who had stayed in the area of origin, and who constantly received new blood from throughout their history, the Sumerians, according to all indications, seemed to have burned all bridges with their point of departure, and they seem never to have received the least ethnic support from that area."

The Sumerians and the Semites "formed the principal elements of the country from before the beginning of history, and together they created their common high civilization," which culminated around the year 3000 B.C. with the Sumerian invention of writing.

Rimbaud: *La morale est la faiblesse de la cervelle.*

The Sumerians were free of the feebling disease of morality. They had no conception of sin. "There was even a goddess whose domain was Love in all the meanings of the term, and she soon became foremost and absorbed all others in her powerful personality: *Inanna / Ištar.*

"For the prostitutes and courtesans of the female sex, we have at least half a dozen different designations of these groups. Some stress their religious character: the *quadištu* were the *consecrated(?),* and the *ištarîtu,* devoted to *Ištar,* emphasized the links to their divine patroness."

Marriage was not necessarily monogamous. The number of a man's concubines were limited only by his wealth. A husband was "free to visit periodically other married or unmarried women."

Women were free to abandon their households. "Others, in particular the *ištarîtu,* were perhaps devoted from their early childhood to *Ištar* and to their vocation, which took them away from union with a single man only in order to offer them to all men." Female homosexuality seems to have been considered no less natural than male homosexuality. "We have at least one record of it, and I have been told that there is a still more explicit one in the Berlin museum that remains unpublished."

Prostitutes, consecrated or otherwise, were distinguished by the manner of their dress and the style of their hair. "The place where they were most easily found, and used, was the tavern (*bît sâbî, bît sâbîti*) and especially the hostel (*aštammu, bît aštammi*) which served as an inn but also played the role of the village pub, and almost that of a brothel, where one could drink and enjoy oneself to one's heart content."

There were also male prostitutes, for men and for women. There were transvestites. There were devotees of every sexual persuasion and *spécialité.*

"These people were also largely connected to *Ištar.*" This was a circumstance that "allowed them to partake in 'abominations' (*asakku*), in other words behavior that is forbidden to common mortals, in order *to delight the heart of the patroness.*"

The excesses of Ishtar "were well known in mythology, and several of them were reflected in her cult. Also known, at least in some places, was an entire liturgy of sacred marriage, the intercourse between a god and a goddess, which was enacted by the ruler and a priestess, perhaps in order to ascertain the fertility of the earth and the herds, and in any case the prosperity of the land. In this tradition there was something that constantly brought up love and its functions, and preserved it, or gave it a naturalism, an ingenuity, and a candor that is for us difficult to imagine."

Love was "presented as being the point of access to a life that is truly cultural and human." Sex "was practiced without constraints and joyously, promoted by all imaginable 'specialists,' encouraged by the gods without the least juridical, moral, or religious restriction—provided only that it did not involve any violence or disorder."

The Sumerians left behind "a certain number of clay figurines where lovers in the midst of sexual intercourse are represented, lying down or standing. Among the latter, at least those figurines where the woman is sodomized while she is drinking beer through a long reed-pipe from a jar, as was the custom in those days, clearly reflect the pleasures of the 'hostel' rather than those of the conjugal bed."

Love was not always rosy, in life or in literature. In *The Epic of Gilgamesh,* the hero's friend Enkidu, nearing his death, looks back with rancor to curse the courtesan of Uruk who long ago had "civilized" him:

Never will you dwell in a harem,
The dregs of beer will stain your beautiful breast,
With his vomit the drunk will splash your attire.

Ishtar was a predatory lover. Gilgamesh himself only barely escaped her caress, which was followed always by her wrath. She had given herself with passion to her first love, the shepherd-king Damuzi, then betrayed him. Any man who lost his virility through battle or illness knew to blame his misfortune on the wicked will of Ishtar.

Babylon: "She made all nations drink of the wine of the wrath of her fornication." Babylon: "Babylon the great, mother of whores and of earth's abominations." Thus the wandering, furying prophet of Revelation, in the time of Domitian.

Ishtar to Esther, *pûru* to *purim*.

Rabbi Moses ben Maimon, better known as Maimonides, the thirteenth-century physician and codifier of Jewish law, asked rhetorically in his *Mishneh Torah:* What is the obligation of the Purim feast?

"That one should eat meat," he said, "and drink wine until he is drunk and falls asleep from drunkenness."

It cannot be known, therefore, how accurately the Masoretic vowel markings and the pronunciations assigned to them reflect the sounds of Hebrew as it had been spoken in biblical days. The vowels interpolated by scholars into other dead Semitic languages must be more conjectural by far. As early as the fourth and fifth centuries, when Latin was still a living language, St. Jerome, St. Augustine, and others were arguing the proper pronunciation of that language. How much more problematic to derive at the pronunciation of a language, a language without vowels, centuries or a thousand years or more after that language had died.

In the Bible, the word *"elohim"* consists only of the letters *aleph-lamed-heh-yod-mem,* equivalent to ALHYM. The *yod*-sound is not represented in the traditional Romanized word *elohim.* The *aleph* was not a vowel, but rather a fast guttural choking of breath that Roman letters cannot approximate. The *o*-sound and *i*-sound were insertions based on a theoretical linguistic restoration of many centuries later. We are left, then, more accurately, with LHYM. This is very close to the Ugaritic *ilhim,* or *elhim*—whose vowels also are based on theory—equivalent to LHM, as found in the phrase for the assembly of the gods. It is clear that the Hebrew word speculatively rendered as *elohim* and the Ugaritic word speculatively rendered as *ilhim,* or *elhim,* are, if not the same word, very close cognates.

It began with Ɛ and Ļ, the earliest known Semitic forms of the Hebrew character *lamed,* the L in LHYM.

Enlil was the greatest of Sumerian gods. In the words of Nancy Sandars, translator of the Gilgamesh epic and other Mesopotamian poetry, Enlil was "air and storm and active power." The worship of Enlil was attested to as early as 2500 B.C., in cuneiform tablets of the Sumerian city-state of Shuruppak, on the bank of the Euphrates in what is now south-central Iraq. Thousands of years later, in the early twenty-first century A.D., ancient Shuruppak, now called Fara, was one of many archeologically rich sites to be ravaged by desecration and looting following the American assault on Iraq.

The Sumerians, who were not Semitic, were absorbed into the first Semitic Empire, the Akkadian kingdom, established in southern Mesopotamia in the late twenty-fourth century B.C. The Akkadians adopted the cuneiform script to write their own Semitic language. They adopted much else of Sumerian culture as well.

The Assyrians established Nineveh and the other great cities of their kingdom in a geographic triangle formed by the Kurdish mountains to the north, the Tigris River to the west, and the Upper Zab River to the east flowing into the Tigris at the southernmost tip. The Assyrians adopted the Akkadian language, and like the Akkadians, they were cultural dependents of Babylonia and came to embrace the Babylonian gods.

Like the treasures of Sumeria, Akkadia, and Babylon itself, most of the artifacts of Assyrian civilization were stolen or destroyed in the rampages of the American military occupation of Baghdad.

In the Akkadian tongue, Enlil became Elil. The two elements of this name—*el, il*—were to be the theophoric source of all Semitic gods. Since the vowels are speculative, the *l* was where gods dwelled.

In Ugaritic, which descended directly from Akkadian, the word for "god" was *el,* or *il*. In Hebrew, as in Phoenician, the word for "god" was *el*. In Aramaic, the word was *elah*.

Deuteronomy, dating to the seventh century B.C., shows the influence of this Aramaic word for "god." Here the form *eloah,* translated as "God," is composed of the Hebrew letters *aleph-lamed-waw-heh,* the first two letters of *elohim* and the last two letters of Yahweh. Deuteronomy also includes reference to astral worship, which the conquering Assyrians brought to Judah in the century preceding that writing of Deuteronomy. *Eloah* is encountered again in the book of Job, which has been dated to the century after Deuteronomy. Here God bears three names: Yahweh, El, and Eloah, a welding of El and Yahweh.

Later, in Arabic, from *al-ila,* "the god," would come the sacred name of Allah.

The *el* was enfolded into names of other Semitic gods as well: Bel, the Babylonian successor to Enlil in the thirteenth century B.C., known also as

Belial, as Baal to the Canaanites, and, much later, in Christian times, Beelzebul, Beelzebub, Baalzebub. The plural of this dark god, *baalim*, occurs many times in the Old Testament, with the same Hebrew plural inflection as *elohim*. Yet while *elohim* is always translated as "God," never as "the gods," *baalim* appears always as "the Baals."

Strange words from the book of Hosea: "And it shall be at that day, saith the Lord, that thou shalt call me Ishi; and shalt call me no more Baali. For I will take away the names of Baalim out of her mouth, and they shall no more be remembered by their name."

A few points about this King James translation. The "thou" that suddenly becomes "her" is assumed to be Israel, the Lord's chosen bride. The Hebrew word transliterated as Ishi means "my man." Nowhere else in the Bible does the Lord seek to be called such, and nowhere else is he so called. As for the word "Baali," it in fact appears in the Hebrew text simply as Baal. This is reflected in the New Revised Standard Version, which is also more explicit in its phrasing "the names of the Baals."

Hosea, who was active in the prophecy racket in the eighth century B.C., is believed to have actually delivered many of the oracles, such as the one just cited, that are attributed to him. Be that as it may, verses such as this don't-call-me-Baal routine serve to illustrate that the Old Testament is in no way a monotheistic work. It is a *monotheizing* work. Monotheism did not exist when the early books of the Bible were written. There would not even be a word to express the concept of monotheism until the dawn of the fifth century A.D., when the word *"unicultor,"* "worshipper of one god only," appears in the late Latin poetry of Prudentius. The books of the Bible move, through the centuries of their authorship, *toward* monotheism.

In 1901, the scholar of myth Edwin Sidney Hartland (1848–1927) coined a strange and beguiling word: "theoplasm." As he defined it, theoplasm is "god-stuff, not a god fully formed and finally evolved." It is a definition that can be rightly applied to the shifting divine force, now plural and now again singular.

The Sole One. Creator of mankind. King of kings. Lord of lords. These are phrases applied to the gods Re and Osiris in the Egyptian Book of the Dead, from the second millennium B.C. Though they are worded specifically in the singular, they are in no way to be taken as intimations of monotheism, only as titles of worshipful or fearful respect. The same is true of similar phrasings in the Bible.

The monotheizing process was a slow and winding journey, ending in theocracy: the mingling of deities into one divine being. God comes to us not ex nihilo, from nothing, but from the gods that preceded Him.

Yahweh—some say this name is of Egyptian origin—was a storm-god, like Baal and Enlil before him. And, like all the gods who have been born of monotheism, he becomes increasingly a god of destruction.

In forsaking paganism, in abandoning the gods and cleaving the sacred into Almighties, man had chosen, raised, and embraced under different names and guises long-sleeping Enyalion, the ancient Cretan god of war and destruction, and had begun to "go down," to use the words of William Blake, "to self-annihilation."

Enyalion. Ad nihil. Annihilation.

The artificial births of the one true God were the true genesis of the fatal disease that is the plague of Enyalion: ψῡχόθρος, the death of the soul. Where once theophany billowed through soul and sky, there now billowed the black smoke of annihilation through soul and sky gone dead. What can be made of words such as "Thou shalt not kill"? They have no meaning in this world and are worthless as poetry.

Theology redacts, revises, implants conditional clauses and circumstantial exegesis. Where once was the Word, there are now words. Where once was the Law, there are now legal definitions, interpretations, and amendments. Where once was the Book, there are now treatises.

The Greek word *"pneuma,"* the divine spirit, the breath of life, also meant flatulence. Thus theology.

The Koran tells that Jews, Christians, and followers of the holy messenger Muhammad were all descended from Abraham. This is the first sacred text to state the common Semitic roots of the three religions. In blood and language, Arab and Jew were indeed kindred Semites.

The fifth sura of the Koran tells of Allah's giving His commandment against murder to "the children of Israel." For "whoever slays a soul," says Allah, "it is as though he slew all men."

Central to early Christianity was agape, the shared feast of holy love.

History attends no love feasts, but it does attest that it was men who were the products of Christian cultures who brought about the greatest feast of death that the world has known: the forty-month period that began in December 1941 with the implementation of the *Nacht und Nebel* order at Chelmno and ended in August 1945 with the bombings of Hiroshima and Nagasaki. Christian cultures in conflict, atom bomb courtesy of the good Jew.

BUT SUZY TELLS IT better herself: "Jesus and I were sitting at your kitchen table, smoking cigarettes, as you and I did so many times after John left. The room was lit by candles and your oven light, and Jesus was dressed in a white robe with a garnet scarf—the image that we in the West see so often. He had long thin fingers and smoked slowly and deliberately. I'm not sure if there was any conversation, but the next image I have was of me straddling him, still at the kitchen table, and grinding on his lap as we kissed. We moved to the bedroom and took off our clothes before we got on the bed. He was thin and pale and had a thin patch of hair between his nipples, thicker hair around his penis, which was also long and thin and curved slightly upward when erect. He wore a gold cock-ring, attached to which was a thin gold chain bearing a small green dragon charm on the end. The chain dangled so that the dragon hit just below the balls, which were tucked tightly to the body, given the current state of arousal. Without foreplay, we fucked on top of your bed, Jesus on top. With every thrust, the dragon would hit the space between my vagina and my asshole, and would slap Jesus's balls on the outward pull. The dream ended before we finished."

N EW YORK COUNTY SURROGATE'S COURT, 31 Chambers Street. February 7, 1929. Examination by Mr. Isidor Gainsburg, Esq., attorney for Mr. Abraham E. Rothstein et al., contestants of the will.

What is your name?
   —Maurice F. Cantor.
And what is your vocation?
   —I am an attorney and member of the state legislature.
And where is your present office address?
   —45 West 57th Street, New York.
And where do you reside?
   —225 West 106th Street.
How long have you had your office there, at 45 West 57th Street?
   —About eighteen months.
Where was your office prior to that?
   —152 West 42nd Street.
Were you associated with or were you there with the attorneys known as or the attorneys' firm known as Fallon & McGee?
   [Objection raised by Senator Thomas I. Sheridan, attorney for Mr. Maurice F. Cantor, Esq. Mr. Gainsburg resumes:]
Can you tell me the month that you moved into 45 West 57th Street?
   —September 1927.
When did you first meet Mr. Arnold Rothstein?
   —About seven or eight years ago.
And when did you become the attorney for Mr. Arnold Rothstein?
   —September 1927.
Where was Arnold Rothstein's office at that time?
   —45 West 57th Street, on the fourth floor.
And what part of the premises did you occupy?

—A suite on the seventh floor.

*Did you become Mr. Arnold Rothstein's attorney under any annual
retainer?*

—Yes.

*What was that annual retainer? When I say what was it, I mean in
dollars and cents.*

    —It was agreed between Mr. Rothstein and myself that I was
to represent him and several of the corporations that he was
interested in, for which I was to receive a compensation of no less
than $7,500 per year, plus expenses.

Was that reduced to writing?

—No.

*Did you ever receive a letter from Mr. Arnold Rothstein to confirm such
an arrangement?*

—No.

*Was there any arrangement as to when you were to be paid your fees
under this annual retainer?*

—No.

How much since September 1927 did you receive from Arnold Rothstein?

    [Senator Sheridan objects. Mr. Gainsburg resumes:]

Would you say it amounts to $20,000?

    [Senator Sheridan objects. Mr. Gainsburg resumes:]

*Give me the names of the corporations for which you say you acted as
attorney, corporations which you say were owned or controlled by Mr.
Arnold Rothstein?*

    —Rothmere Mortgage Corporation, Hooper Realty Corporation,
Lark Holding Company, Beekman Credit Corporation, Rothstein
Brokerage Company, Hotel Fairfield Incorporated. That is all I
can remember at this time.

Were there others?

—Yes.

Who introduced you to Mr. Arnold Rothstein?

    [Senator Sheridan objects. Mr. Gainsburg resumes:]

*Were you introduced by Mr. LeBouef, formerly attorney for Arnold
Rothstein?*

[Senator Sheridan objects. Mr. Gainsburg resumes:]

How long have you been living at 225 West 108th Street?

—Since September 1, 1928.

Where did you live prior to September 1, 1928?

—Hotel Fairfield, 20 West 72nd Street.

And was that owned by the Fairfield company?

—Yes.

One of the concerns that you represented and which was owned by Arnold Rothstein?

—Yes.

Do you know Inez Norton?

[Senator Sheridan objects. Mr. Gainsburg resumes:]

Did you introduce Inez Norton to Arnold Rothstein?

[Senator Sheridan objects. The objection is withdrawn. Mr. Cantor responds:]

—I did not.

Did you know or do you know Inez Norton?

—I do.

When did you meet her?

[Senator Sheridan interjects: "Objected to as incompetent."]

Where did you meet her?

[Senator Sheridan objects. Mr. Gainsburg resumes:]

Was Inez Norton living at the Fairfield Hotel when you were living there?

[Senator Sheridan objects. Mr. Gainsburg resumes:]

Did you meet her at the Fairfield Hotel?

[Senator Sheridan objects. Mr. Gainsburg resumes:]

Are you married, Mr. Cantor?

—I am.

When were you married?

—October 1927.

Now after you moved in, in September 1927, to the premises 45 West 57th Street, and you say you made arrangements with Arnold Rothstein, who was present at that arrangement?

—The arrangement was made by another lawyer. The offer came
to me.

Who was the other lawyer?

[Senator Sheridan objects. Mr. Gainsburg resumes:]

*You say that the arrangement was made by another lawyer. Did that
lawyer bring you that arrangement?*

—He brought the offer to me from Arnold Rothstein.

Did you then see Mr. Rothstein?

—I did.

Did you have a talk with Arnold Rothstein about it?

—Yes.

Who was present when you had that talk with him about it?

—Nobody. Mr. Rothstein and myself.

Where was the conversation held?

—Mr. Rothstein's office.

*And how frequently thereafter, how often, would you meet Mr. Arnold
Rothstein?*

—Almost every day.

Would that include Saturdays and Sundays?

—Yes.

*Can you give us, or tell us, the places where you would meet him, or, we
will put it this way, where you met him oftenest outside of his office?*

—Where I met him oftenest?

Yes.

—At the Fairfield Hotel.

And were those meetings in the afternoon or evening?

—Evening.

*Did you meet him anywhere else other than at the Fairfield Hotel on
72nd Street?*

—I met him a few times at his home.

What address?

—912 Fifth Avenue.

Did you meet him at any other places?

—Sometimes in the barbershop.

What new corporations did you form for him?

—Armor Realty Company. It occurs to me there is another
corporation which I did not mention: the Oceanside Realty
Company was in existence then.

*The Oceanside Realty Company was one of the corporations which you
failed to enumerate. What other corporations can you now recall that
were in existence in 1927?*

—Juniper Realty Company and the Cedar Point Golf Club
Incorporated.

*Can you tell us, in the month of January 1928, how often you and Arnold
Rothstein were together during that month?*

[Mr. Sheridan objects. Mr. Gainsburg resumes:]

*Now can you tell us from memory how often you and Mr. Rothstein were
together, whether it be in the daytime, afternoon, or at night, in the month
of February 1928?*

[Mr. Sheridan objects. Mr. Gainsburg resumes:]

Did you see Mr. Arnold Rothstein in the month of March 1928?

[Mr. Sheridan objects. Mr. Gainsburg resumes:]

And did you see Mr. Arnold Rothstein in the month of April 1928?

[Mr. Sheridan objects. Mr. Gainsburg resumes:]

*And I ask you the same question with reference to the balance of the
months of the year 1928, as to whether or not you saw Arnold Rothstein,
May to December 1928, and how often you saw him during these months,
and when you saw him and where you saw him.*

[Mr. Sheridan: "The objection is limited to any time other than a
reasonable time before the execution of the will of March first or
the second will, executed on November fifth. If counsel wants to
interrogate the witness with reference to these particular dates, all
right." Mr. Gainsburg resumes:]

*Then I ask you, in view of the fact that the objection is limited, I will ask
you whether or not each month you saw Mr. Arnold Rothstein and how
often you saw him in the month of May 1928.*

[Mr. Sheridan objects. Mr. Gainsburg resumes:]

*How often did you see Mr. Arnold Rothstein, if you saw him at all, and
where, in the month of June 1928?*

[Mr. Sheridan objects. Mr. Gainsburg resumes:]

How often did you see Mr. Arnold Rothstein, and where, in the month of July 1928?

[Mr. Sheridan objects. Mr. Gainsburg resumes:]

How often did you see Mr. Arnold Rothstein, and where, in the month of August 1928?

[Mr. Sheridan objects. Mr. Gainsburg resumes:]

And how often did you see him in the month of September 1928?

[Mr. Sheridan objects. Mr. Gainsburg resumes:]

Did you meet Mr. Rothstein and have any conversations with him in the month of October 1928?

[Senator Sheridan: "No objection."]

—I did.

How often did you meet him in the month of October?

—Three or four or five times a week.

Where did you meet him?

—Either at his office or at the Hotel Fairfield.

How late was his, Arnold Rothstein's, office open?

—Until about seven every night.

At that time were you the attorney for Inez Norton?

[Senator Sheridan objects. Mr. Gainsburg resumes:]

Did you receive any compensation from Arnold Rothstein for any services which you may have rendered for Inez Norton either under that name or under any other name?

[Senator Sheridan objects. Mr. Gainsburg resumes:]

Did you in 1928 draw any wills for Arnold Rothstein?

—My office prepared a will.

Did you draw any other wills for Arnold Rothstein?

—I had one other drawn.

You say you had another drawn. Who drew that other will?

—Mr. Abraham Schwartz.

That is the young man who is still associated with you?

—Yes.

And working for you exclusively?

—Yes.

He is a member of the bar?

—No.

He is not?

—Not yet admitted.

So he was a law student at that time?

—Graduate law student.

So, those two wills that you had drawn, neither one was dictated by you personally?

—That is correct.

Please follow me. From November first inclusive to November fifth inclusive, how many times did you see Arnold Rothstein?

—Possibly once.

Possibly twice?

—Possibly.

And when you saw Arnold Rothstein between the first inclusive and the fifth inclusive, possibly once or possibly twice, where did you see him?

—At his office. I might say this: The last time I saw him was on Friday before he was shot.

Will you tell me where?

—At his office.

Did you see him on Sunday?

—I did not.

[Senator Sheridan corrects the record, calling attention to the fact that Mr. Cantor had seen Mr. Rothstein at Polyclinic Hospital on Sunday night.]

And then did you see him again on Monday?

—Yes.

What time of day did you see him on Sunday?

—Around midnight. I saw him midnight, and then I saw him on the hospital operating table a little later.

Did you know Mr. Arnold Rothstein's chauffeur in 1928?

—Yes.

What was his name?

—Gene.

What?

—I think it is Reimer.

But he was known and referred to as Gene?

—Yes.

Did you see Gene between November first and November fifth, both dates inclusive?

—Yes.

When?

—I saw him at the hospital.

That would be Sunday night?

—Past midnight.

After Sunday night, midnight, you and Gene, Gene Reimer, went in a car to your office, 45 West 57th Street?

—Yes.

And whose car was that? Whose car did Gene drive?

—Arnold Rothstein's car.

And how long did you remain with Gene in your office that night?

—About ten minutes.

Did you or Gene during that time that you were there, for those ten minutes, speak with or to Mrs. Carolyn Rothstein?

—Yes.

Who called her, Gene or you?

—Gene. And I spoke to her.

And who spoke to her first, Gene or you?

—I think I did. I don't think Gene spoke to her at all. I think I spoke to her.

Did you ask him to call her?

—Yes.

And then after he called her, did he immediately turn the receiver over to you, or did he actually talk to Mrs. Carolyn Rothstein?

—I said, "Gene, you had better let me talk to her, you are too nervous."

Now during this time, and in the months of September, October, and November, up to and inclusive of November fifth, did you meet and speak with Inez Norton?

[Senator Sheridan objects. Mr. Gainsburg resumes:]

Did you ever discuss with Inez Norton any of the subject matters which you say you discussed with Arnold Rothstein?

[Senator Sheridan: "With reference to the will?" Mr. Gainsburg: "Naturally no." Senator Sheridan: "I object to that. If it is confined to anything with reference to the will, I will withdraw the objection." Mr. Gainsburg: "You understand the question?" Senator Sheridan: "Objected to in its present form."]

Hearing adjourned to Thursday, February 14, 1929, at 10:30 A.M., at the office of Mr. I. Gainsburg, 35 Wall Street.

THE HOLOCAUST

Great guides, great company

Full colour brochures from Midas Tours

www.midastours.com

Check out the website for a full itinerary:

Day 3. This morning we drive out to the Death Camps at Treblinka, where up to 17,000 victims were murdered daily. Returning to Warsaw for the afternoon, we stroll through the pleasant and peaceful Lazienk Park, maybe to the strains of Chopin. Return to our hotel for dinner.

T HE ATOM BOMB WORKED. But we live now in an age in which humanity dares not speak its true name. To employ a nuclear bomb—or, as our political leaders are inclined to say, "nucular"—would not be "humane" (even as humanity, the nature of the species, continues to be defined by the very attributes and acts that it decries *as* inhuman; the Godwinian reproach of "man's inhumanity to man" has become a conceit of our hypocrisy, as *la faiblesse de la cervelle* enters its terminal stages). At Hiroshima, more than a hundred thousand civilians were killed in the span of a breath. Another fifty thousand or more civilians were killed three days later at Nagasaki, again in the span of a breath. But Japan surrendered.

In 1996, the National Defense University of the Pentagon published a book called *Shock and Awe: Achieving Rapid Dominance*. It proposed an absurd new method of military assault that would effect "the non-nuclear equivalent of the impact that the atomic weapons dropped on Hiroshima and Nagasaki had on the Japanese."

A great Gospel song came out of the summer of 1945: "Jesus Hits Like the Atom Bomb." The Pilgrim Travelers recorded it, then a lot of others. Somehow "Jesus Hits Like Shock and Awe" just would not be the same.

When a "Shock and Awe" attack, after much pre–Shock and Awe blustering of threats and warnings, was conducted by the United States against Iraq in March 2003, it worked about as well as the War on Drugs.

Are you old enough to remember that one? It was in June 1971 that the late, great American president Richard Nixon—the only president to be stricken with the biblical wrath of shingles—declared his open War on Drugs, saying at a press conference that drug abuse was "public enemy number one in the United States."

A trillion dollars later, the war is still ongoing and the drug trade has increased remarkably. It has prospered especially where America has invaded. Let us recall the attack of Afghanistan in October 2001—Operation

Enduring Freedom, a last minute name change from Operation Infinite Justice, which it was feared might be offensive to the people being attacked, as they believed that only Allah could dispense infinite justice. Thus Operation Enduring Freedom. And, yes, it can be hard at times to endure freedom as we came to know it in the early twenty-first century. This "operation" is not to be confused with Operation Iraqi Freedom—all this freedom can be not only hard to endure, but downright confusing—or with—ooooooooh, look out—Operation Resolute Sword. The heroin trade was doing well. But in the wake of Operation Enduring Freedom, it did even better. The land devoted to opium-poppy cultivation in Afghanistan grew to more than sixty thousand hectares (almost a hundred and fifty thousand acres), yielding some three thousand metric tons (about three million kilos) of opium tar—and that's a lot of smack—in 2003. But that was nothing compared to the spring harvest of 2004, when about a hundred and twenty thousand hectares (almost three hundred thousand acres) yielded a magnificent six thousand or so metric tons, or about six million kilos of tar. Shake down, mama, there's a party going on.

This Shock and Awe shuck-and-jive turned out to be little more than an expensive fireworks show that served only to rouse the anger rather than to paralyze the will and bring about the immediate capitulation of the attacked country. The small mendacious brat of wealth who presided over this fiasco had once explained:

"When you turn your heart and your life over to Christ, when you accept Christ as Savior, it changes the heart and changes your life, and that's what happened to me."

Why are there no images in paint or stained glass of Jesus Christ puking out his guts?

Julia Day, *The Guardian,* April 10, 2003:

Japanese electronics giant Sony has taken an extraordinary step to cash in on the war in Iraq by patenting the term "Shock and Awe" for a computer game.

It is among a swarm of companies scrambling to commercially exploit the war in Iraq, which has killed more than 5,000 soldiers and civilians in the space of three weeks.

MediaGuardian.co.uk has learned that Sony wants to launch a computer game called "Shock and Awe," having filed an application to register the defining phrase of the coalition's military campaign as a trademark in the US.

It applied to register the term as a trademark with the US Patent and Trademark Office on March 21—just one day after war started. It wants to use it for computer and video games, as well as a broadband game played both locally and globally via the internet among PlayStation users.

The phrase, coined by former US navy pilot Harlan Ullman, was adopted by Washington to describe the fierce bombardment of Baghdad on the second night of the war—the military tactic designed to bully the Iraqi resistance into submission.

However, the crassness of the phrase was seized upon by critics as evidence of US arrogance in a war that the UN, and notably France and Russia, refused to support.

A spokesman for Sony PlayStation in the UK admitted the company might not stock the game in Britain and Europe owing to political sensitivities.

"Sometimes registering trademarks does not necessarily mean the product will be launched. But if it was deemed unsuitable then we might not ship it here," he said.

"If indeed it is related to the Iraqi war rather than just using that phrase, then, yes, it might well be something we would be very sensitive to," the spokesman added.

However, the Sony game is only the tip of the iceberg as the US market is set to be flooded with goods ranging from T-shirts, toys, board games, train sets, sunglasses, mugs and fireworks branded with slogans such as "Operation Iraqi Freedom" and "Battle of Baghdad."

On February 19, 1942, little more than ten weeks after the *Nacht und Nebel* order was issued in Germany, Executive Order 90066 was issued in the United States by the late, great president Franklin D. Roosevelt. Under this order, Japanese and Italian Americans were placed in concentration camps. Germans were overlooked, as they represented the largest ethnic group in America.

Little more than sixty years later, the United States in its "war on terror" would shun any consideration of "racial profiling." Nice war you got there, kid. This so-called war on terror was associated with the late, great American president George W. Bush, who pronounced it in his September 20, 2001, address to American suckers. But we can find it on the front page of *The New York Times* of February 3, 1947: JEWS IN PALESTINE BAR AID TO BRITAIN IN WAR ON TERROR. The use in English of the word "terror" in this sense, referring to a state of things in which the general community live in dread of death or outrage, derives from the period, from about March 1793 to July 1794, of the first French Revolution, called the Terror. From the fifth edition (1798) of the *Dictionnaire de l'Académie Française:*

Terrorisme. substantif masculin. Système, régime de la terreur. Voyez: Terroriste.

The fifth edition of the dictionary was fully completed by 1793, but the Académie Française was suppressed in August of that year by order of the Convention Nationale, thus delaying actual publication of the work until 1798.

In the early twenty-first century, the French coined a word: *bushienne*. The English language could use such an adjective, to connote something that looks like a colorectal polyp, possesses the intelligence of a colorectal polyp, and, yes, is every bit as undesirable and potentially destructive as a colorectal polyp.

There is an old Abbott and Costello routine. Abbott spends the last of their money on a hamburger, leaving Costello with a magazine page on which there is a picture of a steak. As Costello drools at the hamburger that Abbott is eating, Abbott explains that it is all mind over matter. He tells Costello to eat the magazine page. Costello hesitantly brings the page to his mouth. Abbott encourages him, complaining that all he has to eat is a lousy hamburger while Costello has a big beautiful steak. Costello chews the page and swallows.

We have all become Costello. We eat the illusion as we starve. We eat and evacuate "freedom" and "liberty," "compassion" and "justice"—the words, not the real things. The more Abbott says "steak," the less its truth. The more that words such as "freedom" and "liberty"—and "truth"—fill the air like the cloying redolences of cheap plastic deodorizers, the more endangered and suppressed are freedom, liberty, and truth in fact. They become like the "spring bouquet" and "mountain wildflowers" of the deodorizer—a stench of artificiality, a lie. But unlike Costello, we have come to enjoy our meal. We have been conditioned to consume it with a pleasant and politically correct smile. It has become the only blandness our systems can take. And the more that empty words take the place of things—the more they come not to denote, but to supplant—the more that we must distinguish between "good" words and "bad." Not according to poetic or linguistic standards, but rather according to "moral" standards. As words become the closest we come to things themselves, "good" words are to be the whole of our babblement, while "bad" words are forbidden, criminally punished, expelled from society. No "nigger" presently resides in the white community. To have "family values" is good, but we must ensure that no child is brought into a family through "fucking." Through the advances of modern verbal science, we do not have a single "cripple" or "retard" among us. We do, however, have "challenged" persons. Like "used cars," they were here one day, replaced by "pre-owned vehicles" the next. Challenged by whom? I myself was taught never to pick on them.

When Hitler banned smoking in Nazi Germany in the spring of 1939, it was "bad."

When the late, great mayor of New York banned smoking sixty-four years later, almost to the very day, in the spring of 2003, it was "good."

This is because Hitler was "bad," and the mayor, because he was not Hitler, was "good." And it is because the science behind Hitler's ban—the Institute for Tobacco Hazards Research (Wissenschaftliches Institut zur Erforschung der Tabakgefahren)—was "bad," and the science behind the mayor's ban—the World Health Organization, bastion of the postwar antismoking movement—was "good." It was the World Health Organization that warned us in 1955: "Under the influence of cannabis, the danger of committing unpremeditated murder is very great; it can happen in cold blood, without any reason or motive, unexpectedly, without any preceding quarrel; often the murderer does not even know the victim, and kills simply for pleasure." Surely the World Health Organization must be right, even if the results of its own ten-year study on the effects of what it called ETS (environmental tobacco smoke)—results that were not much publicized—failed to show a connection between secondary smoke and disease. There probably was no proof, either, of the connection between marijuana smoking and murder, but surely none will be so foolhardy as to call it myth. Besides, the World Health Organization was always taking out its United Nations wallet and showing everybody all those sad pictures of starving children. Sad pictures of starving children are "good." We should give them all pictures of steaks. But even then, we must see to it that their health is protected from the dangers of exposure to tertiary smoke, which is what happens when you're around somebody who has been exposed to secondary smoke. And even then, the risk of random homicide at the hands of lurking marijuana smokers must not be discounted. If we protect the starving children from these things—it will cost us only pennies a week—we will be "good." Or we could feed them Power Bars instead of pictures, although this would increase the cost to us by several pennies. Power Bars are "good" because they are *nutritious,* more so even than a picture of a steak. Their main ingredient is fructose syrup. Fructose syrup is "good," because we should eat all the sugar we can. Remember: smoke "bad," sugar "good." And Power Bars were invented by a nice man who was married to a *nutritionist.* And he did not smoke, and she did not blow secondary smoke at him or run up a bag of reefer and dismember him. They were "good." And he got rich selling sugar to people, and that is "good." But now he is dead, and that is "bad." He was only fifty-one years old when he croaked, and that is really "bad." I know junkies a lot older than that. Maybe he did not eat enough Power Bars. Or maybe, a long time ago, he was in a room with an ashtray. To feel sympathy for the nutritionist lady is "good." Now she has enough money to give Power Bars to everybody. We want sugar, lady, we want sugar. Mmm. But maybe croaking at fifty-one is not such good publicity for the healthy way of life. Maybe I should market my Duji Wuji Bars: fructose syrup and heroin. Mmm, mmm, good. I want heroin, lady, I want heroin. It is "bad" to want to place your penis into the mouth of a widow and say, "Here, ma'am, suck on this Power Bar awhile." Even to say it or just to think it would be "bad." Our "freedom" is very precious: If you say dirty things around it, or think nasty thoughts around it, it will die. And that would be "bad." Worse even than when the Power Bar man died. You are "bad"—very "bad"—for reading this. You will surely go to hell when you eat your final Power Bar. And you know what's there, don't you? Yes: environmental smoke. One of our "great men" was a man named Rudolph Giuliani. He did not invent the Power Bar, but still he was "great." When he was the mayor of New York, he brought "quality of life" to New York, and, of course, "quality of life" is "good." He did this by outlawing topless bars, which are "bad." Yes, even as a devout Roman Catholic, he had the "courage" to take a stand against God, who surely had done a very "bad" thing when He let Eve traipse around with those things of hers jiggling around. So the "great man" named Rudolph Giuliani made ladies' titties illegal. He was a "brave" man. He was "challenged," yes—so homely that no good-looking woman would give him a good look—but he "overcame" this "challenge." He did this through "just retribution," by casting titties from the garden of the quality of life. But that is not why he was a "great man." He became a "great" man during a "time of great tragedy," when he put on a baseball cap. And because of this, there were many opportunities to grow rich in positions that never would have been offered him if there had been no "time of great tragedy," for a "time of great tragedy" makes "heroes" of men. And though he was, as "heroes" often are, too humble to say it, we can all be assured that, devout Christian that he was, the late, great Rudolph Giuliani got down on his hands and knees every night before he went to bed and thanked God for the "tragedy" that redeemed, raised, and enriched him. I was in a jail cell one night before the "time of great tragedy." I now can see that God had placed me there, to minister to those whose souls had strayed. I had the matches, and they had none. A jail cell is a "bad" place. Written on the walls are all manner of vile obscenities and grammatical errors. But in this cell, in the heart of New York, there was no obscenity, but only, again and again in myriad colors, sizes, and shapes, the phrases KILL RUDY and DIE RUDY DIE. The poor man was considered to be a disgrace not only to the wops, but to races that could brag that they had never even produced one among them such as he. But when the "time of great tragedy" came, all men cast their writing implements aside as there rose among them a cry of "Hail, Rudy, hail!" Embraced then they the "quality of life." Scorned then they the female breast. Out with those cigarettes! Off with their breasts! It was time to fight for "freedom." Let all men hide the truth of themselves within them, and let all men speak only the "truth."

And then, when the great attorney general of the United States of America stood before the statue known as the Spirit of Justice in the Great Hall of the United States Department of Justice—lo and behold—the Spirit of Justice, which had stood there with one breast exposed since the 1930s, had been draped with blue cloth to cover her shame. And it was good. And then at the Super Bowl, in which the Panthers beat the spread, a fair-skinned Negress teat was exposed, and there was much wrath and wailing and fear of justice and begging for mercy in the land. And it was good. And wasn't it a shame the way those awful wogs made women cover themselves with those babushkas and veils or whatever the hell they called them. I tell you, if I were a gal these days, I would watch out for that Resolute Sword.

Unser Führer Adolf Hitler trinkt keinen Alkohol und raucht auch nicht— "Our führer Adolf Hitler drinks no alcohol and does not smoke"—said the inspirational words beneath the picture in *Auf der Wacht* in 1937. "The passion to regulate down to the final detail of people's lives can lead to infringements of personal liberty," said the words in the Philip Morris Europe, S.A., advertisement, associating smokers with Jews and antismokers with Nazis, in the June 25, 1995, European edition of *Newsweek*. As regards New York's late, great mayor, it was a miscalculated analogy on the part of Philip Morris, which relocated its American headquarters from New York to Richmond in 2003, after being ordered that no smoking was to be allowed in the Philip Morris building at 120 Park Avenue.

Why were Nazi antismoking propaganda and the work of the Nazi Institute for Tobacco Hazards Research excluded from the exhibition "Deadly Medicine," mounted at the United States Holocaust Memorial Museum in Washington, D.C., in the spring of 2004? According to the museum's director, the exhibition, opened by the director of the National Institutes of Health, explored "then-contemporary scientific and pseudoscientific thought." What of the Nazi posters that linked smoking with Jews, Gypsies, and other ethnic undesirables? What of the "scientific" studies that educed smoking as a hazard to Aryan strength and salubrity?

And why do even some Jews embrace the word "holocaust" to describe the mass killings of the Nazi regime? This is a word, from the Greek, that is found in the Septuagint to refer to burnt offerings. The sacrifice demanded by the God of Abraham was holocaust. As George Steiner says eloquently in *Grammars of Creation:* "'Holocaust' is a noble, technical Greek designation for religious sacrifice, not a name proper for controlled insanity and 'the wind out of blackness.'" The right word is Shoah, from the Hebrew, *sho'ah,* "great and catastrophic destruction." This was the word first applied, rightly, to the exterminations under Hitler, as in the 1940 booklet *Sho'at Yehudei Polin.* But history, so often ignorant of truth, is more often ignorant of word as well.

But fuck the Holocaust and fuck the führer and fuck the late, great faggot Nazi kike mayor, and fuck all those that pay lip service to Henry David Thoreau's essay "Resistance to Civil Government," or to their own imagined individuality, while meekly obeying whatever regulations authorities impose. No citizen of the United States in the twenty-first century is fit to utter the slightest criticism of those who remained passive during the rise of Nazism and Fascism. If this seems to be an "extremist" statement, let two things be remembered: that extremes are reached through increment; and that the dead cells of liberty, like the tresses of a corpse, seem to flourish awhile after death. A mayor bans smoking in bars and restaurants. A year later he speaks of banning smoking in homes. Each new increment of repression is for our own welfare, our own protection, our own good. As it said on the cover of the Hitler Youth manual, *Du hast die Pflicht, gesund zu sein!*—"You have the duty to be healthy." We must not have "racial profiling." But we must know what books you've been reading. It's all done quite properly, under—but what else?—the Patriot Act. You see, not all books are pablum for the maw of mediocrity. There are these other books, and some of them have these *words,* and sometimes these words are "bad" words, not at all good for you, and sometimes we don't even understand the words—the men, good clean college men, who write the words that come out of our mouths don't even understand some of the words—and that can be a dangerous thing. Is that a sneeze we hear? Yes, that is another bad thing about these musty, dusty old books and their musty, dusty old pages: They can make you sneeze. *Gesundheit*. To your health!

Islam is more honest in its prohibition of killing. Innocent souls must not be taken. Of the first four caliphs who succeeded the prophet Muhammad in the seventh century, three of them were murdered while at prayer. Two of these were killed in mosques: Umar, the second caliph, at the Medina mosque in 644; Ali, the fourth caliph, at the Kufa mosque in 661. Hussein, the grandson of Muhammad, was murdered in Karbala in 680. His killers were soldiers of the caliphate of the Umayyad dynasty, named for Umayya, ancestor of Muhammad.

And who is innocent? He who is killed, for he who is killed is raised to innocence. On one morning a man may sit detestable and detested in an office, with the *baalim* of greed, fraud, and larceny as his only gods. On the next morning, the wrath of Allah may descend on him in flames. Suddenly he becomes an "innocent," a martyr. Again, the great lesson of Christianity. They love you when you're dead. No one is innocent.

Cross, crescent, six-pointed star. They became weapons in the sash of Enyalion.

It is good to kill those who transgress against us. It is beatific, as the Ch'an masters tell us, to kill a god. Deicide, most fair and freeing. As has been written:

> *Fuck the Semite triad, and fuck all the sons of Shem.*
>
> *May the unclean hook-nosed God of the Jews kneel with open mouth before Allah.*
>
> *May vile hook-nosed Allah kneel with open mouth before Jesus.*
>
> *May hook-nosed God, Allah, and Jesus kneel with open mouth before we who have made them.*
>
> *The Levant—Jerusalem—the cradle of the Beast of all evil; the "holy city" of the three monotheisms.*
>
> *Fuck these three Jerusalem cats, fuck the dirt of all Jerusalem.*
>
> *May the true and sacred gods blow them and defiled Jerusalem from the face of this damned and dying earth.*

I THINK I NEED to go back to the doctor. No, not him. The other one. It's like with Anthony. The same thing. First the teeth, then the brain. I can feel it.

B UT WHERE WAS I going with this? Moses, perhaps. Yes, his name was Moshe, likely from the Egyptian nominal suffix. Thomas Mann tells it well, in *The Tables of the Law:* "In the end they gave him a half-Egyptian name, or rather half of an Egyptian name. For the sons of the land were often named Ptah-mose, Amen-mose, Ra-mose: in other words, sons of those gods. Amram and Jochebed preferred to leave out the god-name and simply called the boy Mose."

Or perhaps it was Jochebed, his mother, who was both his father's aunt and his own aunt as well. We are told this in Exodus. But then was written Leviticus, which forbade carnal knowledge between a man and his uncle's wife. Thereafter, in all translations of the Bible, Jochebed was rendered instead the cousin of her wife and son.

To think that people swear on this book—that they have been doing so ever since pre-Norman law—in oath of their truthfulness.

But, no, it was not Moishe or his mother. It was his brother. Yes, his brother. It was all of them: Moishe and Moishe's brother and their God and another Jew who came much later. Yes, that was where I was going with this.

Albert Einstein said, "I cannot believe that God plays dice with the cosmos."

But according to Exodus, dice were indeed the means through which the divine will was revealed. These dice had strange names: Urim and Thummim. Appointing Aaron, elder brother of Moses, to serve as high priest, God instructs Moses to fashion a breastplate: "And thou shalt put in the breastplate the Urim and Thummim; and they shall be upon Aaron's heart." In casting the Urim and Thummim, the will and ways of God would be known.

God crapped out. After being anointed priest, Aaron turned away from him and made the vile golden calf. It was the image of Marduk, the ancient Babylonian god, the bull-calf of the golden son.

S T. AUGUSTINE SAID it late in the fourth century, as Rome lay dying and magic fell to religion. All of Judeo-Christian theology can be set beneath kindling wood, save for these few words: *Si comprehendis non est Deus*—"If you can comprehend it, it is not God."

—◦❧❦◦—

T HALES SAID it better, and long before, in the sixth century B.C. *Παντα πληρη θεων ειναι*—"All things are full of gods."

Nurse Love

—◦❦◦—

ONCE UPON A TIME, when New York City lived and breathed, there was a man marked for death, like us all.

His name was Arnold Rothstein, and he himself was the only God he worshipped, and he was a great and sinful man.

I am not here to make elegy for that city that lived and breathed, am not here to make praise-song of this man. What's dead is dead. I am here—like him, like us all—to make a buck. So let the tale begin, for I feel again an itch to buy my wearied, fleeting freedom from this lost and fallen place.

You sleep with one who has no name and steals your breath. You look at the pulse of your wrist and await. You bear a message for one who is dead. You gather up the small pieces of what used to be.

Did I ever tell you about the night I spent with the human ashtray who was allergic to smoke? Did I ever tell you about the time I stole back my soul with dark and labored breath? The time I stared into the sea and waited? The time there was nothing but rain where the dawn once had slept with a smile on her face? The time I figured it all out, then forgot it? The time I dreamt of you? Well, one of these days, maybe; one of these days.

I T WAS SAID in the twentieth century that Arnold Rothstein's grandfather "had fled the pogroms of his native Bessarabia." In the twenty-
first century, after more extensive research, it was said that Arnold
Rothstein's grandfather "had fled the pogroms of" his "native Russian-
ruled Bessarabia."

This sort of statement, assumptive rather than factual, derives from the
enduring misconception that Jews, unlike other people, never simply
moved—they only fled from pogroms. But Jews, one of the great nomadic
and migratory peoples of history, had traveled the trade routes to China
long before Marco Polo. To be sure, the Jews were expelled from some of
the countries to which they had moved—from England in the thirteenth
century, from France in the fourteenth century—but they were perfectly
capable of locomotion. They even wrote the hit song of that name.

In his essay "Demythologizing the Shtetl," Joshua Rothenberg, a historian of Russian Jewry, wrote: "It is both perplexing and ironic to find so
many clichés about Eastern European Jewry, the 'world of our forefathers,' frozen in so much contemporary writing."

Speaking of the great waves of Eastern European immigration to the
United States that began in 1880, Rothenberg confronts the popular
folklore:

"One commonly finds a sentence like this in many books or articles:
'Jews came to the shores of this country from the ghettos of the shtetlekh
as a result of the pogroms.' Each phrase in this sentence is untrue or over-
simplified to the point of untruth. There were no ghettos in 19th-century
Eastern Europe (except in a metaphorical sense, like the old Lower East
Side of New York). By no means had all Jews come to the U.S. from
shtetlekh; many came from large towns like Warsaw, Lodz, Odessa. And
the pogroms were not the principal reason for emigration: proportionately

more Jews came to the U.S. from Austrian-ruled Galicia—where there were no pogroms—than from Tsarist Russia."

The shtetlach were the Jewish hamlets that lay outside the predominantly Christian villages. The word "shtetl" is Judeo-German—Yiddish, from the German *jüdisch,* "Jewish," as in *jüdisch-deutsch,* "Jewish German." It means "little town," after the German *Stadt,* "town." The word for village, *dorf* in Yiddish, is the same as the German *Dorf*.

Every shtetl or group of shtetlach had its intermediary merchants and representatives, known in Yiddish as *dorf-geher,* "village-goers." The Jewish populations of the shtetlach and *Dörfer* were of such a size as to allow most of the Jews within a local area to know most other Jews within that area.

Rothenberg explains that Central and Eastern European Jews—the Ashkenazim, as distinguished from the Western European Jews, the Sephardim of Spain and Portugal—clearly discerned the difference not only between a *dorf* and a shtetl, but also between a shtetl and a *shtot* (large town, city) and between the ways of life and the social relationships in each of them.

"The contrast between shtetl and shtot is reflected in the respective Yiddish adjectives *kleinshtetldik* (small-townish, provincial) and *groisshtotish* (large-townish, cosmopolitan). When people living in Warsaw or Odessa were characterized as *kleinshtetldik,* everyone understood what attitudes were meant."

Bessarabia, the Black Sea region between the rivers Prut and Dniester, had been a part of Moldavia. Acquired by Russia from the Ottoman Empire in 1812, it became in 1818 an oblast and later a province, within the Pale of Settlement, the western territory of specified provinces and districts in which Jews were commonly required to reside from the late eighteenth century until the Bolshevik revolution of 1917. By 1820, the Pale of Settlement comprised all lands east of the German and Austro-Hungarian empires: Byelorussia (Belorussia, Belarus—all attempts to transliterate a Russian word that meant "White Russia"), Lithuania, Novorussiya (New Russia), Poland, and Ukraine, as well as Bessarabia.

Empress Catherine II, who ascended the throne in 1762, was not impressed with the productivity of the Russian serf system. She had begun life as a German princess, and she wanted German farmers to come to Russia to work her land. In the first year of her reign, in a proclamation circulated throughout Germany, she welcomed "all foreigners to come into Our Empire." Her decree promised much to new settlers: freedom of religion, freedom from taxes for a period of from five to thirty years, freedom from military service, and parcels of free land.

At this time many Germans still suffered from the effects of the Seven Years' War, which had been fought largely on German soil and had ended only months before Catherine's proclamation of 1763. Russia had been an ally in that war against Frederick II of Prussia. The war had laid waste to much of Germany. Land shortages and famines were widespread. Princely rule had grown ever more oppressive. Freedom of religion was restricted: The law of *Cuius regio, eius religio,* established at the Peace of Augsburg in 1555, authorized each prince to impose on his subjects the Christian sect of his choice.

By the end of 1767 German settlers, coming primarily from central Germany, had organized more than one hundred colonies along the Volga River. Extensive German settlements of a second area in Russia, the Black Sea region, began in 1803 when Czar Alexander I, a grandson of Catherine II, issued a similar decree enticing foreigners to settle in south Russia, the region that in 1812 came to include Bessarabia.

Settlers from the southwestern German duchy of Württemberg—from 1806, the German kingdom of Württemberg—were among the first to arrive in Russia, as early as 1763. One of their colonies was settled near the Dnieper in 1780. In the periods 1814–1816 and 1821–1834, immigrants from Württemberg settled mainly in Bessarabia.

The river Danube, the Donau of the Germans, is the second-longest river in Europe, after the Volga, which begins and ends in Russia; and is the only major European river to flow from west to east. The Danube has its source in the Schwarzwald, the Black Forest, which lies in Württemberg and empties after 2,850 kilometers (1,770 miles) into the Black Sea, the Schwarzes Meer, at what was, in the early nineteenth century, the southernmost part of Bessarabia. One of the tributaries of the Danube is the Prut, which rises in the Carpathian Mountains in Ukraine and flows into the Danube near the southern Bessarabian port town of Reni. The Danube long had been an important route between Western Europe and the Black Sea. Caesar knew it as Danuvius; and by the third century, it served as the northern boundary of the Roman Empire in southeastern Europe.

The melancholy beauty of the Danube worked its magic on painters, poets, composers. The *Donaulandschaft bei Regensburg mit dem Scheuchenberg,* a view of the Danube valley by Albrecht Altdorfer (ca. 1480–1538), is considered to be the first landscape painting in Western art.

The majestic and haunting Danube valley inspired the eighteenth-century German poet Friedrich Hölderlin (1770–1843) to beatific madness in his symphonic poem of 1801, "Am Quell der Donau."

This title, "Am Quell der Donau," is translated as "At the Source of the Danube." But to a soul as receptive and a mind as brilliant as Hölderlin's, the noun *Quell,* meaning "source," was rich in evocation, summoning forth not only the *Urquell,* the primal fountainhead, and the strong German verb *quellen,* "to spring from," "to well up," and "to gush," but also the umbrous ancestral resonance of the Old High German *quellen,* meaning "to torture" and "to kill," from the same Teutonic root that brought the words "kill" and "quell" to the English language, in which a "quell," from Shakespeare to Keats, was a slaying or a slaughter and also, in the nineteenth century, a beneficent wellspring, as in Mary Clairmonte's "quell of living water out of which he drew fresh strength." In Hölderlin's poem, these indwellings—the rising and flowing of inspiration from its chthonic source; the dangerous baptism in, and the maddening surrender to, those ungraspable waters of poiesis; the life-giving renewal of having done, of having gushed forth the light of the soul—are all given breath in Hölderlin's simple noun, which he has chosen the Danube to possess.

Hölderlin was born in Württemberg. He was a friend of Hegel's and was Nietzsche's favorite poet.

Johann Strauss's opus 314, "An der schönen blauen Donau," known to us as "The Blue Danube," would remain forever in the breezy air after its first performance, in Vienna, on February 13, 1867.

No one saw beauty in the lower Danube, the desolate region east of where it met the river Prut. The Danube delta was a forsaken wasteland of marsh and swamp. In the seventeenth century, fugitive Cossacks had escaped to the low alluvial islands of the delta, where they had constructed hovels of refuge, elevated by bough and rough-hewn beam, to protect them from tide and storm and flood. In the early nineteenth century, the worn and jagged remnants of these dwellings haunted dead and dying trees.

The Romans often distinguished the lower Danube from the rest of the river, calling it Ister, from a Greek word for the Danube used by Hesiod in the eighth century B.C., long before the Greeks knew of the river's grand full course. The primitive, warlike tribes of Thrace had a colony in the lower Danube region, and the name Ister is of Thracian origin. The name Danuvius is believed by some to be derived from the Thracians as well. Others discern a Celtic origin.

Hölderlin found something in the Danube estuary of the Schwarzmeerküste, but it was not beauty. The hymn known as "Der Ister," which was left untitled by Hölderlin, ends: "The upward / glance spans the between of sky and earth. This / between is measured out for the dwelling of man." In this "between" of death-in-breath, Heidegger found "the 'no-more' of gods who have fled and the 'not-yet' of the gods to come."

It was to the port of Reni in the Danube delta that the German settlers of Bessarabia were delivered after the long voyage down the blue Danube.

Some of them carried Russian passport documents, worded in German, obtained in Frankfurt, where the coronation route of the Holy Roman emperors led to the Danube. Some carried nothing. One way or the other they came to Reni; and from there they traveled north.

Summers in Bessarabia were cool, with daytime temperatures of about twenty-two degrees Celsius, or about seventy-two degrees Fahrenheit. Winters were cold, with temperatures in the sun of about minus three degrees Celsius, or about twenty-seven degrees Fahrenheit. There was not much rain, not much snow: about three hundred millimeters, or twelve inches, a year.

And the wine was good.

Most of the Württemberg settlers, like most of the German settlers overall, were Catholics or Lutherans. The Pale of Settlement was not a distinctly Jewish place. In this territory of approximately a million square kilometers, or 386,370 square miles—more than twice the size of Germany—Jews constituted little more than 10 percent of the population.

Nor was Jewish settlement beyond the Pale unknown. Kharkov, Moscow, St. Petersburg, and other Russian cities where Jews officially were "forbidden" to reside had considerable Jewish populations. In fact, almost 20 percent of the Jews in nineteenth-century Russia lived beyond the Pale. In St. Petersburg alone, the Jewish community in time would number more than twenty thousand. In Kharkov, almost fifteen thousand. In Moscow, ten thousand.

There were sixteen Jewish colonies in Bessarabia. Nine of these were in the Sorok district, north of the Bessarabian capital of Kishinev, near the river Dniester. There were two in the Orgeev district, also north of Kishinev, and two in the district of Belz, northwest of Kishinev. There was a colony in the far northern district of Khotin, another in Bender, to the southwest of Kishinev, also near the Dniester, and another in Kishinev itself. By the mid–nineteenth century, an estimated ten thousand Jews were living in the Bessarabian colonies—a figure that would increase more than twentyfold in the decades to come.

These Jews encountered others of their faith who had settled in the Bessarabian region long before, in the sixteenth century, when it was a part of the Islamic Empire of Suleiman the Magnificent. As was usually true before the early twentieth century, Jews and Christians alike were accepted with greater tolerance by Muslims than they were by one another.

A man named Yoshue Rotshtejn was born in Bessarabia sometime around 1820. According to one document, he was born in 1817 or 1818. Another document fixes the year at 1820. Yet another infers 1822. Other evidence presents the possibility that he may have been born in the southeastern German lands, in the predominantly Catholic kingdom of Bavaria, bounded on the west by Württemberg, and that he came in childhood to Russia with his family.

The place of his birth remains unknown. To be sure, to say that he was born in Bessarabia is to speak without proof, or even without intuition, in any true sense of the word. A lie repeated often enough becomes the truth. I want to believe that I am not in neglect of this theorem, this profound underground fissure on which all history precariously rests. I want to believe that I am not abandoning myself to the accepted, baseless repetitions of the lesser louts who have preceded me with their talk of pogroms and flight. I want to believe that I have discovered a suggestion of substance in the movements of the Bessarabia-bound shadows from Württemberg. But I cannot with honesty say that I do believe these things. What I can say with honesty is that my research in Russia and in Germany has brought me nothing but the worsening of my eyesight and the waste of years of my life. And I did it all for you.

The name of Yoshue—corrupted to Joshua in English—was a good biblical name, the name of the prophet who was chosen by God to succeed Moses.

The name of Rotshtejn was the Judeo-German form of a patronym welded from strong and ancient Germanic elements: *rot,* meaning "red," and *Stein,* meaning "stone."

He saw and survived the cholera plague, the wave of death that swept through Russia in the winter months before the feast of unleavened bread, passing on through Europe and across the Atlantic, where it appeared in New York City in June 1832, brought by stricken ships from England. Cholera had never before come to North America or the Western Hemisphere.

The year of the plague was followed in Russia by the Black Year of 1833: a year without rain and without crops, and thus a year of famine.

Like other boys in Europe, he worked twelve or more hours a day. The Factory Act of 1833 in Britain required laborers to be at least nine years of age. It would not be until 1871 that Prussia passed laws on child labor, limiting the legal workday for children to twelve hours. It was in Prussia, in the Silesian linen industry, that children as young as four years of age were employed. None of these laws was welcomed by working families, who ignored them. Long hours meant more money. Legislation in England, as elsewhere, failed. Six-day, ninety-hour workweeks brought families the only hope of freedom open to them, and they clung to the right to choose their own hours of work. Government dictates in the name of social reform took food from the table and coins from the purse of dreams. No ruler would ever understand work or those whose lot it was to reap the meager grist of their lives through toil.

By the time he reached manhood, Yoshue almost surely earned his wages as a *kapelyushnik,* a cap maker, one of the traditional German trades—*Kappenmacher*—that had been taken up by Jews throughout medieval Europe.

Lev Davidovich Bronstein—Braunshtejn, from the German for "brown" and "stone"—was the son of a successful Jewish farmer in the Pale of Settlement later in the nineteenth century. In his autobiography, written long after he had taken the name Leon Trotsky, he recalled the local *kapelyushnik* of his youth:

> *My uncle's house was almost at the entrance to the colony. At the opposite end lived a tall, dark, thin Jew who had the name of being a horse-thief and of carrying on unsavory deals. He had a daughter—she too had a dubious reputation. Not far from the horse-thief lived the cap-maker, stitching away on his machine—a young Jew with a fiery red beard. The wife of the cap-maker would come to the official inspector of the colony, who always stayed at the house of Uncle Abram, to complain against the daughter of the horse-thief for stealing her husband. Apparently the inspector offered no aid. Returning from school one day, I saw a mob dragging a young woman, the daughter of the horse-thief, through the street. The mob was shouting, screaming, and spitting at her. This biblical scene was engraved on my memory forever.*

In some places, young men who were bashful or feared rejection went to the local *shadchan* and described the woman, either known or unknown to them, that they should like to marry. If successful, the matchmaker would take a percentage of the bride's dowry. This arrangement would inspire the matchmaker to find a girl who was well endowed, in the original sense of that word as well as in other desired attributes. The matchmaker, taking note of the young man's own attributes—age, appearance, money-making ability—would approach the chosen woman or go among the young women of his acquaintance and find one who was willing to wed on the terms the matchmaker offered. The matchmaker was paid when the dowry was established and the engagement was announced. If a girl was exceptionally pretty, or if her family had given her a large marriage portion—certainly if both were true—further negotiations between the matchmaker and his client would be in order.

In 1843 or 1845, Yoshue married a woman named Royze Malke. These are first and middle given names. Royze is Yiddish for the German *Rose,* from the Latin *rosa.* The names Rose and Rosa long had been used by German Christians. When Royze appears as Rose or Rosa in Germany, it is the result of scribes substituting these older and more familiar Christian forms.

Malke is a postbiblical name derived from *malkah,* the Hebrew word for "queen." It appears in Cyrillic as Malka in nineteenth-century Russia; as Malke, Malka, Malche, Melke, and other shapes in Germany. This variety of spellings is largely the result, through the centuries, of the transcription of a Hebrew name into a German form, made more problematic by the fact that Hebrew variations of the name also appear.

These difficulties with Royze Malke's name would worsen. Her first name would appear in documents always as Rosa or Rose, while her middle name would appear as Malke, Mahlke, and Mahlkah, the latter fluctuations having no known historical precedents. In one document, her middle name is said to be Aurelia—the feminine form of the Latin word for "golden"—unknown as a Jewish name in the nineteenth century or earlier.

Royze Malke's maiden family name alternates between Goldstein and Pearlstein. The first of these surnames, from the Yiddish Gol'denshtejn, or its derivatives Gol'dshtejn or Goldshshtejn, is the Jewish form of the enduring German patronym Goldenstein, or Goldstein, from the Old High German words *Gold* or "golden," and *Stein,* "stone." The less common name of Pearlstein, from the Yiddish Perel'shtejn, or its variants Perl'shtejn or Perlshtejn, is again the Jewish form of a German name—Perlestein, Perelstein, Perlstein—from the words *Perle,* "pearl," and *Stein,* "stone." Of these names, Gol'denshtejn is found with frequency among the families of the Kishinev area of Bessarabia.

All of these names—Rotshtejn, Goldshshtejn, Perlshtejn—were borne by Jewish families in Russia. But they were carved, long before, from the rock of the German language. In the forms by which we have come to know them—their old, original forms, save for the Anglicizing of *Perle:* Rothstein, Goldstein, Pearlstein—they are German names, not Jewish names.

Royze may have been older than Yoshue. The possible years of her birth educed from available documents are 1811, 1817, and 1818. But the earliest of these seems unlikely. Examining the divergent evidence in light of what little is known of the common ages of marriage and childbearing in this period, one may approximate that Yoshue and Royze Malke Rotshtejn both had been born late in 1818 and that they were both about twenty-six years old when they were married, in early 1845.

In that western Russian spring, when the rabbi made of them man and wife, the dowry that Royze brought to the marriage would be revealed, as would be the beauty of her dress, which was her mother's marriage dress before her. Yoshue would place a ring of gold on her finger, and the marriage contract would be read aloud, that all might hear the price of Yoshue's indemnity to his bride should he seek divorce. Under the wedding canopy of a prayer shawl hung from four poles, he and his bride would drink wine from the same glass, and he would shatter that valuable glass underfoot. The rabbi's invocation in Hebrew of the *sheva b'rachot,* the seven blessings of the Babylonian Talmud, would cast them as the givers of new life in the granted, fleeting Eden-light of God, who had brought the wretchedness of life and death upon them in punishment for the sin of their forebears, Adam and Hawwa, to whom Eden everlasting was given, and who from Eden by their iniquity were driven.

Blessed art thou, Lord our God, King of the universe, creator of the fruit of the grapevine.

Blessed art thou, Lord our God, King of the universe, who created all things for his glory.

Blessed art thou, Lord our God, King of the universe, who created humanity.

Blessed art thou, Lord our God, King of the universe, who created man in his image, in the image set forth by his plan, and who prepared from himself a structure to last for all time. Blessed art thou, Lord our God, creator of humanity.

May the barrenness rejoice and be glad when its children are gathered back to it in joy. Blessed art thou, Lord our God, who makes Zion rejoice in her children.

May you grant great joy to these dearly beloved, just as you granted happiness to the work of your hands long ago in the Garden of Eden. Blessed art thou, Lord our God, who grants joy to the bridegroom and bride.

Blessed art thou, Lord our God, King of the universe, who created happiness and joy, bridegroom and bride, rejoicing in song, delight and cheer, love and harmony, peace and fellowship. Soon, O Lord our God, may there be heard in the cities of Judah and in the streets of Jerusalem, a sound of gladness, a sound of joy, a sound of the bridegroom and sound of the bride, the sound of rejoicing from bridegrooms at their weddings, and young people at their feasts of song. Blessed are you, O God, who grants joy to the bridegroom with the bride.

That the young people at their feasts of song might one day include a new king, a king of vice and corruption, there was no way of knowing.

A daughter was born to Royze and Yoshue in 1846. They gave her a name that was rare among Jewish families: Yulia. It was a name whose Hebrew characters were pronounced the same as the German name Julia, which came from the feminine Latin septal name of Iulia, also pronounced the same. The name was common among not only Christians in Germany, but Christians in Russia as well. In German, the affectionate form, as might be used with a newborn babe or little girl, is Julchen.

The new family survived the next wave of cholera, which ravaged Russia and Germany in early 1848.

Royze and Yoshue had chosen to give their daughter a beautiful name. But it was a name that was more Christian, more evocative of the European mainstream, than it was Jewish. To their son, who was born either in October 1849 or on April 1, 1850, they seem to have given an unusual name as well. Ludvik, a name not wholly unknown among Jews of Eastern Europe, was a form of Ludwig. It was originally a Frankish name, borne by Chlodwig (456–511), better known as Clovis I, the founder of the Merovingian dynasty. Its elements meant "celebrated in war." Under his long reign, the name had taken Latin aspects: Chlodovicus, Hludovicus. From Hludovicus came the Germanic name Hludwig, and from Hludwig came Ludwig. It was a name common among Christians, rare among Jews.

Things had changed since the days of the early German settlers. The horse-drawn railways belonged to the past. There were steam engine trains now and ever increasing lengths of railroad. In a spring day in 1837, a hundred and more people in the province of Saxony had boarded a train in Leipzig and traveled to the nearby town of Althen. The journey was scarcely more than nine kilometers—fewer than six miles—and the price of even a third-class ticket, four groschen, was the better part of what was left of a workingman's weekly wages after he had paid his state, communal, and seignorial dues. But within two years, the train route was extended all the way to Dresden. By midcentury, there were six thousand kilometers (more than four thousand miles) of wrought-iron rails in Germany: a rapidly growing system that was the heart of all European travel and commerce. One now could go from Kehl am Rhein, near Württemberg, to Paris-sur-Seine in a morning's time, moving at almost a hundred kilometers (more than sixty miles) an hour.

And there were steam engine ships as well. The first of these had crossed the Atlantic sea when Yoshue was a child. It took that wooden ship forty days and more, under steam and sail, to voyage from England to America—longer than it had taken Christoph Kolumbus to reach the New World from Spain on his second voyage, in 1493. The American men who owned that steamship later sent it to St. Petersburg in the hope that Czar Nicholas might buy it. But he would have nothing to do with it, and it ended its days sailing up and down the Atlantic coast of America with its engine removed. The British, however, now had a new sort of steamship, built of thousands of tons of iron, with a big screw propeller that could power it across the Atlantic in little more than ten days' time. Soon after Yoshue's marriage, ships like this had come to set forth from Hamburg under German flag.

And what, since man first set bark on rushing waters, had belonged to the realm of madness—the idea of sailing *up*river—now belonged to the realm of reality. Paddlewheel steamboats traveled *up* the Danube every day.

Only God knew what was to be. But on certain nights, when work was done, a man could see it, the mystery of it, in the gleam of soft-glowing candle or oil lamp.

I T WAS Arnold Rothstein's last day. Arnold Rothstein understood this. What he did not understand was all that had come before this day.

The late autumn sun descended beyond the western river, casting shadows on him.

—o❧❦o—

Nᴇᴡ ʏᴏʀᴋ ᴄᴏᴜɴᴛʏ ꜱᴜʀʀᴏɢᴀᴛᴇ's ᴄᴏᴜʀᴛ, 31 Chambers Street. December 17, 1928. Examination by Mr. Daniel F. Madigan, Esq., attorney for Mr. Maurice F. Cantor, Esq., one of the executors, legatees, and proponents of the will.

What is your name?
    —Elizabeth F. Love.
Where do you live?
    —Hotel Grenoble, New York.
Miss Love, I show you a paper which purports to be the last will and testament of Arnold Rothstein, dated November 5, 1928, and ask if that is your signature.
    —It is.
Did you sign your name as you admitted on the fifth day of November, 1928, to this paper?
    —I did.
Where was this paper signed by you?
    —In the Polyclinic Hospital, on the eighth floor, room F; in Mr. Rothstein's room.
Who was present at the time you signed?
    —Miss Goerdel, the other nurse, and myself and Mr. Cantor.
And the deceased?
    —Yes. He was in bed, naturally.
I show you page nine of this paper that you identified and ask you, did you see Arnold Rothstein make that mark on the paper before you signed your name?
    —Mr. Cantor put the pen in Arnold Rothstein's left hand, and it just remained there very languid, the hand did, and Mr. Cantor got hold of the hand and made that mark.

And when Mr. Cantor entered the room did he have any conversation with you as soon as he entered the room?

—No.

When he entered the room did he stand on the left side of the patient's bed or the right side?

—The left side.

And immediately alongside of the left side of that bed as the patient was lying in bed, was there a small table there?

—Yes.

Between the bed and the windows?

—Yes.

And did you hear Mr. Cantor say, "Arnold, I have your will"?

—Yes.

And did he have any other conversation with the patient of that kind, other than saying, "I have your will"?

—Yes.

What was the other conversation?

—"I am a little late in getting here, but I put in the things you told me to this morning."

What else?

—He said, "Arnold, you know this is your will."

After that mark was made, as you stated, by Mr. Cantor holding Mr. Rothstein's hand, what else was done there at the time?

[Objection raised by Mr. Isidor Gainsburg, Esq., attorney for contestants to the will. Discussion off the record. Mr. Madigan resumes:]

What do you mean by "wiggled his hand"?

—Shook it like this and made the mark.

Is that the mark he made?

—Yes, he made this wiggly mark here.

What did Arnold Rothstein do?

—He didn't do anything.

Did Mr. Cantor say anything to you at the time?

—Well, he told us not to tell what went on in the sickroom.

About the will?

[Mr. Gainsburg interjects: "Don't answer."]

Did you know it was a will?

[Mr. Gainsburg interjects: "Objected to."]

Did Mr. Cantor say that this was the last will and testament of Arnold Rothstein when he asked you to sign it?

—He told the patient, "This is your will, Arnold, this is your will, you know this is your will."

Were the patient's eyes open at the time?

—No.

And you say after that Mr. Rothstein repeated the word "will"?

—He said, "Will."

When he said "Will," did he nod his head or do any overt act?

—No. He just said in a weak voice, "Will."

Did he have his eyes opened then?

—He opened his eyes a little, but he slept most of the time he was there.

Did he look at you?

—No.

In your opinion, was Arnold Rothstein at the time of making this will of sound mind?

—He was irrational most of the time.

How about the rest of the time?

—He seldom ever spoke any word that was any sense to it at all.

How long was he at the hospital?

—Well, I was with him November fifth, and he died on Tuesday morning the sixth, at fifteen minutes after ten.

This will was executed at what time?

—I should say between two and three; sometime in the afternoon between two-thirty and three-thirty.

[Mr. I. Gainsburg, Esq., attorney for contestants to the will, assumes examination of the witness:]

You have been asked a number of questions by the attorney for Maurice F. Cantor, a lawyer and the gentleman who was in Mr. Arnold Rothstein's room and brought this paper that you have been shown, and also by Mr.

Brown, who is also a lawyer and who appears for another Mr. Brown,
whose name is mentioned in the will, and you were asked about the
circumstances in connection with the signing of your name on that paper.
They are offering the will. You, however, have been served with an order
signed by Surrogate O'Brien requesting you to appear as a witness on
behalf of the contestants of the will. You know that, don't you?

—Yes.

What did you say to Mr. Cantor when he asked you to sign that paper?

—I told him the patient was in no condition to sign a will; that he
was irrational most of the time.

And what did Mr. Cantor say to you then?

—He didn't say much at all. He was very nervous and his hands
were shaking.

And what, if anything, did you say to Mr. Cantor after that, before you
actually did sign the paper?

—Well, I told him the patient was very weak and that if I had to
sign the paper, I would sign it in order to get him out of the room.

Were you in attendance on the patient from seven o'clock in the morning
until this hour?

—I was on from seven o'clock in the morning until seven o'clock
in the evening.

That day, Mr. Rothstein had had a blood transfusion?

—At two o'clock.

Would you say how long before Mr. Cantor came in the room did he,
Arnold Rothstein, have this blood transfusion?

—About a half hour, I should say.

Before he had this blood transfusion, had you noticed the condition of his
pulse?

—Yes. It was very weak and very rapid.

And you have been a nurse for how long?

—Eleven years.

He had, to your knowledge, did he not, an operation the evening before?

—He was operated on during the night. On Sunday morning, I
believe, some time after he came in Sunday morning.

Now how was the door? As you came into the room, was Mr. Rothstein facing the door or was his side to the door?

—The bed faced the Hudson River. There were four windows in the room, two facing Fiftieth Street and two the Hudson River.

And his hand remained on the bed?

—Yes. Mr. Cantor put the paper on the bed under his hand.

And then did he lift the hand up?

—Yes.

And then he put the pen in the left hand and it remained stationary with the pen in his hand on that paper?

—Yes.

Now what then did Mr. Cantor do?

—He took hold of the hand and wiggled the hand. With the pen, he made the little mark on the paper.

When Mr. Cantor left the room, was the paper with him?

—Yes. He put the paper in his pocket and left the room.

[Reexamination by Mr. A. H. Brown, Esq., attorney for Mr. Samuel Brown, one of the executors and proponents of the will:]

Were any of Mr. Arnold Rothstein's relatives permitted into the sickroom to see him that morning, the morning of the fifth?

—Yes. His mother was there, and two brothers, I think, were there. Two brothers and his wife were shown in.

Did they speak to him?

—He slept most of the time.

Did Arnold Rothstein speak at all from seven o'clock in the morning of the fifth of November, outside of uttering that one word, "will"?

—He rambled about different things, but we didn't know what he was talking about.

STEAMBOATS UP the Danube, railway steam wagons to Hamburg, steamships across the great Atlantic sea. These things, once unimaginable but now real, nonetheless involved sums that were still unimaginable to a workingman of meager means. But as the old people said: *Wo ein Wille ist, ist auch ein Weg*—"Where there is a will, there is also a way."

Relations between Russia and America were good. Seventy years ago, during the American Revolution, Catherine the Great, in 1780, had issued a Declaration of Armed Neutrality, which gave notice to Great Britain that Russia stood ready to fight on the American side. In the years following the Revolution, Russia had became an important part of American trade. The biggest and best of American ships, laden with cotton, tobacco, sugar, coffee, and other goods, sailed with increasing frequency from the ports of the American eastern coast and West Indies to the northern Russian port of Kronstadt, near St. Petersburg. By 1830, when Yoshue was a boy, American ships had even appeared at Odessa and other Black Sea anchorages. The Russian-American Commercial Treaty, ratified by the Senate in March 1833—the year that in Russia would become the Black Year of famine—formalized the alliance between the two nations. The Russian navy's great steam frigate *Kamchatka* was built under contract in America and launched from Jersey City in the fall of 1840. An American engineer was brought to Russia to supervise the construction of the railway system between St. Petersburg and Moscow, begun in 1842 and completed in 1851.

Russians had come to North America in the eighteenth century and perhaps earlier. Vitus Bering, a Russian mariner who had been born in Denmark, was one of many seaman sent out by Russia to explore the regions beyond Siberia. It was hoped that nearby lands might be found to provide new sources for the Siberian fur industry. On his second expedition, Bering had mapped the Alaskan coast, which was separated from northeasternmost Siberia by the strait that would come to bear his name.

By the late eighteenth century, Russian fur trappers had established a permanent settlement on Kodiak island; and by the turn of the century, the Russian-American Fur Company, a trapping and trading firm whose primary shareholders were members of the czarist family, supported a number of outposts in Alaska. The company's ships began to travel farther south along the Pacific coast—sometimes as far as the Baja California peninsula of Mexico—in search of seal, sea lion, and sea otter pelts.

In 1812, twenty-five Russians and eighty Aleuts established a fortified settlement on the California coast north of the mission town of San Francisco. The settlement, which came to be known as Fort Ross, was named for the motherland, Rossiya. The settlers grew food for the Alaskan outposts, hunted seal and sea otter along the California coast, and conducted trade with the native Californians.

The agriculture of Fort Ross was insufficient, and the Russian-American Fur Company was forced to contract with the Hudson's Bay Company of Great Britain to supply its Alaskan settlements. And the sea otter were fast vanishing due to rapacious hunting. Furthermore, company officials felt that the westward movement of Americans would soon reach the California territory. In 1841—five years before America did indeed take possession of California—Fort Ross was sold to a German-born Mexican named John Sutter. (It was during the construction in 1848 of a sawmill on Sutter's land near the Sacramento River that the discovery of gold would lead to the biggest gold rush in American history.)

With the sale of Fort Ross, the Russians withdrew to Alaska and never returned. So it was that through the mid–nineteenth century few Americans had ever seen a Russian, and few Russians had ever seen an American.

Exceptions were notable. Baron Gustavus Heinrich Wetter von Rosenthal, a German-born subject of Russia who had killed a fellow nobleman in St. Petersburg and escaped to America, had distinguished himself in the Continental army during the Revolution. John Quincy Adams had been a respected figure in Russia during his four years of diplomacy there, from 1809 to 1813. And later there was Senator Arthur Bagby of Alabama, who was appointed minister to the Russian court in reward for his support of the Polk administration. Bagby was a figure of a different sort:

"Preceded by a substantial consignment of diplomatic liquor, he arrived in August 1848 in an alcoholic stupor and sobered up briefly in December for a long-postponed audience with the emperor."

This lovely sentence is from Norman E. Saul's *Distant Friends: The United States & Russia, 1763–1867,* from which I have here stolen much else besides. Professor Saul could have chosen no better phrase for his title, so well does it express the interaction between America and Russia and, simultaneously, the personal as well as physical remoteness between Americans and Russians at this time.

As late as 1840, when Niblo's Garden, at the northeast corner of Broadway and Prince Street, presented an entertainment of Eastern European folk dances, the mazurka was a novelty that soon captured the curiosity of New York, where Russia remained an imagined and exotic land. It would not be until 1867 that the first American passenger ship arrived in Russia, cruising into the Black Sea with Mark Twain aboard.

The figure of George Washington had grown great in Russia. When, in the 1820s, translations of the stories of Washington Irving appeared, to wide appeal, in Russia, the author was referred to as Irving Washington.

In the summer of 1790, a small congregation of Sephardic Jews in Newport, Rhode Island, had addressed George Washington:

"For all the Blessings of civil and religious liberty which we enjoy under an equal and benign administration, we desire to send up our thanks to the Antient of Days, the great preserver of Men—beseeching him, that the Angel who conducted our forefathers through the wilderness into the promised land, may graciously conduct you through all the difficulties and dangers of this mortal life: and, when like Joshua full of days and full of honour, you are gathered to your Fathers, may you be admitted into the Heavenly Paradise to partake of the water of life, and the tree of immortality."

The nature of Washington's response had become legend:

All possess alike liberty of conscience and immunities of citizenship. It is now no more that toleration is spoken of, as if it was by the indulgence of one class of people, that another enjoyed the exercise of their inherent natural rights. For happily the Government of the United States, which gives to bigotry no sanction, to persecution no assistance, requires only that they who live under its protection should demean

themselves as good citizens, in giving it on all occasions their effectual
support.

It would be inconsistent with the frankness of my character not to
avow that I am pleased with your favorable opinion of my Administra-
tion, and fervent wishes for my felicity. May the Children of the Stock
of Abraham, who dwell in this land, continue to merit and enjoy the
good will of the other Inhabitants; while every one shall sit in safety
under his own vine and figtree, and there shall be none to make him
afraid. May the father of all mercies scatter light and not darkness in
our paths, and make us all in our several vocations useful here, and in
his own due time and way everlastingly happy.

And was it not true as well that the Continental Congress had asked
Benjamin Franklin to devise a seal for the United States of America and
that this great American man, in his own hand, had proposed "Moses
standing on the Shore, and extending his Hand over the Sea, thereby caus-
ing the same to overwhelm Pharaoh," with "Rays from a Pillar of Fire in
the Clouds reaching to Moses, to express that he acts by Command of the
Deity," and as motto to this seal, "Rebellion to Tyrants is Obedience to
God"—was this not true?

And the man Thomas Jefferson. His fight for the Act of Religious
Freedom, to establish that freedom and ensure the separation of church
and state, was known to all. Under his act no one would suffer in any way
for his "religious opinions or belief." Under it, no one would "be compelled to frequent or support any religious worship, place, or ministry
whatsoever."

The words of Jefferson's private correspondence were not known. In
one letter, he spoke of Jesus as "the great reformer of the vicious ethics and
deism of the Jews." In another, the Jews of Jesus's time were "a blood
thirsty race, as cruel and remorseless as the being whom they represented
as the family God of Abraham, of Isaac and of Jacob, and the local God of
Israel."

Jefferson had died when Yoshue was just a boy. But to breathe the air
that he and Washington had breathed, the air in which their spirits yet

dwelled—a miracling air. Where in the Europe that Yoshue knew could such men, such spirit, such air, be found?

Wo ein Wille ist, ist auch ein Weg—"Where there is a will, there is also a way."

The steamships bound for New York left from Hamburg. The old three-masted, bark-rigged sail ships still left from Bremen. The steamships made the crossing in two weeks, the sail ships in six. But the sail ships were cheaper. They arrived in Bremen with their between decks loaded with cargo. After the cargo was discharged, crude accommodations were readied for poor travelers seeking outward passage. When the between deck held living human cargo, it was called "steerage class." The worth of incoming cargo was realized on arrival and was thus cared for accordingly. The value of steerage passengers ended with their purchase of a ticket.

The American scientist and explorer Kane Grinnell described a brig on which he sailed in 1850: "The temperature and foulness of air in the between-deck Tartarus can not be amended." Nor, for peasants, could the price be beat—about thirty-five talers. Even that was larcenous: a sum that took advantage of those seeking new life in a new land. Going from New York to Bremen, a proper traveler could sail in a proper second-class cabin for the same price. But many paid a further price for their steerage passage and its "foulness of air," in which disease and sickness thrived. Many died on the voyage from Bremen to New York: forty-five—16 percent of all passengers aboard—on one 1853 sailing alone; lesser numbers on other sailings.

Perhaps Yoshue had been a fool. Years later, the newspaper *Smolenskii Vestnik* would complain of Jews who had been given residence rights as artisans and then operated as moneylenders, tavern-keepers, fences of stolen goods. Perhaps Yoshue should have been one of them. *Fahrgelt,* passage money, would then have been no problem.

But every good fortune bears three curses. The trembling luminant silent song of candle, of oil lamp: All he needed lay therein.

Yoshue and Royze would bring their daughter, Yulia, with them. Their son, Ludvik, would stay behind for now, with kin.

There was no receiving station for immigrants in New York at this time. Castle Garden, in the Battery of southern Manhattan, would become the first such immigrant landing place in 1855. From 1890, when Castle Garden would be shut down, a harbor barge would serve as the immigrant-processing center until the opening of Ellis Island in 1892. But at this early date, there was nothing. Not even a Statue of Liberty at which to gaze. The shipping company representative gave a passenger manifest to the collector of customs, and the immigrants simply disembarked onto the wharves and into the loud rabbling populace of Manhattan.

So it was with Harris and Rosa Rothstein and their little girl, Julia, on an unknown day in the year of 1852.

Nᴇᴡ ʏᴏʀᴋ ᴄᴏᴜɴᴛʏ ꜱᴜʀʀᴏɢᴀᴛᴇ'ꜱ ᴄᴏᴜʀᴛ, 31 Chambers Street. January 9, 1929. Examination by the Hon. Thomas I. Sheridan, attorney for Mr. Maurice F. Cantor, Esq., one of the executors, legatees, and proponents of the will.

What is your name?
 —Martha Goerdel.
And where do you reside?
 —204 West 108th Street.
Were you one of the nurses in attendance on Arnold Rothstein, deceased?
 —Yes.
Did you or Miss Love, which one of you had charge of the case?
 —I did.
How long have you been a nurse?
 —Ten years.
Did you see Mr. Cantor, the man who brought this paper that afternoon?
 —Not until he entered the room.
Did you hear Mr. Cantor say to the deceased, "Arnold, I have your will"?
 —Yes.
What else did you hear him say?
 —Miss Love said, "This man is in no condition," and he said, repeated [it] again.
Did the patient make any response?
 —Not that I could see.
Mr. Cantor took a fountain pen out of his pocket?
 —Yes.
Can you recall now, when he took the pen out of his pocket, was the pen given to either you or Miss Love with any remarks requesting that you place the pen in the hand of the patient?

—It was handed to Miss Love.

What did he say when he handed the pen?

—"Will you put it in his hand?"

What else did he say?

—Miss Love refused.

Then what happened?

—He did it himself.

He placed the pen in the hand?

—Yes.

Which hand?

—The left hand.

What did Miss Love say when she refused to place the pen in his hand?

—She again said, "He is in no condition to sign this will."

Now what did he do, or what took place when the pen was placed in the left hand of Mr. Rothstein?

—You mean Mr. Rothstein?

Yes.

—He made no effort to grasp the pen at all.

What happened?

—He pushed the paper under the hand and placed—

Who is "he"?

—Mr. Cantor, and guided his hand, which was very nervous.

Which was very nervous?

—Mr. Cantor was very nervous, and made the hand make the crooked cross.

Do you know Mrs. Carolyn Rothstein, the widow of the deceased?

—I met her at the hospital.

When?

—When I came on duty.

Did you see her after the execution of the will?

—Yes.

Where?

—She was at his bedside when he died.

Did you have any conversation with her with reference to the will?

—No.

What is the name of the superintendent of the Polyclinic Hospital?

—Mr. Jaller.

Did you speak to him about the will?

—I told him I had signed it, yes.

Did you mention whose will it was?

—Yes.

What did he say?

—"Foolish girl."

In your opinion was this man of sound mind when you signed that will?

—No.

Was the man irrational?

—Yes, most of the time.

Tell me one thing that the patient said that impressed you as being irrational.

—I would not dare repeat it.

HEINRICH HEINE WAS BORN into a Jewish family of modest means in the city of Düsseldorf in 1797. His name by birth was Harry Heine. He took the name of Heinrich when he was baptized as a Christian in 1825. He felt that to be marked as Jew was to be deprived of his rightful place in the European society of arts and letters. He called his baptismal transformation and new Saxon name his *Entrébillet zur europä-ischen Kultur:* his "admission ticket to European culture."

This comes to mind as I wonder how Yoshue arrived at the name of Harris. It is one thing to go, as the poet did, from the Middle English of Harry to the revered Old German of Heinrich, the descendant name of the tenth-century German king and founder of the Saxon dynasty, Henrik the Fowler. It is another thing to leap from Yoshue—leap directly over Joshua—to land in the Hebridean mist of the landed Scotch gentry, upon the tweedy name of Harris. It is a leap that challenges prenominal reason.

"Then came Amalek, and fought with Israel in Rephidim. And Moses said unto Harris . . ."

The name is an old one, formed from the name Harry (originally Herry) and the third-person masculine singular genitive, *his,* which in Gothic, Old Saxon, and Old High German had been formed without the aspirate *h,* as *is.* Thus Herry plus *is* as a possessive suffix became in time Harry plus *is,* or, as it evolved, Harris, meaning "that which was Harry's" or "that which belonged to Harry," such as a son, serf, or slave. As these connotations faded, the given name of Harris struck a distinguished note through the British Isles. It was an almost exclusively British and almost exclusively Christian name.

Was this new name a part of his baptismal transatlantic crossing? Was it seen as an element of his *Entrébillet zum amerikanischen Kappen-machen,* his "admission ticket to American cap making"? I fear that we may never know.

But I can tell you this. By 1855, Harris Rothstein, maker and merchant of caps both secular and sacred, was established at Number 4 Baxter Street in Manhattan.

Harris Rothstein was here when Orange Street became Baxter Street. It was one of the oldest streets in Manhattan, laid out soon after 1664, when New Amsterdam became New York. In the early nineteenth century, it lay in the heart of the city's most notorious neighborhood, known as the Five Points, after the central crossroads at the five corners—the meeting points of three right and two acute angles—formed by the intersection of Orange and Cross streets, the divergence of Anthony Street, and the eastern corner of the triangular wedge between the convergence of Anthony and Cross. Harris Rothstein's address, in lower Orange Street, later Baxter Street, was steps away from this crossroads.

On March 19, 1829, the *New York Evening Post* declared that the Five Points had "become the most dangerous place in our city." A month later, on April 20, the city's police, jail, and bridewell committees jointly reported to the common council that "the Five Points is a place of great disorder and crime, and that it would be particularly desirable to rid the City of the Nuissance complained of."

Five years later, in May 1834, the *New York Sun* presented a hellish vision of "the most disgusting objects of both sexes" reduced by depravity and drunkenness to "a state of misery almost indescribable," in which "the most abominable indecencies of every kind" were "such as few eyes have witnessed."

More than a decade later, things seemed to have worsened. The *New York Evening Post,* January 30, 1846:

> The attention of the public has been called often, of late, to the propriety of opening and widening Anthony street, and it has been urged in favor thereof that it would greatly tend to reform that sink of pollution known as the Five Points. Much as we are opposed to the revival of that system of improvements that has heretofore wrought so much evil in this city, yet if the widening and opening of every street connected with the Five Points would in any wise tend to break up that nest of vipers, and wipe away from the

heart of the city that plague spot, we would not only lift up both our hands in favor thereof, but would be willing that every man, woman and child should be assessed to pay the damages. We know of no place on the earth where there are more wretched beings congregated together than at the Five Points, and what renders it still more abhorrent to the feelings of every philanthropist is that the number, instead of decreasing, is constantly increasing.

Harris Rothstein was a part of that increase, a part of that Five Points population that was seen as barely human: as—the April 1829 reports to the common council—"the most degraded and abandoned of the Species"; as—the *Post,* July 1832—a "race of beings of all colours, ages, sexes and nations."

The neighborhood was further cursed when it was host to the first appearance of the cholera epidemic of 1849, which killed about five thousand of the city's half a million or so residents. The cholera pandemic of 1832, witnessed in Russia by Harris Rothstein, had taken a third of its New York victims from the Five Points.

This population of "the most degraded and abandoned of the Species" that occupied the Five Points at the time of Harris Rothstein's arrival was predominantly Irish. Many of these Irish, who constituted two thirds of the Five Points populace, had arrived from Ireland during or after the potato famine of 1846–1847—which, curiously, had originated in the northeastern United States.

Germans—Christians and Jews alike—were the second-largest element, representing about 15 percent of the Five Points populace. Many of them had arrived from the German states after the failed revolution of 1848.

Native-born Americans accounted for about 10 percent of the Five Points inhabitants. Many of these were freed or fugitive slaves, some of whom had lived through the Five Points race riots of 1834–1835. The discovery in 1854 of the cohabitation and illicit unions in the Five Points of Irish women and black men was a further source of scandal and opprobrium.

Approximately 3 percent of the neighborhood's population were immigrants from Italy.

About 2 percent were Poles, mostly Jewish, who had immigrated after the failed insurrections against Russian rule in 1831, 1846, and 1848.

About another 2 percent were rogue Britishers.

There were fewer than fifty Chinese. Most of these were single men. The eleven Chinese married men found by census takers were all married to Irish women.

It was felt by the city fathers that to change a name was to change the thing itself. This is known in government circles as "metamorphosis through metonomatosis." So it was that on December 30, 1854, the very street beneath the feet of Harris Rothstein ceased to be Orange Street and became Baxter Street. The old name had come to evoke horror. The new name was meant to evoke the noble and patriotic spirit of Charles Baxter, a member of the state legislature who had resigned to enlist in the Mexican War and had been killed in the final battle of the war, at Chapultepec Castle, Mexico City, in September 1847. We cannot be sure that Baxter's spirit was truly noble or patriotic, but we can be sure that practically no one in the Five Points had ever heard of him.

Another casualty provided Anthony Street's new name. William Jenkins Worth, the major general alleged to have been the first American soldier to enter Mexico City in the fighting that took Baxter's life, had died of cholera in May 1849 while in command of the Department of Texas. He is said to have been a Quaker of great arrogance.

As Orange Street became Baxter Street, as Anthony Street became Worth Street, so Cross Street became Park Street. The old Five Points triangle, the wedge of land between the convergence of Anthony and Cross, was Paradise Park. There is still a crossroads where the heart of the Five Points once was. It is formed now by the intersection of Baxter and Worth streets, the divergence of Park Street. And it is five-cornered, owing to a triangular traffic island where Park Street converges with Worth Street, east of Baxter. This crossroads now lies amid the New York County Court House (1926), the Louis J. Lefkowitz State Office Building (1930), the two concrete high-rises of the Chatham Towers (1965), and Columbus Park (1911), the former site of Mulberry Bend Park.

The latter was the city's first project under its Small Park Acts of 1887, and the city paid one and a half million dollars for the property. The methodical razing of the Five Points block—the block bounded by Baxter, Park, Mulberry, and Bayard streets—given over to this park was celebrated by city officials and urban reformers alike; and it was the opening of Mulberry Bend Park, on June 15, 1897, that marked with finality the end of the Five Points. As duly noted in *Appleton's Annual Cyclopaedia and Register of Important Events of the Year 1897,* the establishment of this park had "reclaimed for healthful purposes one of the worst tenement districts in the city."

Standing near where Harris Rothstein once stood, we are today surrounded by city, county, state, and federal government buildings that are less imposing in grandeur than in monolithic mediocrity. We cannot imagine what was here in Harris Rothstein's day. Our imagining has been informed by the folly and falsity of popular romance and entertainments. We know of no one from the Five Points who wrote of the Five Points. We have no representations from life. Except for a few rare views from the late 1860s, the photographs made there, most of them from 1888 and later, are artificially posed. Nothing candid could be captured with apparatus using magnesium flash powder and extremely long shutter speeds. Nor did the photographers seek after true and candid life. They were reformers set on staging propaganda.

We have nothing—no voice, no vision from the *within* of it—through which to distantly sense that place and time. The closest we have come is through archeology.

On May 20, 1991, prior to the construction of the new Daniel Patrick Moynihan United States Courthouse (1994) and Annex (1995), an archeological excavation of the site was undertaken. The area, near the convergence of Pearl Street and lower Baxter Street, had been covered by a parking lot since the 1960s, when the last of the residential buildings had been brought down.

Fourteen city lots within the block were explored. More than a million artifacts were discovered in twenty-two stone-lined and brick-lined privies and cesspools. Much of the work was centered at what was called Feature H, a stone-lined privy in the backyard of what had been 8 Baxter Street, two doors from where Harris Rothstein had been located.

The archeologists were afforded little time, less than eight months, but their work yielded rare artifacts of life in the Five Points. Some forty or more years' worth of pins, needles, thimbles, and cloth of various dates and kinds attested to the longevity and extent of the Baxter Street garment industry, of which Harris Rothstein was a part. There were shards of crockery, clay pipe stems, liquor bottles, perfume bottles, glass urinal vessels used by bedridden syphilitic prostitutes. There were lice combs and spittoons. There was a Staffordshire teacup with the image of the Irish priest Father Theobald Mathew (1790–1856) calling his flock to take the temperance oath. In the hollow of the cup, ever there to meet the drinker's eyes, were the words "Temperance and Industry" and "Industry Pays Debts." From a whorehouse at 12 Baxter Street, there were traces of decayed finches in dainty cages.

Dr. Rebecca Yamin, who directed the analysis of artifacts from the site, observed: "It is not unlikely that the brothel catered to the politicians who worked just two blocks away at City Hall. It would have been easy to combine a visit to a Baxter Street tailor with one to a favorite prostitute."

With the many sewing implements, remnants of woolen rags attested to Baxter Street's importance as a center of garment work.

Most curious were the skeletal remains of a monkey that may have been cast to the privy by an intemperate Italian organ-grinder who lived at 14 Baxter Street.

The artifacts were placed in twelve hundred archival boxes that were stored in the Foley Square Archaeological Laboratory in a sub-basement of Six World Trade Center. Eighteen items relating to the Irish community, including the temperance teacup, were borrowed by the Archdiocese of New York for an exhibit called "The World of John Hughes: New York's First Archbishop." In May 2001, after the exhibit, instead of being returned to the laboratory at the World Trade Center, these eighteen items were transferred to the South Street Seaport Museum. Dr. Yamin said, "They're safer there."

We cannot see what was there in Harris Rothstein's day, but we can be sure that the government buildings of the next century surely represent, in their cold monolithic mediocrity, vaster malfeasance and malefaction than the Five Points ever knew. Harris Rothstein's grandson would drink of that new and hidden knowledge, and of the lost old ways as well.

THERE WERE MORE than twelve thousand needle-and-thread men working in New York in 1855. More than 95 percent of them were immigrants. Harris Rothstein, cap maker, was one of them.

Other Jews in the Five Points, like many of the neighborhood's Irish, were peddlers. Others ran junk shops, pawnshops, or secondhand shops. Most of the secondhand stores in Orange Street were owned by Jews, and many of them were fences.

I owe to Tyler Anbinder's *Five Points* (2001) my introduction to a ninety-page 1916 typescript, *The Autobiography of George Appo*. George Washington Appo (1856–1930), son of a Chinese father and Irish mother, was a professional thief and inveterate opium smoker. "At No. 14½ Baxter St.," he wrote, "was a second hand clothing store owned by a man named Cohen who was a 'fence' and where all the crooks used to get rid of their stolen goods." The address was at the entrance to Donovan's Lane, also known as Murderers' Alley, where Appo lived for a time in 1869. Elsewhere Appo describes a basement opium joint at 17 Mott Street, a basement that later became the all-night restaurant Wo-Hop.

The *New York Evening Post* of January 21, 1854, names a man—Mayer Rosenthal, of nearby 6 Mulberry Street—who, as Anbinder tells us, was reputed to have fenced "half the stolen calico, muslin, shawls, silk, and thread in New York."

Robbery and murder, saloons and stews, defined the Five Points. A writer for the *New York Tribune* near midcentury said of the area that "nearly every house and cellar is a groggery below and a brothel above." Anbinder's examination of the New York district attorney's indictment records has revealed that nearly every building actually did have a brothel. "Bordellos operated in thirty-three of the thirty-five dwellings on Anthony Street between Centre and the Five Points intersection at some point during the 1840s and 1850s. Brothel proprietors were likewise prosecuted in twelve of the fifteen houses on Cross Street between the Five Points inter-section and Mulberry, and in thirteen of the seventeen residences on Or-ange Street from the Five Points intersection to Leonard Street," which itself long had been known for more elegant whorehouses, such as Julia Brown's, at 55 Leonard Street.

As the saying went, in the Five Points, if they were old enough to bleed, they were old enough to butcher. Elizabeth Dayton, a prostitute and brothel keeper in Orange Street, sent her fifteen-year-old daughter street-walking outside the place. Upon her arrival from Ireland, fourteen-year-old Mary O'Daniel was brought into the trade by her aunt Bridget McCarthy, who had preceded her from County Tipperary. Bridget Man-gin's two teenage daughters worked in her whorehouse on Worth Street in 1855. Police earlier had found an eleven-year-old girl working for her. In *City of Eros,* Timothy J. Gilfoyle gives accounts of "homeless nine- and ten-year-old girls peddling sex late at night." The environs of City Hall were the nighttime haunting grounds of many child prostitutes. Several brothels "specialized in ten- to fourteen-year-old girls." The age of con-sent in New York before 1889 was ten.

By the turn of the century, the sex rackets would come to be controlled by Jews. But now, in the years of New York's first archbishop, John Hughes, formerly of County Tyrone, the money side of whoredom be-longed to the sainted Irish.

And the murder rate ascended through the 1850s, as handguns became commonplace.

But to Harris Rothstein, set among the saloons and stews, Baxter Street was the garment district.

At this time, before the sewing machine came into widespread use, tai-loring required little equipment. It would not be until 1857 that the first Singer showroom opened, to the northwest of Baxter Street, at 458 Broad-way. If making caps required little capital in those days before mechanical sewing machines, it brought in little money as well. A standard workday back then began at seven in the morning and ended at six in the evening, with an hour's break at noon. Five hundred dollars a year was a good liv-ing for a workingman in New York in the late 1850s. This is equivalent to about ten grand a year today.

The first Jew to settle in New Amsterdam was Jacob Barsimson. He was an Ashkenazic Jew who came from Amsterdam in the summer of 1654, bearing a *licent brief* passport from the West Indies Company. He was followed later that year by a group of twenty-three Sephardim from a Dutch settlement in South America.

In the summer of 1655, this small group of Sephardic Jews petitioned Peter Stuyvesant, the despotic Dutch governor of New Amsterdam, for permission to purchase "a burying ground for their nation," intimating that they did not wish to inter their dead in the common burying ground. The colonial council responded that, as there were as yet no deaths among the Jews and thus no immediate need of a boneyard, a grant of land would be made to them when "the need and occasion therefor" should arise. Some months later, in early 1656, the Jews repeated their request, and the council granted them "a little hook of land situate outside of this city." This location is conjectured to have been at New Bowery near the "Highway," the later line of Chatham Square, which would become the southeastern corner of the Five Points. All that is known is that the Jews purchased land in the same area in 1681. The graveyard was full by the summer of 1728, and the property was expanded in 1729.

There were problems of vandalism and desecration in the 1740s and 1750s. In the summer of 1746, the *New York Post-Boy* reported: "Whereas some malicious and evil-minded Persons, have lately been guilty of doing very considerable Damage, both to the Walls and Tombs of the Jewish Burying-place, near this City," a reward of five pounds was being offered to anyone who could lead the Jewish community to the culprits. The same newspaper reported in the fall of 1751: "Whereas several evil-minded People, have at sundry Times broke down the Wall of the Jewish burying Ground, and very much damaged the Tomb Stones belonging thereto," it was the intention of the community elders to prosecute the culprits to the full extent of the law.

The first Jewish congregation in New York was Sephardic: The Spanish and Portuguese congregation of Shearith Israel had formed in the late seventeenth century and in the fall of 1700 was deeded property for its first synagogue, in Mill Street, in southern Manhattan near the base of lower

Broad Street. The congregation built a new synagogue, also in Mill Street, in 1729. By the 1750s, Mill Street was known as Jews' Alley.

The Jews' burial ground, at New Bowery near Olive Street, became the sepulcher place of the Congregation Shearith Israel in 1784. Later, in 1823, the congregation sold a part of the cemetery property to Tradesmen's Bank for commercial development. In 1855, the cutting-through of New Bowery took more of the burial ground. Bodies were dug up and removed to a Jewish cemetery on Twenty-first Street. The New Bowery thorough-fare opened in 1856.

New Bowery became St. James Place in 1947, renamed after St. James Church at 23 Olive Street. A part of the Jews' burial ground still exists there, on St. James Place near Olive Street, as the oldest burying ground in Manhattan. Its oldest marker bears the date 1682.

The famous Plan of the City of New York of 1807, engraved by Peter Maverick and published by Isaac Riley, noted the congregation's presence in Mill Street with the simple words "Jews Synagogue."

The synagogue was rebuilt in 1818, and in 1833 the property was sold and a new synagogue was built northwest of the burial ground, on Crosby Street, where the congregation remained until the consecration in 1860 of its new synagogue on Nineteenth Street.

The words of the 1807 map were plain but true. Until 1825, Shearith Israel was the only temple in town. By then, however, the number of Ashkenazic Jews was growing, and in that year there was a secession from the Sephardic congregation. The first Ashkenazic congregation, B'nai Jeshurun, purchased the old African Presbyterian Church in Elm Street, later Lafayette Place, in 1826 and dedicated the synagogue in June 1827. The congregation remained there until 1850, when a new B'nai Jeshurun synagogue was built in Gothic style on Greene Street between Houston and Bleecker streets.

Ansche Chesed, a German congregation, was incorporated in 1830, and in 1849 built a synagogue on Norfolk Street between Houston and Stanton streets. A Polish congregation, Shaarey Zedek, was formed in 1839, drawing members from both B'nai Jeshurun and Ansche Chesed. A German Reform congregation, Emanu-El, was formed in 1845. A secession from B'nai Jeshurun in 1845 brought about the Congregation Shaarey Tefila, embracing the Polish ritual, at 67 Franklin Street, later building its own Byzantine-style synagogue on Wooster Street.

The Shaarey Zedek congregation held its first services in the rented flat of a tenement building filled mostly with Irish immigrants above a ground-floor saloon at 472 Pearl Street. The old thoroughfare of Pearl Street ran north from the Battery. It passed through the Five Points as it veered west at the base of Baxter Street, near Chatham Street, which was the southeastern border of the Five Points and which in the spring of 1886 would become Park Row. The Shaarey Zedek flat was at this southeastern edge of the neighborhood.

Within the year, the congregation moved to other rented quarters in the Five Points, on City Hall Place, a small street that intersected Pearl above Chatham and in 1941 would become Cardinal Hayes Place. From there, Shaarey Zedek took rooms recently vacated by Congregation Ansche Chesed, above the New York Dispensary at White and Centre streets, also in the Five Points. These hallowed rooms had also been occupied by Shearith Israel while awaiting the completion of the new synagogue on Crosby Street. This was in 1833, three years after the dispensary building opened.

Shaarey Zedek remained above the medical clinic for ten years, then bought a building at 38 Henry Street, a former Quaker church that had been owned previously by Ansche Chesed. Later, Shaarey Zedek would erect its own temple.

Like most of the Jewish congregations in New York, those in the area of the Five Points often found it difficult to attract the minimum attendance of ten men, constituting the minyan, required for formal services under Talmudic law. The Sabbath was a good day to make money in New York. If they could afford to do so, some Jews hired goyim, non-Jews, to tend to their business on the Sabbath. The congregations resorted to hiring "minyan men," paying them to attend services as needed to fill the quorum of ten.

As immigrants from Russia, such as the Rothsteins, began to arrive in small numbers in New York, they met with Polish animosity. Many of these Poles were from the province of Posen, which was a part of Prussia under German colonialism. Despite this Germanic affiliation, the Jews from Poland were always regarded as Poles rather than Germans, and they had little in common with their German neighbors in New York. The Polish Jews also felt themselves to be apart from the Russian Jews, especially when these Russian Jews were of German blood and heritage.

I take this from the scholar Hyman Bogomolny Grinstein (1899–1982), specifically from *The Rise of the Jewish Community of New York, 1654–1860,* which was published in 1945 by the Jewish Publication Society of America. It was Grinstein who devoted unknown time to examining the manuscript minute books of the early congregations of New York. And it was Grinstein who found the following resolution of March 17, 1844, duly recorded in Minute Book 2 of the trustees of Congregation Shaarey Zedek: "That no man can become a member hereafter what was a Russian subject eccept [*sic*] which are members at present—they the Russians are allowed to be seatholders only."

Baby, let me hold your seat. That's not Grinstein talking. But, yes, let's talk seats.

When Shaarey Zedek had been formed in 1839, many of the B'nai Jeshurun congregation broke away to join it. I pass to Grinstein:

> *The minutes of Bnai Jeshurun at the time of this rift reveal a struggle to abolish the admission fee demanded of new members. The attempt was partially successful. There had been a sliding scale of fees ranging from $25 to $250. In 1838 and 1839, this was reduced to a flat rate of $5. Even this fee was distasteful to many, since its purpose was to limit the franchise to those able to contribute to synagogue funds. It apparently alienated many seatholders who joined the newly-forming Shaarey Zedek synagogue.*

As for the matter of franchise, I asked a research assistant some time ago if she could please provide me with a succinct history of this word in its synagogal sense. I received the following with some alacrity through the wonder of computer technology. The source of the first citation was a former dean and executive vice president of Columbia Theological Seminary, a graduate of Union Theological Seminary who held a doctorate in religion from Princeton University:

If the new congregation from the same denomination up the river or down the road could be compared to an additional franchise *of the same kind of fast food (and McDonald's hamburgers taste the same even though the manager and interior decoration are different), then the introduction of a religious competitor within town is more comparable to an outlet for a truly competing brand with its different but substitutable good in the place of the one currently being purveyed. Thus the Quakers in 17th century Salem, Massachusetts were regarded with the same dismay and suspicion that the McDonald's* franchise *owner displays toward the new Pizza Hut in town.*

Hmm. The other citation was of a graver nature and regarded the Congregation Shevet Achim Chaverim kol Israel d'Bet Abraham: "Due to financial difficulties, the congregation debated merging with the Beth Israel Synagogue in 1981, but decided against it. In 1984, they were unable to prevent a Dunkin' Donuts *franchise* from being built within inches of the synagogue building."

And then I paid her.

Meanwhile, back in *The Oxford English Dictionary:* "franchise," noun, sense 4: "The freedom of or full membership of a body corporate or politic; citizenship." The two citations from the nineteenth century instanced deprivation of, and admission to, the franchise.

Back to Grinstein:

Of all the secessions, the most remarkable took place at B'nai Jeshurun in 1845. When its founders withdrew from the congregation they did so over one of the very questions they had raised against Shearith Israel twenty years earlier, namely [get the doughnuts] limitation of the franchise! Now these men who had fought such a limitation made a complete turnabout. They decided that seatholders were not to be admitted to membership automatically, but were to be accepted only upon a two-thirds vote of the general membership. One reason for this was that the English Jews at B'nai Jeshurun feared the growing power of the non-English Jews, just as the ritually Sephardic Jews at Shearith Israel had feared the rise of the Ashkenazim twenty years earlier.

And so it was in the Five Points, the neighborhood that New York looked upon as the warren of the damned. The wooden buildings where the likes of Harris Rothstein and the whores and the fences and the thieves and the drunks and the peddlers and the pawnbrokers and the rest of them lived and worked were decaying and rotting and listing and ready to fall. Many of these old structures of beam and plank had been built in the previous century. Measuring about twenty feet wide and thirty feet deep, these low-ceilinged two-story structures of tinder and dank had been constructed to accommodate single families but since had been partitioned and repartitioned by landlords to accommodate multiple tenant families. If they were fortunate, landlords and occupants alike, these sagging houses would lean here and there against a house of stabler brick rather than slouch one against the other.

It was to the cramped quarters of tenement houses such as these that the slang word "slums" was first applied, in England, in the early nineteenth century. Only later, in the 1820s, did the phrase "back slums" arise to describe gatherings of slum houses. The phrase usually appeared as "back slums of London." In the 1840s, again in England, it becomes simply "slum." At the same time, the word "tenement," as in "tenement house," acquires a bad connotation. In 1855, a "model" tenement house is erected in New York by the Workmen's Home Association, on Elizabeth and Mott streets: six stories, eighty-seven three-room apartments supplied with Croton water and lighted with gas. It is a failed attempt to redeem the thing and the word. In a few years, the six-story building degenerates into one of the worst slum houses in New York. There were to be no more "model" tenements, only tenements. In 1873, James Russell Lowell speaks of "the slums and stews of the debauched brain."

And so it was in the Five Points. The Polish hated the Germans, the Germans the Poles. The Irish hated the blacks, the blacks the Irish. The Jew looked down on the Christian, the Christian on the Jew. Only the noble Italian was above reproach. Your monkey, she's bad, your monkey, she go *bascemen*.

Everybody hated the Chinese, and the Chinese, ever willing to oblige, reciprocated. Even before Manhattan had a Chinatown proper, Horace

Greeley's *Tribune* of December 26, 1869, would feature a multiheadlined article: "Our Pagan Population. The Chinese Considered without Reference to 'Caste.' Among the Dens of Baxter Street—A Celestial Habitation. Opium Smoking."

The *Tribune* story offered not only "A 'Pigtail' Interviewed," but also the first known location of an opium den in New York—14 Baxter Street. Again: that rich, lost tale of lower Baxter Street. If only the excavations of 1991–1992 had been allowed to seek further into that tantalizing richness beneath and beyond the cloacae.

The fever of public indignance grew as the habitués of the opium dens became ever less confined to the Chinese, whose souls were as naught in the scales of American values.

By 1890, the Irish population of the Five Points area would fall to 10 percent. Italians would dominate, representing about half of the population, with Jews representing almost 20 percent and Chinese about 5 percent.

As the New York City census of 1890 was conducted by police during the time of the Chinese Exclusion Act, the ten-year moratorium on Chinese immigration passed by the United States Congress in the spring of 1882, there is good reason to believe that many Chinese may have shunned the census. Despite the Exclusion Act and the restrictions that followed its expiration, it would be the Chinese who inherited the neighborhood. By the end of the century, the Five Points would become Chinatown.

In the late nineteenth century, immigrant movement veered north and northeast of the Five Points, to what some would call the "Lower East Side." This phrase was unknown and unuttered to anyone at the time. In the late twentieth century, there were still old-timers who divided downtown— the only town they acknowledged—into the "Village" and the "East Side." These simple words were all that were. To refer to these two districts as anything else was to reveal oneself as a true *cafon* to these men. As late as 1923, when Jacob Magadiff's *Der Shpigel fun der Ist Sayd* (*The Mirrors of the East Side*) was published, it was still called the East Side, or, as Magadiff had it in Yiddish, *der Ist Sayd*. The phrase "Lower East Side" did not gain currency until later in the 1920s. It appears in Herbert Manchester's *The Lower East Side and the Citizens Savings Bank,* a pamphlet published by the Citizens Saving Bank in 1930. Forget about the "East

Village." This phrase was not turned until the 1960s. Ed Sanders's Fuck You Press (1962–1967) published the first issue of *Fuck You: A Magazine of the Arts* (1962–1965) "at a secret location on the Lower East Side" in the spring of 1962. The first issue of *The East Village Other* (1965–1971) was prepared for press in the late summer of 1965. Sanders's "secret location," his Peace Eye Bookstore, the former storefront of a kosher butcher shop at 383 East Tenth Street between Avenue B and Avenue C, moved in 1967 to 147 Avenue A, another storefront, which had just been vacated by *The East Village Other*.

The East Side became the Lower East Side sometime in the years 1920–1929, and the Lower East Side became the East Village sometime in 1963–1965.

The East Side, the old-timers would say: "That's where Billy the Kid come from."

And it was indeed where the Kid come from. He was born there, Henry McCarty, in the fall of 1859, likely on Allen Street or Greene Street, not too far from the B'nai Jeshurun synagogue.

It is at the Green Street synagogue that we encounter a glimpse of Harris Rothstein at this time. From the congregational register of Congregation B'nai Jeshurun:

> *Rothstein, H.*
> *Admitted 1860.*

He and his family had moved from Baxter Street to Stanton Street in 1856. As far as the streets of New York went, Stanton Street was a relatively new one. It had been opened, along with Orchard Street, in 1806. Orchard Street had been named for the beautiful garden groves of the James De Lancey estate, which had occupied more than a hundred blocks of the East Side in the eighteenth century. Stanton Street had been named, for unknown reasons, for a foreman who had worked on the estate. It was said by the historian William Smith (1728–1793) that the colonial assembly convened on December 6, 1757, "in an out-house occupied by the overseer" of De Lancey's "farm upon the skirts of the town." Maybe Stanton was that overseer.

From Stanton Street the Rothsteins had moved in 1857 to Pearl Street, then in 1858 to Monroe Street. They were living on Monroe Street when Harris's name appeared in the B'nai Jeshurun register book. These moves were of slight distance but much moment, for they took Harris Rothstein and his family out of the Five Points.

Harris had his own cap-making shop now as well. It was located in 1860 down at 140 Broadway, between Liberty and Cedar streets. Farther up Broadway, the Singer sewing machine company had begun something called the hire-purchase plan. You gave them some money, took the machine away in a wagon, then paid the balance over a period of time. The machinery helped you make more money, and the extra money helped you pay for the machine. The hire-purchase plan would soon be everywhere, not just for sewing machines but for everything. The installment plan, they would call it. Céline, *Mort à credit*. It became the American way of life. Death on the installment plan.

A new home, a new shop, a new machine, a new membership in the congregation, even if he never went. And new life, too. Another baby boy.

L AW OFFICES OF Mr. I. Gainsburg, Esq., 35 Wall Street, February 14, 1929. Continuation of examination of Mr. Maurice F. Cantor, Esq., by Mr. Joseph P. Segal, Esq., counsel with Mr. I. Gainsburg, Esq., for contestants of the will.

As a matter of fact you spent a great deal of time with the deceased in conference, did you not?

—Yes.

You also spent a great deal of time with the deceased in social intercourse, did you not?

—Quite some time.

How often did you and your wife and other people, friends, spend at home?

—During what period?

During the period of his acquaintance, beginning about the fall of 1927?

—We had dinner with each other quite often. Sometimes twice a week, sometimes once a week, sometimes three times a week.

Were other people present on those occasions?

—Sometimes, yes.

Who?

—There were occasions when, several occasions when Miss Norton and her son were present. There were occasions when her son was not present.

Aside from those meetings during dinnertime, would you and the deceased, alone or together with others, meet socially—I mean, in your apartment or in the apartment of the deceased—at any time?

—While being at the hotel he might casually drop into my apartment for two or three minutes or five minutes, by no appointment, just drop in, he being at the hotel almost every day.

Did you meet in Miss Norton's apartment in the hotel?

—Yes, I saw him there several times. I would say that I saw him in Miss Norton's apartment many times during the six months or so before his death. Six or eight months before his death. That is all he knew her that I know of.

What business, other than real estate, was the deceased engaged in to your knowledge?

—Making of loans. Buying up paper.

You mean negotiable paper?

—Yes.

Anything else?

—Rothstein-Simon, in which he was interested, had an extensive insurance business.

You know, do you not, that the deceased spent considerable time playing cards?

—I know that he did not.

[Senator Thomas I. Sheridan, counsel for Mr. Maurice F. Cantor, speaks to Mr. Cantor. Mr. Segal: "Object to the senator instructing the witness. The witness is an attorney and I believe he knows without being instructed as to what to testify to; and, furthermore, if he was not an attorney he could not be instructed." Senator Sheridan: "Let the record show that my interruption was merely for the purpose of correcting the witness when he said he knew that the deceased did not play cards. I said that all he could testify was whether he saw the man play cards or whether he saw him refraining from playing cards, and when he volunteered the statement that the deceased did not play cards he ought to be careful of what he is talking about." Mr. Segal resumes:]

In your meetings with the deceased, whether during business hours or socially, did you at any time discuss with him the person of Inez Norton?

—I did.

How many times?

—Quite often.

Did you and he at any time discuss the person of Mrs. Carolyn Rothstein?

—Yes.

Did you and he discuss at any time the person or persons of his brothers?

—Yes.

Did you at any time discuss the subject of the persons of his parents?

—Yes. His father.

How often was that discussed?

—Quite a few times.

During what time?

—His father came to the hotel on several occasions and visited with him while I was present.

Do you remember the time?

—Summertime. 1928.

Did you and the deceased at any time discuss the person of his sister, Mrs. Lustig?

—Nothing other than he had a sister, and that she was married to Mr. Lustig.

What was the education of the deceased, to your knowledge?

—I don't know.

Did he never tell you about that?

—No.

[February 21, 1929. Continuation of examination of Mr. Maurice F. Cantor, Esq., by Mr. Joseph P. Segal, Esq., counsel with Mr. I. Gainsburg, Esq., for contestants of the will. Mr. Segal resumes:]

Were you the attorney for Inez Norton at any time?

—Yes.

When?

—The last of March 1928. I became attorney for her in a matter.

Did Mr. Rothstein engage you to act as attorney for her?

—He did.

Did you and the deceased discuss the person of Mr. Wellman at any time?

—Yes.

What was Mr. Wellman's connection with the deceased?

—He was a term construction manager of certain developments, real estate developments, owned by one of Mr. Rothstein's corporations.

Have you met Mr. Wellman in the presence of the deceased at any time?

—I have.

Where?

—In Mr. Rothstein's office or at the Fairfield Hotel on several occasions.

Were you present at conversations?

—Yes.

What were they about?

—On one occasion Mr. Rothstein interviewed a construction superintendent. A question came up as to whether or not a superintendent should be engaged to become associated with Mr. Wellman in the so-called Juniper development.

Did you and the deceased discuss the person of Sam Brown at any time?

—Many times.

When did you have the very first conversation with the deceased regarding the drawing of any will for him?

—December 1927.

Did you in that month prepare one?

—The will was started to be drawn in January and was completed in February.

I didn't ask you that. Did you prepare one in December of 1927?

—No, not in December.

When did you first meet with Miss Inez Norton?

—The end of March 1928.

Did you introduce Inez Norton to Arnold Rothstein?

—I did not.

Where did you meet her the first time?

—At my office.

Does your wife know Inez Norton?

—Yes.

On the night when the deceased was taken to the hospital, Sunday night, what time did you learn of the matter?

—Around eleven o'clock.

From whom?

—A police officer called me on the telephone.

You know the name?

—No: would not give me his name.

How long after that did you meet Gene the chauffeur?

—I met him at the hospital lobby after I had spoken to Mr. Rothstein, which would make it a little after midnight.

And how long did you remain at the hospital?

—I left there after midnight and came back again. About a quarter of one or one o'clock.

And after that how long did you stay in the hospital?

—About two hours, maybe more.

At that time, you had the will in your pocket?

—Yes, when I came back I had it, the second time.

And when did you come back after that?

—The next afternoon, about one o'clock.

And you stayed there from one o'clock until the will was executed?

—Yes.

Was there anybody around the room of the deceased, any of his relatives, brothers, sister, mother, father, or wife?

—At the far end of the hall, as I recall, there was Mrs. Abraham Rothstein, who I met there for the first time and only time. Mrs. Carolyn Rothstein. And Sidney Stajer. Later in the room adjoining Mr. Rothstein's room I met several others of the family: I think it was Edgar Rothstein and Mrs. Lustig.

And during that time that you just described when you saw those various persons, you had the will in your pocket?

—Yes.

Did you say anything about having the will in your pocket?

—No.

[Examination of Mr. Cantor by his counsel, Senator Thomas I. Sheridan:]

In the month of December—

[Mr. Joseph P. Segal: "I object to the senator asking any questions of the witness whatever. This is not an examination of the proponents, but only on behalf of the contestants." Senator Sheridan: "You object to my asking him any questions?" Mr.

Segal: "I object to your asking him any questions whatever unless the Surrogate rules otherwise." The parties proceed before the Hon. James A. Foley, Surrogate, for a ruling on the objection. The Surrogate: "I hold that the party who is being examined here is entitled to bring out such facts, in as brief fashion as possible, in explanation of the testimony that may have been given to questions that were put to him by counsel for the contestants, and to testify to any material, relevant, or competent fact within the scope of the examination. Objection overruled." Senator Sheridan resumes:]

In the month of October 1928 did the deceased speak to you about changing his will?

—He did.

Have you the stenographic notes of the will of November fifth, 1928?

—I have.

How long did you have the paper that was signed on November fifth in your possession prior to November fifth?

—About two weeks.

When you say in your possession, was it on you personally or in your office?

—In my office.

In what part of your office?

—In the safe.

Where did you get that paper on November fourth?

—I got it at the office after I left Mr. Rothstein.

About what time?

—About twelve-thirty.

Was there anybody with you at that time?

—Yes.

Who?

—Gene Reimer.

And who is Gene Reimer?

—Chauffeur for Mr. Rothstein.

In the month of October, did you show the deceased the will that was finally signed on November fifth?

—I did.

When was that?

—That was on October twenty-ninth.

Do you recall the time of day?

—About seven P.M.

Was there anybody else present when the paper was read by the deceased?

—Mr. Schwartz and myself were in the office when Mr. Rothstein read the will in my office.

Do you recall the date in the month of October when you had your discussion with the deceased with reference to this will?

—On October nineteenth Mr. Rothstein asked me to make a change in his former will. On October twenty-second, the will was drawn in my office.

And on the twenty-ninth?

—He read the will.

On November fourth, between the hours of eleven and twelve-thirty, when you were at the Polyclinic Hospital the night he was shot, did you have a conversation with the deceased, yes or no?

—Yes.

Did you have a conversation with the deceased at the Polyclinic Hospital, the night he was shot, with reference to the will?

—Yes.

At the time that you called at the hospital the night he was shot, November fourth, who was in the room with the deceased?

—Dr. Hoffman and Patrick Flood.

Who is Patrick Flood?

—A detective.

Of the New York City Police Department?

—Yes.

Who else, if you recall?

—A couple of the doctors whose names I do not recall, and a nurse or two nurses whose names I do not recall. There were about ten people in there altogether.

Did you return to the hospital?

—I did.

Did you see the deceased any time that morning and between the hours of one and three?

—When I came back to the hospital he was on the operating table.

The next time you saw him was late the next afternoon?

—Around three o'clock.

Did you meet Mr. Brown at any time at the hospital?

—I did.

Did Mr. Brown go into the room of the deceased?

—No.

Did you see if he met Inez Norton any time at the hospital during the time the deceased was lying there?

—No.

Do you recall whether she was there?

—I do.

Was she there?

—No. I might add that orders were issued not to admit anybody outside of certain people.

You stated, Mr. Cantor, that the first you knew about the shooting of the deceased was when you got a phone call from a policeman about eleven o'clock?

—Yes.

How do you know he was a police officer?

—He said he was. He told me he was in a pay station. I wanted to call him back, and he said he would not stay there but for a second, that Mr. Rothstein told him to call me up.

Now, in your conversation with Mr. Rothstein on the nineteenth with reference to the change in his then existing will, did your conversation take place in his office?

—Yes.

Did you make any memorandum or note of the change?

—I did.

And you have turned it over to me?

—I have.

On the twenty-ninth of October 1928 did you personally submit the changed will to Mr. Rothstein?

—In my office.

Yes or no, did you show it?

—Mr. Schwartz did in my presence.

Was the will executed that night?

—It was not.

A BRAHAM ELIJAH ROTHSTEIN WAS BORN at 237 Stanton Street on November 24, 1856. Harris Rothstein opened a cap shop downtown, at 120 John Street, a brief stroll from Burling Slip and the East River seaport. This was a significant move, bringing his enterprise well beyond the Five Points.

In 1857, he moved his family from Stanton Street to 445 Pearl Street. Running north from the Battery, Pearl Street passed through the Five Points as it veered west at the base of Baxter Street. But the Rothstein family's new address was below Chatham Street, the Five Points' southeastern divide.

Nothing remains today of the life that was in this little stretch of Pearl Street. It lay southeast of what is now the United States Court House Annex (1995). One Police Plaza (1973) and the thirty-two-story equipment-switching tower of the New York Telephone Company (1976) led to St. James Place, which in Harris Rothstein's day was the New Bowery road. There are housing projects: the Alfred E. Smith Houses (1952), the Chatham Green Apartments (1961). The city in 1870 would start buying properties from South Street to Chatham Street on which to build the Manhattan side of what it called the East River Bridge. Today it is the Brooklyn Bridge highway system, which grew and grew and grew in the age of the automobile, that overwhelms the area more than the bridge itself.

In Harris Rothstein's day, if you wanted to go to Brooklyn, you took a boat. But who would want to go to Brooklyn?

It was said in that twentieth-century age of automobiles that Abraham Rothstein was "born on Henry Street, on the lower East Side." In the twenty-first century, after more extensive research, it was said by another writer that Abraham Rothstein was "born on Henry Street, on the Lower East Side." Again, that underground fissure upon which all history precariously rests: "A lie repeated often enough becomes the truth." I'm telling you exactly what I told my ex-wife: Believe nothing unless you hear it from me.

A BRAHAM ELIJAH ROTHSTEIN PRESENTS a curious figure. The father, who himself has forsaken the name of the prophet Joshua, gives his son the name of the patriarch of Genesis and the name of the prophet Elijah, faithful keeper of God's true word.

There was a fairy tale published in Venice in 1557. It bore the title *Peregrinaggio di tre giovani, figliuoli del re di Serendippo*. It appeared under the name of Christoforo Armeno, who described himself as the translator of the tale from a Persian original. A version of the fairy tale was published in London in 1722 as *The Travels and Adventures of Three Princes of Sarendip,* now said to have been translated from Persian into French by Chevalier de Mailly and "thence done into English." From the name of the fanciful land of Sarendip, recalling it from memory as Serendip, Hugh Walpole coined the word "serendipity," which he first shared in a letter to a friend in 1754. The word gained no real currency until the twentieth century.

It is a serendipity—a true serendipity, an affluence leading not to discovery, but to nowhere—that these names of patriarch and prophet were also in the American air of the 1850s. Abraham Lincoln, soon to be the patriarchal figure of a new age, delivered his legendary Lost Speech at the Illinois State Republican Convention in the spring of 1856, when Rosa Rothstein was pregnant with her son. *Moby-Dick* had been published in the fall of 1851, when its author, Herman Melville, was only thirty-two. One of its most memorable chapters, "The Prophet," told of a demented wharfside seer called Elijah. The book was generally dismissed—"so much trash," in the words of a critic for *The Athenaeum* of London—and both Melville and his novel faded slowly from the public mind. He had been born downtown, on Pearl Street, and he would return to work downtown as a clerical drudge in the Customs House on Wall Street, dying his sad death in 1891. *Moby-Dick* had sold, or failed to sell, for a dollar and a half a copy, then less. In the early twenty-first century, copies in fine condition would fetch a price of from seventy-five to eighty-five thousand dollars.

Abraham Elijah Rothstein. It has been written of him:

Orphaned by his father's death, he had left school to support his mother and his brothers and sisters. He had operated a dry goods store, then entered the cotton-converting business. He had been very successful. He was a rich man.

He was also a man of simple, fixed belief. He believed in The Law. The Law of his faith and the law of his country. He was a disciple of orthodoxy. He was a good man.

A testimonial dinner was given in his honor in 1919. It marked his efforts—and success—in settling a major dispute in the New York City garment industry. He had been chosen by both sides to act as arbitrator because both sides trusted him completely.

Among the guests who honored him at the dinner were Alfred E. Smith, then governor of New York, and Louis D. Brandeis, an associate justice of the Supreme Court of the United States.

After others had talked about him, he talked a little about himself. His talk was brief. "My father," he said, "bequeathed me a way of life. He taught me, above all, to love God and to honor Him. Secondly, he taught me to honor all men and love them as brothers. He told me whatever I received I received from God and that no man can honor God more greatly than by sharing his possessions with others. This I have tried to do."

This was the man whom Governor Smith called "Abe the Just."

This was the man of whom were told innumerable stories of charity, years of public service, rectitude and selflessness.

Let us pause a moment to bow our heads and to reflect on the fact that this testimonial dinner of 1919 never happened.

The source of these idealizing words is a book by Leo Katcher (1911–1991) called *The Big Bankroll: The Life and Times of Arnold Rothstein*. First published by Harper & Brothers in January 1959, it is generally considered to be the classic biography of Arnold Rothstein. I remember reading and enjoying it a good many years ago, when I was even more stupid than I am today.

"Abraham Rothstein lived his private life, like his public one, in strict accordance with The Law. He obeyed the Decalogue. No one commandment above any other, but all with his entire belief."

And it goes on.

Let us see what years of further research have brought to light. This is from a book published in 2003:

"He made a very comfortable living. But far more noteworthy than the living Abraham made was the *life* he made. He loved his life and practiced his trade according to the faith of his fathers."

This too goes on:

"He attended synagogue, observed the Sabbath, lived according to the Decalogue—and was soon known to all who knew him (and to many who didn't) as 'Abe the Just.'

" 'My father taught me a way of life. He taught me above all to love God and to honor Him. . . .' "

I turn to a third source, in which this Moses-making achieves a new aspect:

"Abraham had one of those dark, haunted Jewish faces that seemed to disappear with the last century"—this is from 1998—"or else survived just long enough to die in Treblinka or Auschwitz. He had a beard, a nose, eyes. By certain friends he was called Abe the Just. A dinner given in his honor in 1919 was attended by Governor Al Smith and Judge Louis Brandeis. Whenever a Protestant politician had trouble with the poor, downtown Jews, they sought the advice of Abe the Just."

A daily Yiddish newspaper, *Der Morgen Zhurnal* of New York, published a photograph of Abraham Rothstein in 1929. It is the only picture of him that I have ever seen. He does indeed have eyes and a nose. He wears a dark suit, white shirt, and dark bow tie. His hair is gray and white and neatly trimmed. He has a mustache, which is darker and also neatly trimmed. There is the hint of a slight smile on his face and in his eyes. If he has a beard—it is hard to tell—it is a very modest trace of an aristocratic goatee. There is no resemblance between him and his son Arnold.

To be sure, Abraham Rothstein did upon his demise receive the standard good-Jew obituary in *The New York Times,* as done up so well many years later by Philip Roth in *Sabbath's Theater*. It is here that "Abe the Just" seems to have his nativity.

> A nineteen-week strike affecting more than 40,000 garment workers was brought to a close in November, 1926, through the efforts of Mr. Rothstein, Brooklyn Borough President Raymond V. Ingersoll and Dr. Henry Moskowitz. The settlement was hailed as one of the most equitable compromises ever effected between capital and labor in an industry that had been almost destroyed by constant warfare.
>
> In the next month, serving with George Gordon Battle and the late Louis Marshall, Mr. Rothstein was called upon to bring the warring parties together in another cloak-and-suit workers' dispute. The leadership of the Garment Workers Union and the submanufacturers controlling the union chose him as a "just man" acceptable to both sides.
>
> Mr. Rothstein served in these arbitrations without compensation. In his decisions, he said, he followed the principles laid down by Abraham Lincoln, whose life and sayings were eagerly read by him.
>
> In the cotton goods business, Mr. Rothstein became known as "Abe the Just."

He was, of course, a "leader in philanthropic work" and "a constant benefactor of Beth Israel Hospital."

Years later, David Dubinsky (1892–1982), a former president of the International Ladies' Garment Workers' Union, told his autobiography to A. H. Raskin (1911–1993), a former chief labor correspondent for *The New York Times*. As Dubinsky recalls the strike of 1926, his praise for Abe the Just is well potted and contributes an embellishment—Abraham is now a Talmudic scholar—but the truth breaks from the pot:

> *They turned to a retired manufacturer, A. E. Rothstein, whose philanthropic activities and basic decency had earned him great respect. This scholarly man had a son, Arnold, who had established himself in*

New York's underworld. He was in everything from white slavery to dope. Despite his great power, his brothers and sisters would have nothing to do with him; but the father would let him come to his home occasionally to visit, hoping perhaps that he might eventually reform.

In truth, it appears that Arnold was very close and very kind to his brothers and his one sister.

And who was it who called upon whom? Wasn't it Abraham the father who often came to the Fairfield Hotel seeking audience with his son?

When the Communist strike leaders came to the elder Rothstein, he said he was too removed from activity in the employer association to be of great help as a peacemaker. But he put them in touch with one of the most prominent manufacturers, who minced no words in telling them that the man they ought to see was not the father but the son. The younger Rothstein was more than happy to help. Maybe he thought his father would be pleased that he was doing something constructive for a change. More probably, this astute manipulator saw a chance to muscle in on the garment industry. That was exactly what his lieutenants, Louis "Lepke" Buchalter and Jacob "Gurrah Jake" Shapiro, did after Rothstein himself was murdered in a midtown hotel barbershop in 1928.

It's better not to ask about the barbershop.

In the strike, Rothstein's first assignment was to persuade the Legs Diamond gang to stop working for the employers in helping to smash picket lines and intimidate the union members. A telephone call took care of that.

Jack Diamond, one of the eminent sociopaths of the age, worked for Arnold.

With the industry's goons gone, the Joint Board decided it could stop paying off Little Augie's mob. But Little Augie had other ideas, until he too got a phone call from Rothstein. That took all the mobsters out of the picture. At that point Rothstein demonstrated that he had a lot of muscle not only with the hoodlums but with the employer associations as well. He got the bosses and the Joint Board together, and in a short time the essence of the settlement had been worked out.

Charles S. Zimmerman, who worked with Dubinsky in the International Ladies' Garment Workers' Union, also remembered "the help Dubinsky has talked about from Rothstein's son."

In 1941, *The Needle Trades* by Dr. Joel Seidman was published as the first volume in a series Farrar & Rinehart called "Labor in Twentieth Century America." Seidman made no mention of Abe the Just in his study of the garment industry. He says only: "While negotiations were in progress with the inside manufacturers, it became known that the notorious gambler, Arnold Rothstein, had been acting as mediator at the request of the left-wing leadership. On November 12, after twenty weeks of striking, an agreement was reached."

The fiction of the upright father and the errant son is out of time: shabby stock from the trinket bin of folklore and popular history. We seek truth and meaning from the lost or shadowy precincts of the past. An absurd pursuit, as we cannot even find these things in the present, which lies—in both senses of the verb—clearly before us. In this search we feel more comfortable with set pieces of fable than with fragments of fact, for fragments can cut and gash and present themselves in isolation from the other, lost fragments of the unknowable whole.

We are drawn to the neatly wrapped sweet that can be grasped by the child's-clutch of our understanding. And we call it history. The fragment can tear and bloody that small, soft clutch.

But a fragment of real history—and thus, by nature, real mystery—is tool as well as weapon: a tool with which we can dig our way to the moment of the present. We should not subscribe to the confectionery lies called history any more than we should subscribe to the confectionery lies of a politically correct and ordered present. We should not even look back. The past, like our shared future, is a common grave, nothing more. All the wisdom that the past ever held is in every passing breath. And wisdom is devastating in its deliverance.

H ER OWN EYES FOLLOWED his as he turned from her and walked away. She glanced to her companion and smiled.

"Those eyes of his," she said. "He must know it. They're like the eyes of a falcon. You can't see through them to the heart, but there's something about them, something you see in the eyes of falcons and eagles and hawks and such."

"Now tell me, my dear Miss Audubon," her companion said. "What might the difference be between the eyes of a falcon and the eyes of a griffon-vulture?"

❦

Office of the Chief Medical Examiner of the City of New York, Borough of Manhattan. November 6, 1928. Case Number 6293.

NOTICE OF DEATH

Reported by Brown Telegraph Bureau and Dr. O'Hare, Polyclinic Hospital, Precinct No. 9.

Name of Deceased: Arnold Rothstein.

Residence: 912 Fifth Avenue.

Age: 46.

Color: White.

Date of Death: 11/6/28—10:22 A.M.

Place of Death: Polyclinic Hospital.

Body now at: Morgue.

Reported Cause of Death: Gunshot wound of abdomen.

Remarks: Shot by unknown assailant at Park Central Hotel on 11/4/28.

D R. CHARLES NORRIS JR. graduated from the Columbia College of Physicians and Surgeons in 1892. At that time, and for years to come, the coroner system was still in effect in New York City, as throughout America. The coroner's chief function was to hold inquest on the bodies of those supposed to have succumbed to unnatural causes. Coroners often had little or no medical training. In the spring of 1771, the New York coroner Thomas Shreve invoiced the common council the sum of sixty-six pounds for performing twenty inquisitions in the past year. He listed each deceased person and his verdict on the invoice. The coroner attributed one death to "the hand of God." As the coroner's invoice shows, it was a lucrative office. In the next century, there was a back-and-forth ferry traffic in cadavers between Manhattan and Brooklyn, allowing two fees to be certified for the coroner's investigation of the same corpse. Inquests were often negligent or cursory, little more than educated guesses.

To replace the incompetence and knavery of the coroner system, New York was the first city in America to appoint a chief medical examiner. Dr. Charles Norris Jr. was a highly experienced and respected pathologist when, at the age of fifty, he became the first chief medical examiner of New York City, in 1918. He has been remembered as a dignified gentleman in a frock coat, strong-minded and steadfast.

The city mortuary, in Bellevue Hospital, was located near the East River, at First Avenue and Twenty-ninth Street, close to where it is today. In 1928, during Prohibition, the office of the Fidelio Brewery was proximate to the office of the chief medical examiner.

AUTOPSY

Case No. 6293.

Approximate Age: 46 yrs.

Approximate Weight: by scale 169 pounds

Identified by: See Below.
Stenographer: W.J.F.

I hereby certify that I, Dr. Charles Norris, have
performed an autopsy on the body of Arnold Rothstein at
the city mortuary on the 6th day of November, 1928, at
11:30 A.M. hours after the death, and said autopsy
revealed:

Body is that of a middle-aged white male, appearing to
be the age given, scale weight 169 pounds, 5 feet 7
inches in height, well formed, well developed.

Body is warm, no rigor mortis, well muscled and well
built.

There are numerous freckles, yellowish in color,
especially numerous on the upper arms, and there is a
very distinct greenish discoloration with cyanosis of the
forehead, less over the face.

The hair on the head is brown, medium brown, no gray
hairs. Eyebrows scanty. Pupils equal, 1/4 of an inch,
iris is dark brown, conjunctiva somewhat suffused. There
are two small linear abrasions on the pina of the nose,
one, on the left side, the longer, 4/10 of an inch in
length, and one on the right side, 2/10 of an inch in
length.

Nose natural, lips natural, four days' growth of hair.

There is a false rubber plate in the upper jaw. Lower
jaw shows goldwork, right lower lateral incisor, and also
goldwork on the canines. The premolars are absent. The
first molar is present. Left lower all absent.

There is a very considerable swelling of the chest
with numerous puncture marks (hypodermic). The abdomen is
swollen, and there is discoloration, yellowish.

There is an abdominal incision extending from the
pubes upwards 8 1/2 inches in length, 1 3/4 inches to the
right of the navel. The upper end of this wound is

sutured with a running chrome silk in the skin and four rubber retention sutures. Lower end is packed with gauze and with rubber drains.

In the penis there is a catheter retained by tape. Foreskin cut.

Also, staining of the adjacent portion of the thighs below Poupart. The pubes have been shaved.

No marks or bruises seen anywhere.

Fingers natural. Also hands.

There is a superficial excoriation in the middle and upper surface of the right calf.

The posterior surface of the body is natural. Shows only a slight postmortem hypostasis fairly well marked on the neck.

There is a puncture mark on the outer surface of the left elbow and also the middle of the right elbow joint.

There is a single bullet wound situated in the right belly, 3 1/2 inches to the right of the midline, 38 1/2 inches above the right heel, 2 1/2 inches in front of the right anterior iliac spine and 1/2 inch above it. The wound is elliptical in shape, 6/10 of an inch in length, with the outer border somewhat paler than the inner, 3/10 of an inch in breadth and the upper and outer portion of same shows an abrasion on the outer edges and it is red in color. The borders are also red. No powder grains in the skin.

Abdominal fat is 1 1/2 inches in thickness.

Along the line of the surgical incision, the muscles are somewhat softened and slightly infiltrated with blood and on the outer surface of the rectus there is a distinct layer of exudate, pale greenish in color.

The omentum is large, softened over the entire surface. In places, is injected. The peritoneal cavity contains very little blood stained fluid, collected in the dependent portion.

The guts are very warm.

No serosa of the small intestine. There are a few films of blood. The liver is well above the border; 2 inches. Diaphragm, left 4th space, right 3rd space. The anterior surface of the right ventricle is somewhat flattened. The pericardial cavity contains only a small amount of clear fluid, say 5 cc. There are a few adhesions posteriorly upper and lower lobes of the left lung. The right pleural cavity is free from fluid and adhesions. Mediastinal fat in excess. Slight excess of epicardial fat, especially along the groove.

Right lung weighs 470 grams, left lung weighs 570 grams. Lower lobe of the left lung is poorly aerated, somewhat lumpy, dark bluish red on the surface. Numerous dense patches of adhesions posterior surface, upper portion of the lobe. The lung is wet, upper lobe is congested. Frothy fluid in the bronchi, slightly bloodstained. Right lower lobe is dark blue, seen on the surface. Slightly lumpy. Dark bluish red in color. Upper and middle lobes somewhat frankly emphysematous. Upper lobe shows a few small blood spots (aspiration of blood).

Heart weighs 310 grams. Valves natural. Aortic, except for yellowish placques in the dark segment, natural. Mitral valve and left ventricle somewhat opaque. No foramen. Aorta at ring 2 3/10th inches. Intima is distinctly yellowish, somewhat sticky. Few more definite placques just above the ring. Coronaries are natural. Left ventricle normal, contracted as to muscles, 7/10 of an inch. Muscle is without visible fibrosis. Mesentary is fatty. Numerous areas of infiltrated blood.

On removing the intestine, a long, rather wide rectal tube is found inserted at a point below the sigmoid. There is a considerable amount of exudate about the area of the appendix which has been removed and there are

numerous sutures at the point in the mesentary and the
ileo-caecal region and the caecum itself.

Spleen weighs 130 grams, no adhesions, number of
yellow areas, 3/10 of an inch in diameter. On section,
also shows numerous yellowish areas. Otherwise natural.

Liver weighs 1730 grams. Pale brown, with a few paler
or anaemic spots. On section, is distinctly yellowish. No
lobulations. Gall bladder is small, pear sized. Black
bile. Mucous membrane is natural. Pancreas is natural in
size and configuration. Firm. Left adrenal is flat. Cortex
one millimeter, yellowish in color. Somewhat dark.

The left kidney is replaced by fat. No distinct kidney
tissue is made out in the gross. There is, however, a
very small renal artery.

The vena cava and the aorta are natural and without
wounds. On the intima of the abdominal aeorta in two
places, there is a reddish colored blood not adherent.
There is a marked excess of peritoneal fat in the right
kidney, which is very considerably enlarged, 6 inches in
length by two inches in breadth. Pale in color. Cortex is
thickened. Capsule free, surface smooth. Few superficial
scars on the surface. Pelves and ureters natural. No
wounds.

4 1/2 inches to the left of the posterior middle
gluteal fold, in the left buttock at a point 2 feet 8 1/2
inches above the heel, a bullet is found beneath the
skin. It is a 38 lead long, riflings red from base, right
to left.

There is an extensive suturing of the anterior surface
of the urinary bladder to the right of the midline. There
is an E & E wound with the "in" on the center of the
bladder near the midline, "out" or exit at the base of
the bladder through the trigonum and the left lobe of the
prostate. Mucous membrane is hemorrhagic about the point

of entrance. Prostate is natural. Also the rectum. The stomach is distended with a large amount of yellowish fluid. Mucous membrane is pale, otherwise is natural.

Duodenum is normal. Small gut, upper part of the small gut contains yellowish chyme about 1 1/4 inches, greenish chyme below this. There is some blood mixed with the contents of the small and large guts in the lower ileum and the caecum. There is a side to side anastomosis, an entero-caecal anastomosis with the stump of the small gut invaginated and sutured and the lower extremity of the caecum likewise invaginated and sutured. These two guts are sutured side by side, and an opening connects the ileum of both intestines. The large gut below this contains pasty partially formed slight brown feces.

Testicles are natural. Tubules pull out scantily.

Tract of the Bullet

The tract of the bullet is about one foot in length, from right to left and backwards, downwards about 6 inches. The bullet wound of entrance shows the direction of the tract, namely the upper, and short end of the wound shows a scraping of the skin, downward through the abdominal muscles, through the caecum, the urinary bladder, the left lobe of the prostate, pelvis and then out to the muscles through the obturator foramen, where the bullet is found, after passing through the gluteal muscles. The base of the bullet was marked with a single scratch-mark, for purposes of identification.

Scalp natural. Calvarium natural. There is a slight pial oedema. Brain vessels at the base are thin and delicate and smooth. No sclerosis. On section, the brain is natural. Base of the skull is natural. Sinuses at the base, including the middle ears and mastoid anthrum natural. The skull is rather thin, 3/16th of an inch in the frontal region, 5/16th in the occipital region, and about 1/8th of an inch on all sides. Brain weighs 1400 grams.

Anatomical Diagnosis

BULLET WOUND OF THE BELLY CAECUM URINARY BLADDER PROSTATE PELVES AND LEFT BUTTOCKS:

SUPPURATIVE PERITONITIS AND MYOSITIS:

PULMONARY CONGESTION AND OEDEMA: COMMENCING BRONCHOPNEUMONIA:

SEPSIS AND SHOCK.

Cause of Death

SEPSIS AND SHOCK: Bullet wound of the belly, large gut, urinary bladder, prostate, and pelves; Homicide.

Clothes

High tan shoes, marked Robert Whyte, 38 West 45th Street, New York.

Fancy multicolored tie. Label: F. Georges, Boulevarde des Capucines, Paris, France.

Blue garters. Lisle socks with white soles.

Turned-down blue Lane collar 15 1/2, laundry mark 2633, covered with dry vomitus.

Blue coat with red pin-stripes. Label: William Wallach, New York. With vomitus on the collar and shoulders. There is a single hole just below the front edge of the lower pocket. No flares. Trousers of the same material. On the right side, upper portion, there is also a hole which passes through the label of the tailor attached to the pocket: William Wallach, New York. Custom Tailor. Arnold Rothstein, 10/29/27.

Vest of the same material, stained with vomitus.

Silk shirt. Label: Harry Beck, Custom Shirt
Manufacturer. With the initials A.R. and a hole in the
corresponding position.

Coat, trousers, and shirt marked. C.N. 11/6/28.

Identifications

William S. Davis, Shield 2943 of the 9th Precinct to
Drs. Norris, Gonzales, and Vance, 11/6/28 at 12:15 P.M.
as the same body that he saw in the employees' entrance
of the Park Central Hotel, 56th Street and Seventh
Avenue, standing up, holding his side, about 10:45 P.M.,
November 4, 1928.

Deceased refused to say who shot him. Shot by unknown
person or persons. No arrest.

Also by Edgar, brother of the deceased, of 255 West
End Avenue, to Drs. Norris, Gonzales, and Vance at 1:15
P.M., November 6, 1928.

Charles Norris
Chief Medical Examiner
City of New York

—⊶⊷—

NEVER TRUST a loving God.

Dousing the Glim

N EW YORK WAS something. At 271½ Water Street, on the East Side, north of Peck Slip and a block east of Pearl Street, stately, plump Christopher "Kit" Burns ran a saloon and liquor shop from which a narrow winding passage led to Sportsman's Hall.

There was an elliptical pit in the ground, about ten feet long and six feet wide, surrounded by a two-foot fence and circled by rows of seats, accommodating some of the few hundred that could be crowded into the hall.

Sportsman's Hall offered four sporting events: rat killing by a weasel, rat killing by a dog, rat killing by a man, and dogfighting.

Kit, whose face was booze-red and scarred with smallpox, had come to New York from Ireland during the potato famine. He had brought with him a love for whiskey and fighting dogs. His favorite dogs stood stuffed at either end of the bar. There was Jack, a black-and-tan terrier who once had killed a hundred rats in six minutes and forty seconds, and at the other end there was Husky, a blooded bulldog who had the distinguished honor of "going out game," killing his last opponent before dying himself from the wounds inflicted on him by the conquered.

Sportsmen complained that rat killing by a weasel was too slow, as the weasel, who was a natural-born rat killer, devoted too much time to the chase. Rat killing by a dog was better spectacle, and it made for better gambling, as the event consisted of two matches of dog against rats—these two matches constituted a "ratting match"—and the dog that killed the greater number of rats won the contest. It made for an exciting game, as experienced dogs could often kill a rat with a single, snarling bite, and a "green" dog on his first time out could be a bookmaker's surprise.

As for rat killing by a man, Burns often found it difficult to find a man willing to get into the pit, chase down a big fat river rat, seize it, and take off its wild, vicious head with a chomp of the jaw. Some men would do anything for a bottle. But such men were not always adept in the pit, and a man with delirium tremens and nothing but a few wobbly teeth pitted against a mean and muscular rat could make for interesting gambling. Long-money bettors cheered whenever the rat took a piece of hand, lips, cheek, or nose. Burns himself professed distaste for this type of contest. He was a man for dogfighting. This was where the sport was, and this was where the money was. The prize purse for a winning dog could run as high as a thousand dollars. The wagers that passed through bookmakers' hands could run to far more.

Before each fight, dogs would be bathed in hot water and "tasted," to ensure that they were not doped: coated with some substance that might poison and weaken an opponent. There were men for hire who were expert at "tasting." These tasting men could detect a substance by licking and nibbling at the hair of a dog's coat.

The bane of Sportsman's Hall and other such establishments was a tall, slender man named Henry Bergh (1811–1888). He was a member of the New York City aristocracy, the son of Christian Bergh, who had been one of the biggest and wealthiest shipbuilders in New York. After his father's death, in 1843, the younger Bergh became a man of leisure, dabbling in the arts and touring Europe. As befitting the life of an aristocrat, he was appointed in 1863 to a diplomatic post at the Russian court of Czar Alexander II. En route to America on his return from Russia, he stopped in London, where he met with the Earl of Harrowby, president of the Royal Society for the Prevention of Cruelty to Animals. In New York City, in 1866, Henry Bergh founded the American Society for the Prevention of Cruelty to Animals.

In November 1866, a little more than seven months after Bergh's organization was incorporated, the *New York Herald* printed an article decrying the brutality of dogfights. Mention was made of a dogfight held earlier that month at Sportsman's Hall. The *Herald* called for Bergh and the police to put an end to such savagery.

Burns held a ratting match later in the month. Ward politicians and justices protected men such as Burns, as they protected all vice. This was their job. It was what they were paid to do. Legal actions brought against Burns and others were dismissed by justices who said they found nothing wrong with deriving a bit of entertainment from "the fine sport of dog-fighting."

The first annual report of Bergh's society, published in 1867, reported a legal victory in the case of one David Heath, who was sentenced to ten days in prison for beating a cat to death. Upon hearing the verdict, Mr. Heath "remarked that the arresting officer ought to be disemboweled," at which point a twenty-five-dollar fine was added to his punishment.

But Bergh was persistent and a master of public notice in his crusade to protect what he called the "mute servants of mankind." Burns and his fellows hated this wealthy fop who had nothing but time and money on his hands. "Wouldn't he kill a rat if he found one in his cellar?" Burns said of Bergh, to a reporter from the *New York Tribune* in September 1868. "*I know rats*. I know they're vermin and they *ought* to be killed; and if we can get a little sport out of their killing, so much the better." William F. Howe (1821–1900), a skilled and flamboyant defense attorney who was later known as "the Father of the Criminal Bar," was the lawyer who defended Burns against Bergh. With fine rhetoric and complete legal irrelevance, Howe told a judge that if Bergh had his way, New Yorkers might soon be looked upon as criminals for knifing open an oyster and eating it alive.

Raids became increasingly frequent, amid warning cries from the bar and passageway to extinguish the lanterns in the pit hall: "Douse the glim!" Burns was arrested for the last time in November 1870. The case never went to court. Kit Burns died on December 18, a few weeks after the arrest, just shy of his fortieth birthday.

Bergh turned his attention to the city's cockfighting saloons. In early 1871, a reporter from *The New York Times* found fifty-year-old Mike Reynolds, an eminent cocker who ran a joint on Third Street. He was described as "bleary-eyed," emerging from a binge, and free with his rancor. In his Southern manner he alluded to the political power of the cockfighting fraternity. He said the cocks that Bergh had confiscated were caged up in Bergh's office "a-fattenin'." Then he raised his voice: "Hang Bergh, the superannuated old thief."

The "superannuated old thief" was about eight years older than his denouncer.

Baseball had been played since the early years of the century. It is telling of baseball's future as a "good, clean" sport that in the celebrated game of June 19, 1846, between the Knickerbocker Ball Club and the New

York Club, played in Hoboken, the New York Club pitcher, James Whyte Davis, was fined six cents for swearing. Now the game was increasingly promoted as a more salubrious alternative to the sporting events of ratting matches, dogfights, and cockfights. A man could drink his booze and beer and smoke his cigars out in the open air while watching the game, and of course he could bet on it. In fact, as men such as Abraham Rothstein's son would learn, it was easier to dope a ball game than a ratting match. But where the hell was the blood?

As early as the fall of 1867, a writer in the *New York Evening Telegram* mourned the loss of what was vanishing before him. "The irrepressible suppressor" Henry Bergh, he said, was a destroyer of "the good old times." It was a shame: "There is no amusement to be had nowadays."

I am grateful to Martin and Herbert J. Kaufman, whose study of "Henry Bergh, Kit Burns, and the Sportsmen of New York" was published in the *New York Folklore Quarterly* of March 1972.

Still, as bloodshed for profit faded in the 1870s, the saloons of New York were still places where a soul could always find a passage to hell. Bars were the temples of degeneracy, of *joie de vivre* and *joie de mourir*. Drinking, smoking, gambling, wenching, were what bars were all about. This continued to be true for more than a century.

The Bells of Hell, the last public joint in the old tradition, closed on July 26, 1979. Fred Tamburri, last great after-hours proprietor, passed away on June 7, 1986. By the summer of 1988, almost all of the old-style neighborhood bars, social clubs, and gambling joints were gone. Giuliani became mayor of New York in January 1994, and he finished off what was left of real life. Like the reformer Fiorello La Guardia, who had served as mayor from 1934 to 1945, Giuliani persecuted his own kind. A Jew named Bloomberg followed him in 2002. As there was little left in the post-mortem city to offend the new mayor's delicate sensibilities, he outlawed smoking in bars. Welcome to the mall of mortuary mediocrity. The end.

It was not only booze—any kind of booze—that one could get back then.

There was opium. Sweet breath of the lady, most beautiful gift of the gods after life and love.

There was the alcoholic tincture of opium called laudanum, which had gained popularity in the early seventeenth century. Drunkard's dream, housewife's dram, calmative of the crying child.

There was morphine. First extracted from opium in 1803, first commercially manufactured by E. Merck & Company of Germany in 1827, and first rendered injectable in 1843, morphine had grown widespread in America since the Civil War, when it was routinely used to treat the injured. The hypodermic needle had been invented for morphine injection in 1853.

There was cocaine, which had been isolated in pure form from coca leaves in 1844. In France in 1863, the year after Merck produced its first quarter pound of cocaine, a young Corsican pharmacist named Angelo Mariani patented Vin Mariani, a Bordeaux wine containing six micrograms of cocaine per liquid ounce. By the end of the decade, American competitors were selling a stronger version, with more than seven micrograms per ounce. Merck's cocaine production in 1883 rose to three quarters of a pound. The next year it rose to well over three thousand pounds and in 1886 to well over a hundred and fifty thousand pounds.

When Ulysses S. Grant lay dying in 1885 in upstate New York, he was treated with injections of good brandy and morphine as well as cocaine. Down in New York City, his treatment was other people's pleasure.

Opium to be smoked. Absinthe and laudanum to be drunk. Morphine to be drunk or shot. Cocaine to be shot, snorted, or drunk from bottles of infused Bordeaux or the vials of liquid cocaine extract that Parke-Davis manufactured. And very soon heroin. Morphine's synthetic daughter fair would be introduced to the market, by the Bayer Company, in 1898, the year before it introduced aspirin to the pharmaceutical trade.

A Bayer Web site celebrating the centenary of aspirin declared, "We are proud of Aspirin." There was no similar celebration of the centenary of heroin, no declaration by Bayer stating, "We are proud of Heroin."

And, except for those Chinese opium dens, it was legal, all of it. Some indulged, many didn't. They called it freedom, and they called the bars dives. Now everything's illegal, and they call it freedom. It's easier for me to kill you on the subway and get away with it than it is for me to smoke a cigarette on the subway and get away with it. A cigarette takes six minutes.

OTHER MEMBERS of the Rothstein family began to arrive in New York. In 1858, a relative named Henry was a part of the Harris Rothstein household on Pearl Street. Henry was in business with a man named Abraham Raffel in a cap shop, Rothstein & Raffel, at 47 Maiden Lane, close to the shop that Harris had opened on John Street. By 1859, Harris moved his family to 131 Monroe Street, an East Side address, north of Rutgers Street, that no longer exists.

By 1860, he moved across the street to 129 Monroe. By 1862, he moved to the next block, first to 185 Madison Street, then, by 1863, to 91 Madison. He moved his place of business in 1859 from John Street to 140 Broadway, on the east side of the thoroughfare, between Cedar and Liberty streets; then, in 1862, across the road to 139 Broadway; and, in 1863, to 119 Broadway, a block south, at Pine Street. In 1864, the Rothstein family moved to 117 East Thirty-ninth Street, and the shop moved north to 338 Broadway, near Worth Street. Within the next year, the Rothsteins moved to 160 Allen Street, between Rivington and Stanton streets.

The location of Harris Rothstein's shop changed frequently: to 478 Broadway in 1870; to 431 Broome Street in 1871; to 119 South Fifth Avenue—formerly Laurens Street, later West Broadway—in 1874. But the Rothstein family remained at 160 Allen Street for more than a decade, from 1865 until 1875.

On March 3, 1861, Alexander II of Russia signed the Emancipation Manifesto, which abolished serfdom. Serfdom and slavery were essentially the same. A slave was personal property. A serf was required to work for a master who did not own him outright, as the serf was considered to belong to the land. Slaves could be bought and sold. Serfs were passed on with the estate from one landowner to the next. In theory, a serf could buy his freedom by paying off his indebtedness to his master, but this was all but impossible, and slaves and serfs alike found their freedom only rarely.

At the time of the Russian emancipation, about 20 percent of the Russian population lived in serfdom. In the United States at this time, about 10 percent of the population lived in slavery.

By this time, bondage was outdated in the agricultural industry and economy of the South. Steam-powered machines worked far more efficiently, far more productively, than slaves. The cotton gin—"gin" being a shortened form of "engine" that dates at least to the early fourteenth century—could separate cotton-wool from its seeds about fifty times faster than slave labor. But plantation slavery was not the only form of slavery in the South. Many well-to-do individuals, including a number of freed slaves, owned one or a few slaves. Cotton gin or no cotton gin, the "peculiar institution" was a part of the fabric of wealthy Southern life, and it was held by wealthy Southerners to be a part of the fabric of the United States as well. Washington, Jefferson, Franklin, the rest of them: They all owned slaves.

Abraham Lincoln was inaugurated on March 4, 1861, the day after Alexander II abolished serfdom. Lincoln wanted abolition in the United States as well. Following his election, seven Southern states had seceded from the Union and formed their own Confederacy. Other states would join them in the new year. The first of the states to secede had been South Carolina. In the month before Lincoln's inauguration, an unarmed merchant ship bringing supplies to the garrison at Fort Sumter had been fired on from the shore batteries of Charleston Harbor. In April, after the inauguration, the Confederacy attacked Fort Sumter itself.

The years of the Civil War were the most violent that the country knew. September 17, 1862, was the bloodiest day in American history: Six thousand men and boys who were alive at dawn on that day were dead by nightfall, at the Battle of Antietam Creek. Some seventeen thousand more lay wounded. There were more American soldiers killed on this day than at Normandy on D-Day of 1944; more than were killed in the years of the War of 1812, the Mexican War, and the Spanish-American War combined.

On January 4, 1861, Rabbi Dr. Morris Jacob Raphall (1798–1868) of Congregation B'nai Jeshurun preached a sermon at the Greene Street synagogue. It was under Rabbi Raphall's ministry that Harris Rothstein had joined the congregation in the previous year. In his sermon, the rabbi censured those who would abolish slavery.

"How dare you," he exclaimed, "denounce slave-holding as a sin?" Slavery, he said, was not a sin in the Bible, and as the Bible was the highest law, there could be no justification for speaking of any "divine law" against it. He invoked "Abraham, Isaac, Jacob, Job—the men with whom the Almighty conversed," reminding his flock that "all these men were slave-holders."

The rabbi's words were given much circulation and were said to represent the Jewish view of slavery. But they did not. There was no Jewish view of slavery any more than there was a gentile view of it. The abolitionist rabbi David Einhorn was forced to flee Baltimore in 1861 because of his preaching against slavery. From his pulpit in Philadelphia, Rabbi Sabato Morais, a defender of orthodoxy, also declaimed against slavery. Jews served as officers and enlisted men in the armies of both the Union and the Confederacy. (See Robert N. Rosen's book *The Jewish Confederates*.) The Union commanders, like many Christian abolitionists in the North, showed a good deal of hostility for Jews. An order by General Ulysses S. Grant called for the expulsion in 1862 of all Jews from Kentucky, Tennessee, and Mississippi. General Henry W. Halleck saw "traitors and Jew peddlars" as one and described "the Israelites" as "an intolerable nuissance." Both these generals believed that profiteering Jews were in control of the black market in Southern cotton that thrived during the Civil War. Later, in his campaign for the presidency, Grant would say that his order for the expulsion of Jews was written by a subordinate officer and that he had signed it without reading it. He carried the Jewish vote and later appointed several Jews to high office in his administration.

The price of cotton in 1860 had been pretty much what it had been for the last ten years: about twelve cents per pound. The price of scoured wool had been pretty much what it had been for the last ten years: about a dollar a pound. During those black market years of the Civil War, the price of cotton rose to more than ninety-five cents a pound and the price of wool to almost a dollar and eighty cents a pound, driven to some extent by the need for soldiers' woolen uniforms and coats. It would be another ten years, including a financial panic and a depression, before prices showed a stable decline. Meanwhile, the income tax that Lincoln had levied to get war money—3 percent on annual incomes of six hundred dollars or more—would not be repealed until 1872. These were not the best years to be a stitcher of cotton goods or woolen caps.

From *A Century of Judaism in New York*, a history of Congregation B'nai Jeshurun by Dr. Israel Goldstein that was published by the congregation in 1930: "When the Civil War broke out, Dr. Raphall affirmed his loyalty to the cause of the Union." His son Alfred served in the Union army, became a captain, and lost an arm at Gettysburg. Rabbi Raphall gave an address on Lincoln at the B'nai Jeshurun synagogue on April 19, 1865, following the president's assassination. Little Abraham Rothstein was eight years old then. But by this time, B'nai Jeshurun had left Greene Street and moved into a new synagogue uptown, on Thirty-fourth Street between Broadway and Seventh Avenue.

Today the presidential staff includes a deputy assistant to the president and director of speechwriting, a special assistant to the president for economic speechwriting, a special assistant to the president and deputy director of speechwriting, a special assistant to the president and senior speechwriter, an executive assistant to the director of speechwriting, and a speechwriter for the First Lady. But long ago, before fatuous, disingenuous men mouthed the fatuous, disingenuous words of others, there were statesmen who spoke from within, and there was something within them. To read Lincoln's Second Inaugural Address, delivered on March 4, 1865, is to feel the power and immensity of what once was and of what has been lost. The Civil War ended on April 9. Lincoln's life ended a few days later.

Some months earlier, on November 21, 1864, he had written a letter to his friend Colonel William F. Elkins:

We may congratulate ourselves that this cruel war is nearing its end. It has cost a vast amount of treasure and blood. The best blood of the flower of American youth has been freely offered upon our country's altar that the nation might live. It has indeed been a trying time for the Republic; but I now see in the near future a crisis approaching that unnerves me and causes me to tremble for the safety of my country.

As a result of the war, corporations have been enthroned and an era of corruption in high places will follow, and the money power of the country will endeavor to prolong its reign by working upon the prejudices of the people until all wealth is aggregated in a few hands and the Republic is destroyed. I feel at this moment more anxiety than ever before, even in the midst of war. God grant that my suspicions may prove groundless.

These visionary words have had great and increasing currency for many years. They have been recalled in speech making in the United States Senate and included in *The Lincoln Encyclopedia* of Archer Hayes Shaw. So-called liberals and libertarians have found in them a bedrock on which to raise their own voices. Educators, authors, reformers, have called our attention to them again and again.

But Lincoln never knew these words, which first were attributed to him in a promotional pamphlet published by the Caldwell Remedy Company on May 10, 1888. Lincoln's former personal secretary John G. Nicolay was known to have confronted George C. Hackstaff of the Caldwell Company regarding the propriety of counterfeiting a Lincoln quotation to sell patent medicines. Robert Todd Lincoln dismissed the letter as a forged imagining. Furthermore, he wrote in 1917, "I have no recollection of any personal friend of my father named Elkins."

But the lie often repeated becomes history, and the snake-oil pitchman's forgery of yore becomes the inspirational gospel of a posterity that sees itself as worldly and wise.

THE RAVAGED AND conflagrated cities of the South remembered battles. New York remembered the riots of the summer of 1863, when federal authorities tried to put the draft into effect in New York City.

Enacted by the Thirty-seventh Congress to increase the ranks of Union fighting men, the Enrollment Act of 1863 subjected to conscription all males between the ages of twenty and forty-five. Under the act, a man could avoid service by paying three hundred dollars to a substitute who would serve for him. This is what men such as John D. Rockefeller and future president Grover Cleveland did. But this kind of money—equivalent to about forty-five hundred dollars today—was well beyond the means of most workingmen.

A mob of these men, stirred by a group of Irish-born laborers, attacked the draft headquarters and burned and pillaged homes, stores, hotels, and saloons. The mob overpowered police, firemen, and militia for days.

The New York City historian Francis Morrone described Isaac Newton Phelps Stokes (1867–1944) as a "self-deprecating patrician polymath and reformer," a gentleman "effete in manners, aristocratic in temperament, and humble to a fault." Born to a family of wealth, architect and scholar I. N. Phelps Stokes had been raised in the large brownstone at the southeast corner of Thirty-seventh and Madison Avenue that became the home of J. P. Morgan Jr. and is today a part of the Pierpont Morgan Library. He studied under some of the most celebrated professors of Harvard's golden age, including Charles Eliot Norton. He took Josiah Royce's course on Literary Aspects of the Bible, which fifteen years later stirred T. S. Eliot's interest in primitive ritual. After further studies at the École des Beaux-Arts in Paris, Stokes returned to New York from his three years abroad, where with his friend John Meade Howells, the son of novelist and editor William Dean Howells, he entered a competition for the design of the University Settlement Society building. The young architectural firm of Howells & Stokes won. Their Settlement House, built in 1898 of lime-stone and red brick, still stands at the corner of Eldridge and Rivington streets.

The consuming labor of Stokes's life was the monumental six-volume work called *The Iconography of Manhattan Island, 1498–1909*. Begun in 1910 and completed in 1928, it is a work of opulence in every way. Of the first edition, published by Robert H. Dodd in the years 1915–1928, there were three hundred and sixty copies printed on English and Holland handmade paper and forty-two copies on Japanese vellum, each large quarto volume bound in leather and gilt-stamped cloth with an individual slipcase. The collection of innumerable photo-intaglio reproductions, many of them gatefold, and colortype photographic plates made in Vienna has not been surpassed. Nor have the painstakingly detailed and docu-mented chronology of more than two thousand pages, the index of nearly four hundred three-columned pages.

It is a work that is without equal. I think of the greater and vaster, but many-handed, work, begun under James A. H. Murray (1837–1915), of *The Oxford English Dictionary,* the thirteenth volume of the first full edi-tion of which was published in 1933, after almost seventy years' labor. I think of the twenty-nine volumes of the eleventh edition (1910–1911) of the *Encyclopaedia Britannica,* again greater and vaster but many-handed, under Hugh Chisholm (1866–1924). I think of the six volumes of the *En-ciclopedia Dantesca,* under Umberto Bosco (1900–1987), published by Treccani in 1970. But I can think of no other American work like Stokes's.

Here he is at the outset of his "Topographical, Biographical, and His-torical Data" relating to "The Castello Plan Showing the City of New Amsterdam in the Year 1660," a map reproduced in five plates, the last of which enumerates the land's buildings and lots: "Block A, No. 1: Lodowyck Pos, cabinet-maker, and captain of the Rattle Watch bought this house and lot from Jan Martyn, May 21, 1655, for 600 florins ($240.), to be paid in equal installments of 200 florins each, the first, however, to con-sist of two cows. When the second payment became due, Martyn sued for it, May, 1656, alleging that the cows had not been delivered." This is from volume 2, page 215. He arrives at the last of his "Locations Beyond the Wall" on page 341, ending with the note "Now, part of Trinity Churchyard." The index, in volume 6, refers us, by description and date, to other factual entries concerning Lodowyck Pos and Jan Martyn that are to be found in the main historical chronology.

The name Rothstein, alas, is to be found nowhere. Still, I here should like to use Stokes's words. His lucid perspective, historical accuracy, and subtly elegant prose distinguish him.

Monday, July 13, 1863:

Before the day was over, gangs of thieves had joined the crowd and availed themselves of the general disturbance to reap a harvest of plunder. While the up-town mob was destroying a brownstone block on Lexington Avenue, a detachment of marines, some fifty in number, with muskets and blank cartridges, was sent to quell the riot. The mob, informed of the soldiers' coming, tore up the rails of the Third Avenue street-car line, so that the marines were forced to leave their car at 43rd Street, where several thousand men, women, and children stood ready to meet them. As the marines advanced, they fired their blank cartridges at the mob, which immediately rushed upon them, broke up the little band, seized their muskets, trampled the men under foot, beat them with sticks, and laughed at their impotence. Several of the marines were killed, and all were terribly beaten. From this moment, the spirit of the mob changed. Mere resistance was no longer thought of; attack became the watchword.

The mob was particularly infuriated against negroes. Restaurants and hotels whose servants were of this race were taken possession of by the rioters, who smashed windows, destroyed furniture, maltreated guests, and tried to kill the fleeing servants. No coloured person's life was safe. In the afternoon of this day (Monday), the mob attacked and burned the Colored Half Orphan Asylum, a substantial building which had been erected a few years before on Fifth Avenue between 43rd and 44th streets. About the same hour, an attack was made on the armory in Second Avenue at the corner of 21st Street, the object being to obtain the muskets and rifles which the government was known to have stored there. The squad of police that had been stationed there to prevent a successful attack was overpowered, and

forced to retire; the building was fired, and soon fell, a mass of black-
ened ruins.

   During the remainder of the Monday, and for the next three days,
the riots continued. Disturbances occurred in various parts of the city,
from Second Avenue westward to the North River, as far north as
Harlem, and as far south as Mulberry Street. During this time, business
was almost entirely suspended throughout the city. Railroads and om-
nibuses stopped running, the stores on Broadway and on the avenues
throughout the greater part of the city were closed, and prowling gangs
of ruffians made the streets unsafe. The number of rioters killed by the
police and soldiers is unknown, but it was estimated at between four
and five hundred. The number of persons killed by the mob was eigh-
teen, of whom eleven were coloured. The number of buildings burned
by the mob, from Monday until Wednesday morning, was more than
fifty, and included, besides the Colored Half Orphan Asylum, two po-
lice stations, three provost-marshal's offices, and an entire block of
houses on Broadway. A large number of stores and dwellings were
sacked, though not burned, and their contents destroyed or carried
away. The entire amount of property stolen or destroyed amounted to
upwards of one million two hundred thousand dollars.

New York State governor Horatio Seymour "appeared on the steps of
the City Hall, made a few conciliatory remarks to the crowd, in which he
addressed them as 'friends,' and announced that he had sent his adjutant-
general to Washington, to confer with the authorities there and get the
draft stopped. Gradually, the activities of the rioters lessened."

A lot of people had moved out of New York City during the years of
the Civil War. The city's population had grown almost tenfold in the first
half of the century: from sixty thousand or so souls in 1800 to over half a
million in 1850. The following years had seen growth to 814,254 in 1860,
then a decrease to 726,385 in 1865. Within the next five years, however, the
population surpassed nine hundred thousand, then grew slowly in the next
decade to surpass a million by 1880. Twenty years later, after waves of mi-
gration from Eastern Europe and Italy, and after the outlying counties had
been incorporated as the boroughs of Brooklyn, Queens, the Bronx, and

Staten Island, the population of New York City approached three and a half million. More than a million of these were Jews. This increase would continue, and the Jewish population of the city would not fall to under a million again until the early years of the twenty-first century.

Jews had represented less than 1 percent of New York City's population at the turn of the century. By the eve of the Civil War, their number had risen to about forty thousand, or about 4 percent of the city's population.

Some of these Jews were important figures. Benjamin Seixas and Ephraim Hart were among the founders of the New York Stock Exchange in 1792. Mordecai Manuel Noah (1785–1851), a defender of the slavery system and a founder of Tammany Hall, was elected high sheriff of New York in 1821, surveyor of the port of New York in 1829, and judge of the court of sessions in 1841. The publishers Naphtali Phillips and Naphtali Judah were also influential in the Tammany Society in the early decades of the century. Mordecai Myers was elected to the state assembly in 1829. Daniel Jackson was a broker and banker. Bernhard Hart was honorary secretary of the New York Stock Exchange from 1831 to 1853. August Belmont represented the interests of the Rothschilds in America beginning in 1836. Emanuel B. Hart was elected to the House of Representatives in 1851 and also held the posts of surveyor of the port and president of the board of aldermen. Early in the Civil War, Joseph Seligman's firm, J. & J. Seligman & Co., sold federal bonds in the astonishing sum of two hundred million dollars.

The richest Jews, like the richest Christians, lived in the area slightly below and slightly above Wall Street. The copper merchant Harmon Hendricks, considered to have been the richest Jew in early-nineteenth-century New York, lived at 61 Greenwich Street. John Jacob Astor (1763–1848), an immigrant from the German territory of Baden-Baden, near Württemberg, was a Lutheran. But he learned it all from a Jew, Hayman Levy, who gave young Astor a job in his fur-trading business.

August Belmont (1816–1890) and Joseph Seligman (1819–1880) were among the first of the immigrants from Germany whose families came to define the aristocracy of Jewish wealth and society in New York in the nineteenth century. Both Belmont and Seligman arrived in America in 1837. The Lehman brothers began their American journey as pork-eating, slave-owning cotton merchants in Montgomery, Alabama, in 1844. Emanuel Lehman opened the brothers' New York office in 1858. Meyer Guggenheim (1828–1905) arrived in America in 1848, Solomon Loeb (1828–1903) in 1849. These and other immigrants became patriarchs of the social set recounted in Stephen Birmingham's *"Our Crowd": The Great Jewish Families of New York*.

Belmont arrived rich, a financier with the resources of the Rothschilds at his disposal. The banking house of the Rothschilds was not only the foremost Jewish financial firm in Europe, it was also the world's largest private bank. The power that the Rothschilds had invested in this short, stout, ill-mannered man was a source of much speculation and many rumors. His real name was August Schönberg, but he was set on not being a Jew and thus changed the "beautiful mountain" of his name from German (*schöner Berg*) to French (*belle mont*), a ridiculous move in light of his harsh German accent. He carefully chose from Christian society a Christian wife, Caroline Slidell Perry. When John Jacob Astor had died in 1848, leaving a fortune of some twenty million dollars, six Episcopalian clergymen had conducted his funeral. Thus when Belmont married, it was by an Episcopal minister at Grace Church. He and his new wife lived in the grandest mansion in New York, at 109 Fifth Avenue.

But most of these men arrived poor. A few of them, such as Seligman, who gave his farewell oration from the University of Erlangen in classical Greek, were men of erudition. More of them were not.

The aristocracy of families they engendered was an exclusive one. As Birmingham writes, "In New York, it would become a matter of some consequence whether such and such a family, with a German-sounding name, had been a true *native* German family, like the Seligmans, or a stranger from the east, passing through."

Regardless of their German name and blood, Harris Rothstein and his family would be looked down upon as strangers from the East, passing through on their way to America.

Alexander II, who had abolished serfdom, had also instituted many reforms regarding the Jews, attempting to better allow their assimilation into Russian society. Alexander II was assassinated in March 1881. Confusion reigned throughout the country. Revolutionaries called on the people to rebel. The regime was compelled to protect itself, and the Russian government found a scapegoat: the Jews.

The Jewish communities in Russia fell victim to looting, rape, and murder. These pogroms were suppressed only when world pressure was brought to bear on Alexander III. The world at large never before had heard the word "pogrom." It was a Russian word that meant "devastation" or "destruction." But by March 17, 1882, the *Times* of London declared that "the 'Pogromen' (riots against the Jews) must be stopped."

The czar then enacted the laws of May 3, 1882. Canceling the reforms of Alexander II, these so-called May Laws restricted Jewish movement and settlement to the Pale, revoked all deeds and leases held by Jews outside the Pale, and prohibited Jews from trade on Sundays and all Christian holidays. Pogroms continued to flare.

Elsewhere in Europe, there were other new words. The term *"Antisemitismus"* had recently appeared in a pamphlet by Wilhelm Marr (1819–1904) called *Der Sieg des Judenthums über das Germanenthum* (*Jewry's Victory over Teutonism*). Though it was a misappellation—Arabs, for example, were every bit as Semitic as Jews—the word was not as harsh as the more accurate *Judenhass* ("Jew-hatred").

The pamphlet was published in 1879, the year that the journalist Marr founded the Antisemiten-Liga, which sought to oppose "with all lawful means, the further displacement of Germanism by Judaism, by making its task to force the Semites back into a position corresponding with their numerical strength by liberating Germanism from the oppressive weight of Jewish influence in social, political, and ecclesiastical matters, and by securing for the children of Teutons their full rights to office and dignity in the German fatherland." Marr's pamphlet went through a dozen editions in six years. In his later years, Marr dissociated himself from what he called the "business of anti-Semitism." The term that he had brought to the language appeared in English in the London *Athenœum* of September 3, 1881, which noted that "Anti-Semitic literature is very prosperous in Germany." Several months later, in February 1882, the same periodical referred to "these days of anti-Semitism." The term seems then to have slumbered for more than half a century, until the summer of 1935, when it again was applied to events in Germany.

Konstantin Petrovich Pobedonostsev (1827–1907), the lay head of the governing body of the Russian Orthodox Church and adviser to Alexander III, formulated the objectives of Alexander III's government when in 1898 he told a Jewish delegation: One third of Russian Jews will perish, one third will flee the country, and one third will convert and be completely dissolved in the Christian population.

Before the assassination of Alexander II and the enactment of the May Laws, the Jews of Russia represented less than 10 percent of all immigration from the empire. Beginning with the first waves of 1882, Jews represented more than 80 percent of all immigration from Russia. More than two million Jews left Russia in the years 1882–1914. Most of them came to America. Between 1880 and 1900, the population of New York City more than doubled, from under a million and a quarter to almost three and a half million. The immigrant Jews from Eastern Europe were a great part of this increase, followed by large numbers of Italians from the famined South of their land. Over a million Jews came to the United States in the years 1882–1910.

The epithet "wop" was first used among Italians to refer to other Italians. The root of the word is ancient, the Latin *uappu,* which was used literally to describe wine gone bad, but which was also used figuratively as early as the first century B.C., by Horace, to describe a good-for-nothing, a worthless character. From *uappu* came the Sicilian *vappu* and *guappu,* which connoted arrogance, bluster, and maleficence entwined. It was these Sicilian words that were commonly used to describe the work bosses who lured their greenhorn *paesani* into servitude in New York City in the late years of the nineteenth century and the early years of the twentieth.

In New York and other American seaports, the lowly labor of the Italian immigrants' servitude—the dockside toil and offal hauling that others shunned—came to be called, after the work bosses, *guappu* work; and eventually the laborer himself, and not the boss, was known as *guappu.* The peasant immigrants' tendency to clip the final vowels from standard Italian and Sicilian—as in *paesan'* for *paesano*—rendered *guappu* as *guapp',* which was pronounced, more or less, as *wop.*

The word appears, as "wap," in *Courts, Criminals and the Camorra* by Arthur Cheney Train (1874–1945). This book was published in New York by Charles Scribner's Sons in 1912. "There is a society of criminal young men in New York City," writes Train. "They are known by the euphonious name of 'Waps' or 'Jacks.' These are young Italian-Americans who allow themselves to be supported by one or two women." They are, he writes, "one variety of the many gangs that infest the city."

Jack London writes in 1913, in *John Barleycorn,* of a financial desperation that had driven him years earlier to seek "work as a wop, lumper and roustabout."

A Vocabulary of Criminal Slang by Louis E. Jackson & C. R. Hellyer, a slim volume published in 1914 by the Modern Printing Company of Portland, includes the entry "*Wop,* noun. Used principally in the east. An ignorant person; a foreigner; an impossible character."

But not just any foreigner. "He's a wop," wrote P. G. Wodehouse in 1915. "A wop, a dago." Lest there be any misunderstanding: "An Italian." This was the year that Irving Berlin wrote the song "Hey, Wop," recorded by Rhoda Bernard for Pathé and by George Thompson for Edison. It was with a wop song that the Russian-born Jew Irving Berlin began his illustrious career, in 1906. Berlin—he was still Israel Baline then—was eighteen years old, working as a singing waiter at the Pelham Café, a saloon with an upstairs brothel. Located at 12 Pell Street in Chinatown, the Pelham was run by a shady Russian Jew whose swarthy complexion had led him to be known as Nigger Mike Salter.

Some time ago, I found the following statement in a history book about Italian immigrants to America:

> *When the Croton Reservoir was being built in 1895 to meet the needs of New York City, a public notice recruiting laborers for the project was circulated through newspaper advertisements and handbills. It listed a daily wage schedule of three groups:*
>
> *Common labor, white $1.30 to $1.50*
> *Common labor, colored $1.25 to $1.40*
> *Common labor, Italian $1.15 to $1.25*

I had never before come across this intriguing "wage schedule." I made up my mind to see a copy of the original. Perhaps the author had a copy. He was a man with a PhD whom *The New York Times* praised as presenting his data "with scholarly precision." Then, after a moment, it struck me. This was the stuff of folklore and fantasy. The construction of the Croton Reservoir had been completed fifty years earlier, in 1842. The construction of the New York Public Library on the site of the reservoir did not begin until 1899. I wrote to the author, asking him for the source of his "wage schedule," and received no reply. I have since seen this fictive schedule reproduced in another book, citing the book in question as its source. Again the lie repeated becomes history, its precision praised; and again I tell you: Believe nothing unless you hear it from me.

So it was with the word "kike": an epithet first used among Jews to refer to other Jews. For in the late-nineteenth-century immigrant tide from Eastern Europe, the Jewish aristocracy of New York, and the established and aspiring Jewish middle class as well, found a subset that could be looked down upon. These newly arrived refugees all seemed to bear names such as Lansky, Pohalski, and far lengthier, multisyllabic configurations that boggled mind and tongue, all of them ending in the same phonetic particles. Thus the derisive term "kike," perhaps originally pronounced with the final vowel voiced, as a long *e*.

As hard as they tried, members of the Jewish aristocracy could not penetrate the precincts of the gentile aristocracy of New York society. Boss Tweed's New York Railway Company was incorporated in the spring of 1871 to build an elevated railroad—a "viaduct railway," it was called—that was to run the western length of Manhattan beginning at Chambers Street. Tweed installed one of his judges, Henry Hilton, as president of the company. August Belmont sat with William Waldorf Astor on its board. But Belmont remained constantly frustrated in his desire to gain invitation to the Astor family's social functions. Joseph Seligman's appointment in the spring of 1875 to the city's first rapid transit commission was much noted. Yet two years later, Seligman was denied admission to the Grand Union Hotel in Saratoga Springs, one of the celebrated summering places of New York society.

As their moneyed entrée to gentile high society was again and again rebuffed, the Jewish aristocracy, as much as they may have given in charity to immigrant causes, seemed increasingly to find solace in disdain for the less fortunate. From the *Encyclopaedia Judaica:* "The two groups—the prosperous and Americanized 'uptown Jews' and the alien and plebeian 'downtown Jews'—confronted and interacted with one another." One found no "kikes" at the Harmonie, the exclusive club that the Jewish aristocracy had established in 1867 on Forty-second Street near Fifth Avenue.

The popular 1887 guidebook *Wonders of a Great City* devotes a chapter to "the Children of Abraham":

"The people of Israel are very numerous," begins the chapter. "A portion of them are intelligent, respectable and wealthy. The leading bankers are Jews of this class; so are the importers, who have almost wholly monopolized a large portion of the foreign trade. But the Jews of the lower class are disagreeable, and their presence a nuisance to any Christian neighborhood. If they get into a block, they infest it like the plague." The guide cast his gaze downtown: "Portions of the city on the east side are wholly given over to this nation."

The word "kike" does not appear in print until 1904, in *The Show Girl and Her Friends* by Roy L. McCardell, who in 1900 had been the first salaried writer of moving picture scenarios. *The Show Girl and Her Friends* was the sequel to McCardell's 1903 *Conversations of a Chorus Girl.* McCardell was born in Maryland on June 30, 1870. He was a boarder on Fifty-second Street in Manhattan in 1930 and is believed to have died after 1940. His last book, *My Uncle Oswald,* the sequel to *My Aunt Angie,* was published in New York by Farrar & Rinehart in 1931.

Appropriated by gentiles—obviously by 1904, as witnessed by the Testimonium McCardellium—the word was used in reference to all Jews. The same is true of the word "wop" as appropriated by the lesser races and used in reference to all Italians.

As for the German Jews, other Jews called them *yekkim,* a Yiddish term from *Jacke,* the German word for "jacket": a synecdoche of the formal garments that were worn by many of the stiff-looking *Jüdisch-Deutsche.*

The only significant epithet to appear later than "kike" is "mocky," which does not come to view until 1931, when Damon Runyon introduces it in *Collier's* to say that "calling Jewish people mockies, or Hebes, or geese" is "disrespectful." *The Oxford English Dictionary* suggests a possible etymology from Yiddish, *makeh*, "a boil, sore." But it seems far more likely that the word derives from the vulgar New York gentile pronunciation *ya-mock-a* of the Yiddish yarmulke.

Personal correspondence and diaries of the period need to be examined for the East Side likes of a Lord Byron, who, beholding humankind, saw, as he wrote to the Reverend Francis Hodgson in 1811: "The rest of the world—niggers and what not."

This much neglected field cries out for more research and attention. Funding is desperately needed. Especially as regards the geese.

We have read the foreboding words of Abraham Lincoln—or, as it were, George C. Hackstaff of the Caldwell Remedy Company—on the eve of the Civil War's end. I. N. Phelps Stokes looks back on, not forward to, the era of corruption that followed the war.

"At the close of the war," writes Stokes, not Hackstaff,

> *a low standard of ideals and of political morality made it possible for men high in the nation's councils and government to form dishonorable connections with business enterprises. The condition in the nation had its counterpart in the state and in the city. In New York this was the period of the most serious and far-reaching corruption that the city had ever known.*
>
> *Political corruption was an evil of long standing in New York. As has been shown previously, it was the outgrowth of conditions that began to develop as early as 1821, and was rendered more easily possible by successive changes in the city's government made by the Legislature. The chief effort of the Whigs, who controlled the state, was to lessen the influence of the Democratic majority usually given by New York City. To this end, but excusing themselves on the ground that their action was designed to end corruption and secure efficiency, they transferred as much of the city's government as they could to commissions whose members were appointed by the Governor. As a result, the actual control of the city rested at Albany, and not in New York itself. The effect of this transfer was to make two centres of corruption instead of one. In 1857 another change was made when the Legislature formed a Board of Supervisors for the County of New York. The city and county were*

coextensive, but by this act a separate government for each was created. That the Board of Supervisors might be non-partisan, it was arranged that it should be composed of an equal number of men from each of the two great parties. The board was made strictly subordinate to the Legislature in Albany, for it had no power to tax. It could only ascertain and levy the taxes decreed by the Legislature. This arrangement made it possible for the dominant power at Albany and the faction in control at New York to work together for a division of the spoils.

Under Fernando Wood, who had been twice mayor before he was elected to a third term in the fall of 1859, corrupt methods were developed to an extent hitherto unknown, and virtually all the schemes for controlling elections and robbing the city used by Tweed and his confederates a few years later were practiced, although on a much more moderate scale. Corruption was even more prevalent during Wood's third term than it had been in his earlier administrations. It was openly charged that he sold the office of city inspector, and more notorious still was the fraud connected with letting a five-year contract for cleaning the city streets to Andrew J. Hackley. The criticism of the press, which under normal conditions might be trusted to call public attention to such flagrant abuses, was silenced by the payment to the newspapers of large sums of money for "advertising." The outbreak of the war served to aid the designs of those who were robbing the city treasury, in that it distracted public attention from them.

In the campaign for the election of mayor in 1861, Wood was determined to stand for re-election, although Tammany, which had opposed his election two years before, again refused to support him, and nominated C. Godfrey Gunther. A non-partisan movement to oppose the forces of corruption appeared in the People's Union, composed of Republicans and Democrats. It nominated George Opdyke, a Republican, who was elected by a small plurality. In 1863, C. Godfrey Gunther, the candidate of the "McKeon Democracy," was supported by some Republicans and some Democrats, and was elected mayor. In 1865, Tammany succeeded in electing as mayor John T. Hoffman, a man of some popularity and considerable ability. During his administration, the frauds and thefts continued, but he became more and more popular.

The Tammany Society made him great sachem; the Democratic State Committee wished him to be its candidate for governor in 1866, and he was re-elected mayor in 1867 by a much larger majority than he had received in the preceding contest.

The number of votes cast in this election showed the astonishing increase of 22,779 over the number cast in the election for mayor two years before. The reasons for this were apparent to all, and included repeating, false registration, cheating in the count, and, most important of all, illegal naturalization. In the Supreme Court and the Court of Common Pleas citizens were being turned out sometimes at the unprecedented rate of a thousand per day. This was the work of three corrupt judges—Albert Cardozo, George G. Barnard, and John H. M'Cunn—who, in turn, were the puppets of William Marcy Tweed, the man who had made himself master of the whole corrupt system in New York. Up to this time the city had been controlled by a group or "ring" working through Tammany Hall; it was now controlled by a one-man power, the "boss," who was as much of a dictator as the most arbitrary despot.

Tweed was born in New York in 1823, and was of Scotch parentage. His father brought him up to the trade of chairmaker, but he was early attracted by politics, and entered on that career as a volunteer fireman, becoming foreman of the American, or "Big Six," Fire Company. At the age of twenty-nine he went to Congress as a Democrat, but served only one term, as he preferred to devote himself to the field for which he was best fitted, that of municipal politics. He filled many positions in the city and county. In 1852–3 he was alderman of the Seventh Ward; in 1857–8 he was commissioner of public schools; in 1858–70 he was supervisor of the County of New York; and in 1870 he became commissioner of public works. He was, also, nominally deputy street commissioner, a position to which he had been appointed in 1863. In addition, he was a state senator in 1868–9. Besides building these public positions, he was prominent in Tammany Hall. In 1861 he was elected chairman of the Tammany General Committee, and it was while holding this position that his despotic actions earned him the title of "boss." Later, he succeeded Hoffman as grand sachem of Tammany. The other important members of the "ring" were A. Oakley Hall, who was elected mayor in 1868; Peter B. Sweeney, chamberlain of the city and treasurer of the county, and Richard B. Connolly, comptroller. In 1869 Tweed was virtually in control of the state as well as the city government, for he had secured the election of John T. Hoffman to the office of governor in the preceding year, and in 1869 the Democrats were a majority in the State Legislature.

In that year New York taxpayers knew that they were being robbed by a corrupt government, but they were apparently helpless. The public might have risen and driven the "ring" from power had it not been supported by the intricate political machinery of Tammany Hall, which maintained its power through its popularity with the poor. It provided work for the able-bodied, food for the hungry, and care for the sick. In return, it demanded and received the votes of its protégés.

Stokes's narrative moves deftly toward the demise of the Tweed ring. We should stop here, however, where Stokes's prose eddies at a phrase of moment: "the intricate political machinery of Tammany Hall, which maintained its power through its popularity with the poor." Or, elementally: which maintained its power through the poor. Think about it.

The sawbuck in the barroom, the newsboy job for the kid, the tip of the hat and pleasant word, the cigar slipped into the pocket, the Thanksgiving turkey, the word of intercession that bore result, the gift of swag, the sympathetic ear, the douceur, and the humble answered prayer. Of such were steadfast human allegiances made.

A vote was like a single penny in the pocket of a man: insignificant and all but worthless to him, but valuable to he who could gather and amass the individual pennies from the pockets of the many. In a democratic system, votes were the sustenance of corruption, and the spoils of office were such that it served one very well to give a man a lavish return on his penny.

The ward boss was where the neighborhood could see him—and where he could see the neighborhood. It was through him that votes brought benefit. It was through him that democracy worked. Those who delivered were those who received.

When the ward boss and his cronies no longer walked among them, there would be no one to protect them or their jobs, and their penny votes, no matter which way they were tossed, would yield them the same thing: nothing. The stranger's hollow promise from on high would replace the familiar helping hand. "The people" would become an abstraction.

That time would not be upon them in their lives or their children's lives. For now, the neighborhood people were safe. The ways of the Tweed ring seemed to profit all men. If a company presented a claim to the city for work done in the amount of five thousand dollars, the head of the company would be told that the claim could not be paid. He would also be told, however, that if the company submitted a new claim for fifty-five thousand dollars, the amount would be paid. Thus the company got its five thousand, and the extra fifty thousand would be distributed to members of the ring, to each his just due according to his station, with a bit of the money seeping down to be distributed, in this manner or that, among the penny voters. On Christmas Day 1870, Tweed himself gave fifty thousand dollars to the poor of his ward and a thousand dollars to each of the aldermen of the various wards to buy coal for the needy.

In 1871, *The New York Times,* under proprietor George Jones and editor Louis J. Jennings, began to expose the ways of the Tweed ring. Cartoons in *Harper's Weekly* directed at the Tweed ring by Thomas Nast gained international attention. Tweed attempted to bribe both Jones and Nast, then ordered the Board of Education to reject all bids for school books from Harper & Brothers.

As the exposure and the outrage of concerned citizens grew, prosecution was inevitable. Some of the ring fled to Europe. The judges Barnard and M'Cunn were impeached. Their cohort on the bench, the Sephardic Jew Albert Cardozo, escaped impeachment by means of his timely resignation. The Benjamin N. Cardozo School of Law of Yeshiva University today bears the name of his son (1870–1938).

William F. Havemeyer, a reform candidate, was elected mayor in 1872. After long delays, the trial of William Marcy Tweed came to court in early 1873. The jury was discharged when members were unable to agree. Tweed was released, arrested again, and stood trial by a second jury. He was found guilty and sentenced to twelve years' imprisonment. He was released by the court of appeals, which found a technicality of his sentencing to be irregular. Arrested yet again in a civil suit by the city, he escaped to

Spain, where he was recognized from the many caricatures of him that had been published and was returned to New York. He died in the Ludlow Street Jail on April 12, 1878.

Tweed was dead, but Tammany Hall was not. Soon there would be a new cry among the people: "To hell with reform!"

Years of economic depression followed the financial panic of 1873. As Stokes says of the celebratory year of 1876: "The centennial of national independence came when the gloom of hard times still hung over the land."

ABRAHAM ELIJAH ROTHSTEIN BECAME a Bar Mitzvah, a son of the commandment, in the fall of 1869. His elder brother, who had been left behind when his parents had come to America, arrived in New York, twenty years of age, going by the name of Louis Rothstein and evidently in full command of the King's English.

It is not known who answered the door of the Rothstein flat at 106 Allen Street when a federal census taker called on June 18, 1870 or who answered the census taker's questions. According to the census, Harris, Rosa, and their daughter, Julia, had been born in Bavaria. But Julia, her husband, and their son were living with her parents and young Abraham on Allen Street, and Julia is entered twice in the census: once under her father's name, where her place of birth is given as Bavaria, and again under her husband's name, where her place of birth is stated as Russia.

In the next federal census, Harris and Rosa would be born in Russia. After that, they would be born in Germany. (Perhaps of relevance here is the fact that Bavaria had become a part of the new German Empire in 1871.) In the end, they would settle on Russia. Harris and Rosa moved through time as well as through space. Harris, fifty years old in June 1870, is fifty-eight in June 1880. Rosa, fifty-three in 1870, is sixty-two in 1880.

Abraham, whose age is wrongly stated as twelve (he was thirteen), was still in school. It is likely that he also attended Sunday school classes at the B'nai Jeshurun Sunday school, at the Greene Street synagogue. Begun in 1862, with Miss Louisa Bildersee volunteering as the first principal, the congregation's Sunday school program was now in its eighth year.

In 1876, the Rothsteins moved from 160 Allen Street to 185 Henry Street, between Jefferson and Clinton streets. By this time, nineteen-year-old Abraham was working with his father in the cap shop at 142 South Fifth Avenue. The family moved again, to nearby 270 Madison Street, in 1877. The shop was relocated as well, to 79 Greene Street, the street that

B'nai Jeshurun had left in the spring of 1864 because "the neighborhood was deteriorating." In fact, the neighborhood was in the heart of a growing garment center.

The new shop had a new name: H. Rothstein & Sons. Both of his boys were with him now, making caps on Greene Street.

The shop would move again—to 63 Crosby Street, between Spring and Broome streets, in 1882; to 109 Greene Street, between Spring and Prince, in 1887; to 171 Mercer Street, between Houston and Bleecker streets, in 1888—but H. Rothstein & Sons would remain in business until 1890. Throughout those thirteen years, Harris, Louis, and Abraham would work side by side, making those caps.

Leo Katcher writes of Abraham:

He lived in accordance with the religion and the customs of the people. Even in relation to his marriage. As was customary, it had been arranged for him. In only one aspect was it different. He saw his bride for the first time on his wedding day. But that was a matter of geography.

There were not many Jews in the United States in 1878. Those who did live in the United States retained ties with their home cities and provinces. These ties were centered in the various lodges and societies which had headquarters in every major American city. But the main office was always New York.

The secretary was the guiding hand of these organizations. He kept in touch with the old country as well as the new. He was the keeper of vital statistics, of births and deaths, marriages and confirmations.

A good part of his income derived from a side line. He acted as shadchen, or marriage broker. He was Cupid's transmission belt. His records told him when a youth or maiden had reached marriageable age. And he was always ready to locate a proper mate.

There came a time when the secretary visited the home of Abraham's mother. Was it not time for Abraham to take a bride? The mother agreed that it was. Then she listed her son's virtues and asked, "Can you find a maiden who would make him a proper wife?"

The secretary nodded his skullcapped head. "I can. It may take time, but I can."

He went to his office and searched the records. Among them he found the name of Esther Kahn, daughter of Simon and Reba Kahn. The Kahns had come to the United States from the same Bessarabian town as had the Rothsteins.

The secretary told Mrs. Rothstein, "The Kahns are good, religious people. They are learned. And they are successful. Simon Kahn has prospered and will be able to provide a fitting dowry."

There was nothing exceptional about this, dowry giving was customary.

Mrs. Rothstein agreed that Esther Kahn would make a most suitable wife for her son.

Now the secretary began a correspondence with Simon Kahn. Kahn agreed that it was a fitting time for his daughter to be married. There were some upright young men in San Francisco whom he had under consideration. However, he was open to any suggestions from the East.

It took three months for arrangements to be completed. At the end of the period Esther and Abraham were betrothed. And, for the first time, they communicated directly with each other, exchanging photographs and stilted phrases.

Since Simon Kahn was to bear all the expenses of the wedding, it was natural that the ceremony should take place in San Francisco.

It had been planned that Abraham would have three days to spend in San Francisco between his arrival and the marriage. Flat wheels, engine failures, and other mishaps ate up the three days. Abraham reached San Francisco just four hours before the time set for the ceremony.

There was barely time for him to meet the girl he would soon be taking to wife. Shyly he exchanged a few words with her in the presence of her parents. He just had time to see that she was a slight girl, of medium height, with lustrous olive skin and oversize brown eyes that filled the top half of her face. Her hair was blue-black.

She saw a thin, gentle-looking young man with a shy smile. His voice was soft and his manner comforting.

They had this brief moment together and then Simon Kahn took his soon-to-be son-in-law in hand. They sat in the curtained, high-

ceilinged parlor of the Kahn house where Abraham had his first, and only, drink of hard liquor.

In a short while the Kahn family, friends and Landsleit, gathered for the ceremony. The young couple stood beneath the wedding canopy, still strangers, as the rabbi recited the words of the marriage ceremony. At its end, a glass was placed on the floor and the rabbi told Abraham to shatter it. He brought his foot down hard, and the glass splintered.

The rabbi said, "So long as this glass remains splintered, so long shall you two be joined in marriage."

The pair were man and wife.

Years later Esther said, "When we married, we did not love each other. How could you love a stranger? But all the material for love was there. I respected Abraham. I knew he was a good man or my father would not have approved of him. From the first moment he was gentle to me and considerate. Love, of course, came later."

The day after the wedding, the couple left for New York. Ahead was a long journey. For Abraham, it was a journey home; for Esther, it was a journey away from home to a strange world. She was leaving her family, her friends and her youth behind. It saddened her.

Abraham said, "I promise that you will return here many times."

She accepted the promise on faith. She felt that Abraham never made a light promise, for a promise became a debt. And he believed in paying his debts.

Eight days later they were in New York.

Abraham, before leaving, had found a home for them. It was a brownstone on Forty-seventh Street, just west of Lexington Avenue. The neighborhood was quiet, far removed from the business section. And there was a synagogue only a few blocks away. At that time the district in which they lived was part of Yorkville.

Esther came to this new home in the strange city of New York, a city about which she knew little. When she saw it, it overwhelmed her.

Leo Katcher was from Bayonne, which was good. But he went from Bayonne to Hollywood, which is not good. There is a grain of truth in what he wrote about Abraham Rothstein, but that grain is lost within the weft and warp of fabrication.

There is no evidence that Abraham Rothstein's marriage was a *shidduch,* a union arranged through a *shadchan,* or marriage broker.

The maiden name of Abraham's wife was not Kahn, and her parents were not named Simon and Reba.

We are told of "flat wheels, engine failures, and other mishaps." However, this was a time before automobiles: The steel wheels of railroad trains did not get flats.

Abraham Rothstein never lived on Forty-seventh Street, and as a common cap maker, he did not live in one of the dark brown sandstone residences that then defined stately living. He lacked even the means to live in one of the new style of multiple-dwelling buildings that had been introduced from Europe within the past decade. They called them "apartment houses," and people living in them called their homes "Parisian flats." In truth, Abraham Rothstein and his wife moved in with Abraham's parents at the tenement on Madison Street.

And it is not true that Forty-seventh Street was then a part of Yorkville, which extended along the East River from Sixty-ninth Street to Ninetieth Street.

As for Esther's reflections on love and the description of her in youth—I like especially the "eyes that filled the top half of her face"—these are fictions more to be pitied than punished.

Some months before the publication of Katcher's book, he was credited with providing the story for the 1958 moving picture *Party Girl,* directed by Nicholas Ray.

Other writers have built on the legend that Katcher did much to invent.

We read that in the early twentieth century, "through the Bessarabian Landsmannschaft, an immigrant social group comprised of those who came from the same areas of the Russian Pale, Abraham met Esther. The elder Rothstein"—the writer speaks of Abraham—"had such Jewish communal attachment that he vigorously participated in Landsmannschaft meetings although both he and Esther had been born in America."

In Katcher, Abraham finds his wife through the secretary of one of "the various lodges and societies which had headquarters in every major

American city." This secretary locates the marriageable daughter of a family in San Francisco who comes "from the same Bessarabian town as had the Rothsteins."

Jewish businessmen such as Motche Goldberg and Abe "the Rabbi" Ratelles, known as white slavers, would establish a trade route between New York and San Francisco. In her memoir, the San Francisco madam Nell Kimball (1854–1934) recalled the early westward whore drives of the New York flesh barons and how "the rage for redheaded Jew girls took on in the town." But unlike Motche and the Rabbi, marriage brokers are not known to have worked both coasts.

Later writers, seeking to give substance to Katcher's unnamed society, have identified it as the Bessarabian Landsmannschaft. But most of the *Russlanddeutsche* were Christian, and their homeland organization, the Landsmannschaft der Bessarabiendeutschen, was Christian as well.

In 1871, Czar Alexander II had revoked the preferential rights and privileges that had been given to the German colonial settlers by the manifestos of Catherine II and Alexander I. The emigration of Christian Germans from Russia began at that time, more than a decade before the Jewish emigration from Russia that followed the pogroms of 1881. The majority of Germans who immigrated to America from the Bessarabian, Black Sea, and Crimean regions of Russia settled in the Dakotas.

Ingo Isert, director of the Heimatmuseum der Deutschen aus Bessarabien in Stuttgart, states that there was no Landsmannschaft der Bessarabiendeutschen yet in existence in the 1870s, in either New York or anywhere else in the world. The *Bessarabiendeutsche* in America were "represented" through German-language newspapers in the Dakotas, such as the *Dakota Freie Presse,* which was founded in 1874.

Only when Jewish emigration from Russia grew in the decades after 1881 were any Landsmannschaften to be found among the *russlanddeutsche Juden* of New York; and there is no evidence of a Bessarabian Landsmannschaft for Jews in America until the twentieth century.

So much for young Abraham Rothstein's vigorous participation in Bessarabian Landsmannschaft meetings that did not exist. So much for the little marriage broker from the Bessarabian society who nods his skull-capped head in Rosie Rothstein's kitchen.

I expend so much time here not because the details of a long-ago marriage are of any meaning, but to show that the cellular core of what we call history—knowledge itself—is diseased. It is not the artful novelist who has blurred the divide between fiction and fact: It is the professor of learning, the peddler of secondhand misknowing. The more we "know," the less we *know*. It is better to keep away from words, "facts," "knowledge." They are almost always the carriers of disease.

Love, of course, came later.

The elder of Abraham's siblings, Julia, had married a man named David Pohalski on May 13, 1866. He was a twenty-four-year-old Jew from Russia. They were married at the flat at 160 Allen Street, by Reverend Judah S. Kramer, the *chazzen*, or cantor, since 1858 of Congregation B'nai Jeshurun. On August 10, 1867, Julia gave birth at the Allen Street flat to a son named Moses. Her husband, David, had no job at the time. In the next year, David found work as a "segar manufacturer"—a cigar maker—and he moved his little family to a flat at 83 Rivington Street. There, on December 30, 1868, Julia gave birth to a second son, named Benjamin. They returned to live with her parents and brother Abraham on Allen Street.

Abraham's brother, Louis, would marry a young lady named Pauline Chuck on June 20, 1880. He was thirty. She was twenty-three, born in New York to immigrant parents, Henry and Esther Deborah Aaron Chuck, who lived on Cherry Street. The marriage would be performed by Rabbi F. de Sola Mendes of Congregation Shaaray Tefila, which had been formed in a secession from B'nai Jeshurun many years before. Louis had moved out of the Madison Street flat earlier in 1880, and his flat at 235 East Thirtieth Street would be his family's home. A male child would be born in late May 1881 and would die of convulsions at the age of a day. A second son, Raymond, would be born in 1882 and would live. Then there would be Stella in 1884, Abram in 1886, Miriam in 1890.

These are simple neighborhood marriages. Why then would Abraham, the youngest of the three siblings, the only one of them born in America, go to San Francisco to marry? If he was fixed on marrying the daughter of a couple of German Jews from Russia, surely he could have found such a woman right there, on the East Side, especially as this quest would have meant that the woman herself did not much matter as long as she fit the ethnic profile.

It was another Jew, born the same year as Abraham, in the never known but beloved *Vaterland* of his heritage, who would come up with something called *der Ödipus-Komplex*.

Jacob Solomon Rothschild was born in 1817 in the former Polish territory that lay within the Pale to the north and northeast of Bessarabia. The river Dniester was the natural border between Bessarabia and Podolia—Podolien, in German—the southernmost Russian province of that former part of Poland. In Russia, he married a teenage girl named Minna. She had been born there in 1820, and she was illiterate. Together they had three daughters. The first of them, Jennette, was born on July 20, 1839. Sarah was born a decade later, then Gilda two years after her. In the early 1850s, Jacob and Minna and their daughters immigrated to America and settled in San Francisco. A fourth daughter, Esther, was born in San Francisco in September 1860.

Jacob S. Rothschild was a merchant, and he did well. He owned his home, at 267 Tehama Street, where Esther was born. In 1860, the year his wife gave birth to Esther and his eldest daughter gave birth to a son, Jacob declared a personal estate of two thousand dollars in addition to the house, whose value he declared to be a thousand dollars. He became a naturalized citizen in 1867. The family moved to 120½ Turk Street, then to 527 Post Street. By the late 1870s, when he and Minna and Esther lived at 705 McAllister Street, his general-merchandising firm, at 511 Market Street, went by the name of J. S. Rothschild & Co. His teenage daughter, Esther, went by the name of Essie.

We do not know how the marriage of Abraham Rothstein came to be. He or his father may have wholesaled woolen caps to Jacob Rothschild. Abraham may have met Jacob's daughter when her family came to New York. Harris Rothstein and Jacob Rothschild may have known each other from the other side. There is, in fact, evidence suggesting that Harris and Rosa may have been living in the Polish part of the Pale when their daughter was born. Perhaps the two couples and their daughters had come over on the same boat. We do not know.

We do know that Abraham Rothstein was in San Francisco in the late summer of 1879, as Essie Rothschild's birthday approached. By this time, travel across country was no longer the travail that it had been. In the year of the nation's centennial, 1876, the Transcontinental Railroad Company had inaugurated direct service from New York to San Francisco. The trip was made in record-breaking time: eighty-three hours and thirty-nine minutes, which was just under three and a half days.

From the *San Francisco Evening Bulletin* of September 5, 1879, under "Marriages":

ROTHSTEIN-ROTHSCHILD—In this city, September 3, Abraham Rothstein, of New York, to Esther Rothschild, of San Francisco.

Abraham returned with his bride to New York. They lived together at 270 Madison Street with his parents and his elder brother and a twenty-seven-year-old Irish maid named Mary O'Rieley. Essie—Esther, Ishtar—was pregnant by October's end. The child, a son, was born in the Madison Street apartment on July 18, 1880. They named him Bertram.

The crowded tenement conditions in the old neighborhood grew increasingly worse. It would come to be that one fourth of the city's population lived on only one twentieth of the city's land, in the congested southern wards of the East Side, the area bounded by Catharine Street, the Bowery, Third Avenue, Fourteenth Street, and the East River.

(Catharine Street was laid out and named for Catharine Rutgers in the mid–eighteenth century. Only in the mid–twentieth century did it come to be misspelled, as Catherine Street, with an *e* instead of an *a*. Some years later, the city placed a street sign at the northeast corner of Grove and Bleecker streets, on which Bleecker Street was misspelled as Bleeker Street. One day I saw a cop standing under the sign, unable give an inquiring passerby proper directions to West Tenth Street, which was not only just a few blocks straight away on Bleecker Street, but also where the nearest police station was.)

After the birth of their son, Abraham and Essie moved to 325 East Twentieth Street, ten blocks south of where Louis and Pauline Rothstein now lived.

My friend, the writer Frank Fortunato, tells me: "325 East Twentieth

Street doesn't appear to exist any longer. The majority of the street is taken up by the educational complex of Public School Number 40, Simon Baruch Junior High School, and its playground. The tenements are actually above and behind a grocery store that has a First Avenue address, 349.

"The street is most distinguished not by its pre- and pubescent students, all of whom remarkably eat pizza and scream at each other, but as a conduit to the FDR Drive, three blocks east, running through the canyon of the 1940s Metropolitan Life Insurance Company's housing project Alphavilles that are Stuyvesant Town to the south and Peter Cooper Village to the north. These extend from First Avenue to Avenue C and the Franklin D. Roosevelt East River Drive, Stuyvesant Town occupying the area from Fourteenth to Twentieth streets, and Peter Cooper Village, the area from Twentieth to Twenty-third streets. Writing in *The New Yorker* in 1948, Lewis Mumford (1895–1990) referred to these many acres of red-brick buildings as 'the architecture of the police state.' This stretch of the East River Drive was completed in 1942. The housing projects, begun in 1943, were completed in 1947."

In the spring of 1881, Esther became pregnant again. It was to be another son. He would be born on a Tuesday, and he would die on a Tuesday. The day of his birth was January 17, 1882. They named him Arnold.

Fʀᴏᴍ 325 ᴇᴀsᴛ ᴛᴡᴇɴᴛɪᴇᴛʜ Street, the Rothsteins moved to 191 East Seventy-sixth Street. Louis Rothstein and his wife moved into 325 East Twentieth Street when his brother moved out. Abraham Rothstein and his family moved again, to 1835 Lexington Avenue, near 114th Street. This avenue had been extended through Harlem in 1873, and the East Side elevated railroad had reached Harlem in 1880. From Harlem, they returned to 325 East Twentieth Street, where Louis and his family were still living. Abraham and his family moved next to 328 East Forty-third Street, where their son Arnold had his fifth birthday. The family moved then to 327 East Eighty-second Street, where they remained through 1890, when they moved down to 951 Lexington Avenue, near Seventieth Street. (Louis Rothstein and his family took over the residence on Eighty-second Street.) From there, they moved to a house at 165 East Seventy-eighth Street. These uptown East Side addresses lay outside the precincts of the Jewish aristocracy, which occupied the territory from East Sixtieth to East Eightieth Street between Fifth and Park avenues.

Through these years, Abraham and Louis Rothstein continued to work downtown at their father's cap shop. The old man was now in his seventies: fifty and more years a cap maker, first in the old country, then in the new. These men, these young men like his sons, they did not know what it was like when your hands were the only machinery you had. Pedal and treadle were your own will. And, sooner or later, all of this broke down like so much junk as well. By 1892, it was time to quit.

When Harris Rothstein retired from work, Abraham and Louis opened their own shop, at 114 Greene Street, near where the old B'nai Jeshurun synagogue used to be, near where they had worked with their father five years earlier, when he had the shop across the street, and where they had worked with him back before that, at the first shop on Greene Street, in the years before Abraham's marriage.

But Abraham and Louis were no longer simple cap makers. They had a partner, Jacob Edward Ryttenberg. The firm of Rothstein Bros. & Ryttenberg was in the "cotton goods" business.

Throughout the 1890s, into the new century, the garment industry in New York became increasingly the domain of Eastern European Jews and their children. It was during this time that the phrase "sweatshop" came into use on the East Side. The *Westminster Gazette,* London, November 2, 1895: "All but fifteen of the 385 wholesale clothing manufacturers in New York have their goods made in 'sweat shops.'" Abraham and Louis Rothstein were a part of this growing domain.

Esther gave birth to a third son, Edgar, on September 1, 1883, when the family was living in Harlem. A daughter, Edith, came in November 1886, at the East Forty-third Street home. Another daughter was born there sixteen months later, on March 7, 1888. She was named Sarah Miriam, after Essie's sister. But Sarah Rothstein lived little more than four years. She died of heart failure brought on by pneumonia, on May 24, 1892, at the house on Seventy-eighth Street. A year before, on March 11, 1891, Essie had given birth on East Seventy-eighth Street to her fourth son, Jacob Solomon Rothstein. He was named for her father, who had passed away on December 22, 1883, at the age of sixty-six. Jack was the last. After the death of little Sadie, there were no more children.

Sarah's death was followed by more death. The autumn of 1893 was a season of constant mourning, shivah unto shivah. Harris Rothstein had been taken from his home at 160 East Seventy-first Street to Lebanon Hospital in the heat of August, suffering from uremia. He went on September 15. Then, on October 11, Essie's mother, Minna, died in San Francisco at the age of seventy-three. Rosa Rothstein succumbed to cerebro-spinal meningitis, fell into a coma, and on October 29 followed her husband down that blue Danube. Arnold's twelfth birthday, eight weeks later, cannot have been a happy one.

It was in 1895, while the family was living on East Seventy-eighth Street, that Arnold Rothstein became a Bar Mitzvah.

The cornerstone of the new B'nai Jeshurun synagogue, on Madison Avenue between Sixty-fourth and Sixty-fifth streets, had been laid in the summer of 1884, and the synagogue had been consecrated in the spring of the following year. Abraham Rothstein had belonged to the Congregation B'nai Jeshurun since childhood. Both he and the synagogue of his congregation had now moved uptown, afar from their roots in the downtown East Side. This was a time of religious disquiet for many New York Jews, as the Reform movement spread from Europe to challenge the orthodoxy of congregations such as B'nai Jeshurun. For B'nai Jeshurun, the turning point was to come in 1906. The gifted young British rabbi Joseph Mayor Asher, who took leadership of the congregation in 1901, was a strong believer in the Orthodox ways. But even he could not still the heterodox voices of those who believed that Reform, a freeing of the old strictures, would bring renewal to a congregation whose members showed increasing apathy to the traditions of their forefathers. Some of the congregation went so far as to suggest that English prayers should be introduced in addition to the regular Hebrew service. Rabbi Asher would have none of this.

"Where are our children? Have French and music completely ousted religious instruction? These very children who refrain from coming to our religious schools will when they become men and women, be ashamed of their religion or probably of their own ignorance of its tenets.

"The attendance in our Hebrew School is pitifully small," he rebuked. "Services have barely any worshippers. Were it not for our 'minyan men' we should have been unable to conduct the services. Our ritual is attractive, and it is hard to understand why we cannot have our pews filled. Have all the Jews in this metropolis ceased to attend synagogue?"

In 1906, when Rabbi Asher's term of office expired, he refused to be considered for another term and instead became rabbi of another, strictly Orthodox congregation. Until then, and for a time after, men such as Abraham Rothstein stood strong for the old ways at B'nai Jeshurun. Then they, too, like Rabbi Asher, moved on.

The Hebrew classes of which Rabbi Asher spoke were conducted separately from the B'nai Jeshurun religious school, which had been active under the same principal, Morris S. Wise, since 1871. We do not know if the young Arnold Rothstein ever yielded to paternal demands that he attend Mr. Wise's religious school or if he was one of those errant children the likes of whom Rabbi Asher later spoke.

"Natura abhorret vacuum," says Rabelais's drunkard begging wine for cup and gut. But it is not so much nature that abhors a vacuum, but rather journalists and popular historians. Most of what has been written and believed about Arnold Rothstein derives largely from several standard sources, bought wholesale and embellished through the years. The authors of these sources, or their editors, abhorred a vacuum. When there was no wine, they made it in the basement.

The first of these sources is a book called *In the Reign of Rothstein*. Eleven books by Donald Henderson Clarke (1887–1958), most of them pulp novels, were published by the Vanguard Press of New York from 1929 to 1951. *In the Reign of Rothstein* was the first of them. It was published in January 1929, barely eight weeks after Arnold Rothstein was murdered. In a letter to Clarke of April 22, 1947, the editor James Henle wrote regarding a deadline: "But, Don, times have changed since you and I pushed *In the Reign of Rothstein* through the Wolff plant in four weeks. Now it takes four or five months to get a book from the manuscript stage to publication date." If it took a month for the book to be printed by the firm of H. Wolff, this means that the book was researched and written in a matter of weeks after Rothstein's sudden and unexpected death. At this time, Clarke recently had been released from the care of Bloomingdale Hospital for Mental and Nervous Disorders, formerly Bloomingdale Lunatic Asylum, in White Plains, New York, which he had entered, "with pint," in the summer of 1927. He had a job writing moving pictures for Metro-Goldwyn-Mayer, but he earlier had been a reporter for the *New York World*. It was the clippings library of the *World* that provided Clarke with most of the material he tore through to produce *In the Reign of Rothstein*.

The second source is a ten-part series of articles, "Rothstein: Mathematician of Crime," that appeared in the *New York Telegram* in early November 1929. Joseph Lilly, the author of the series, was a staff writer for the *Telegram*. In his conjuring of Rothstein's childhood and adolescence, Lilly states that "Arnold was born, the first of four children," in a brownstone on East Forty-seventh Street, where the family lived for "about ten years." Arnold's father, Abraham, was "born on Henry St." Lilly likens the elder Rothstein to "his ancient namesake" and tells of his "intensely religious, human, and lovable life." He is a man who "deals much of his charity secretly. For instance, he pays the monthly rent for a score or more families through an official of Beth Israel Hospital, who acts as his agent and thus keeps his identity secret." One day, "in the winter," Abraham "removed his overcoat on the street and placed it on a beggar's back." Arnold Rothstein was "precociously shrewd" as a boy. "Like Pythagoras, Tex Rickard, Bertrand Russell and Jesse Livermore, he was born with what some call a head for figures." The author invites us to ponder with him: "Did Abraham's strictness, his generosity, his wide embracing love, tend to develop Arnold's waywardness? Or vice versa." Of course, "the reaction of the city upon a boy in his teens in the mauve decade was very different from what it is today. Lads of 13 hung about billiard rooms." There is mention of the "psychological compensation" that may have informed Arnold's life. When we read that the young Rothstein attended Public School Number 87 at Amsterdam Avenue and Seventy-seventh Street, where "he comported himself well," and went on for two years to Boys' High School at Forty-eighth Street near Sixth Avenue, there is a desire to take these details at face value. Any fact-checker would accept them, on the grounds that they had been published in a reputable journal and not been contradicted elsewhere. But we must not: Because so many of the statements that surround them have been made in the basement, we must look on these with suspicion as well.

The stock tendency to see "Arnold in great contrast to his father, fabled for his uprightness," as the *Telegram* series has it, is by now overly worn. The legend of the elder Rothstein—"Abe the Just"—also has a source in an article that appeared, in Yiddish, in *Der Morgen Zhurnal* of Sunday, November 18, 1928. The article is titled אָרנאַלד ראָטשטײן װערט געעהרט אַלס װיכטיגער כּלל־טהוער פֿאָטער פֿון, which translates as "Arnold Rothstein's Father Is Honored as an Important Community Activist." (In the Hebrew characters of the Yiddish, the family name is rendered in its old form, as Rotshtejn. The name Arnold, a Germanic Christian form of the Hebrew Aaron, the name of the brother of Moses, is rendered here in Yiddish as Arnalt.) These columns of Yiddish newsprint in *Der Morgen Zhurnal* were occasioned by celebrations at Beth Israel Hospital and the Jewish Center of Abraham Rothstein's seventieth birthday. Much is made of Abraham's "great charitable activities of many years." He is "the old benefactor" and "the great contributor to charities." He was born to "an ultra-

Orthodox, poor, Jewish family," and "he stayed with his strict Jewish values. All his life, he has been an Orthodox Jew in the finest sense of the word." The article shares space on the page with "The Cry of Suffering of the Jews of Yemen," the day's radio listings, also in Yiddish, and an advertisement for a Grand Street finance company offering money at 6 percent. The truth is that, at the time of both the *Morgen Zhurnal* and *Telegram* articles, Abraham Rothstein, publicly celebrated for his "secret" charity, was fighting in court for control of his late son's will, in which he was not named.

The book *Now I'll Tell,* by "Carolyn Rothstein (Mrs. Arnold Rothstein)," had a publication date of May 3, 1934, preceding by weeks the release date, May 26, of the Fox moving picture version of *Now I'll Tell,* with Spencer Tracy as the Rothstein character, who in the moving picture bears the name Murray Golden and little semblance of reality. The back of the book's dust jacket advertises *Murder among the Nudists* by Peter Hunt, author of *Murder for Breakfast.* Circumstantial evidence in the papers of Donald Henderson Clarke, now in the Columbia University Rare Book and Manuscript Library, suggests that Clarke was also instrumental to this book, which, like Don Clarke's books, was published by the Vanguard Press. While this book contains some interesting recollections by Arnold Rothstein's widow, it should be remembered that she lived apart from him for much of their marriage. "Mrs. Rothstein"—her real name at the time was Behar—never tells us when she was born or what her maiden name was, which are not good signs in a memoir, but does tell us that she was born and raised "in an old-fashioned house in Gramercy Park" and that a certain stage show in which she appeared was "the comedy hit of the season," neither of which statements is true. In fact, the first sentence of the book is a lie about her age. But such statements are telling of the light that she intends to cast. She also was a contestant in court of her husband's will.

These "sources" are gathered and improvised upon in the fantasia of *The Big Bankroll: The Life and Times of Arnold Rothstein,* written by Leo Katcher in 1958 and published by Harper & Brothers in January 1959. Since then, Katcher's book has been accepted and used as the standard reference. Its invented dialogue places it well in the realm of parody, and I have wondered if Katcher ever laughed aloud as he wrote it.

Katcher tells us that dark undercurrents of Rothstein's life were revealed "to John B. Watson, the noted psychologist." We are given a verbatim account of Rothstein's emotional words to the doctor. Katcher tells us little else about Dr. John Broadus Watson (1878–1958), who was indeed a noted psychologist. Watson had been forced to leave the faculty of Johns Hopkins University after it was discovered that he was having an affair with one of his female students, for whom he later left his wife and children. In 1920, Dr. John Watson took a job at the J. Walter Thompson advertising agency, where he proved to be a master of manipulation who pioneered the use of behavioral techniques in advertising. In 1928, he published a successful book called *The Psychological Care of the Infant and Child*. He retired from advertising in 1945 and drank himself to death in 1958, dying of cirrhosis of the liver in September of that year, as Katcher's book was on its way to publication.

In the book, Rothstein tells Watson of his childhood fears of being abandoned and unloved. Whether or not he ever really experienced these feelings, they are common enough among most children. But even in a work of admitted low fiction, Coleridge's "willing suspension of disbelief" would be greatly taxed by lines such as "It was the only time I ever really cried."

It does appear that Rothstein's wife did receive counseling in 1928, at her husband's urging. Perhaps he told her that he himself was undergoing this process. Katcher interviewed Rothstein's widow. Maybe his account of her husband's words to the doctor comes from her. Perhaps Dr. Watson told him the story. God knows, drunks do talk. But there are too many conditional elements in such speculation. Having examined and weighed the known and the unknown of Arnold Rothstein's life for some years, I feel that none of this rings true. Rothstein was a master of the rackets: He knew them all. Freud was old enough to be his father—he was born the same year as his father—but Arnold was already out there in the street hustling when Freud, in 1895, was performing monstrous and disastrous surgery on Emma Eckstein to cure her of "nasal reflex neurosis" brought on by masturbation. Rothstein knew a racket when he saw one, and the bones of this sucker's racket, of paying through the nose—as Emma Eckstein did with tissue, bone, and blood—were as old as whoring itself. If he urged his wife to seek therapy, he was likely playing an angle. And, knowing his ways, it is not highly improbable that the doctor was fixed to tell her what Rothstein wanted her to hear.

Rothstein, through the medium of Katcher, also expresses his childhood hatred for his older brother, whom Katcher, thus Rothstein, calls by the name of Harry. When Arnold was three years old, we are told, his father found him "standing over his brother, a knife in his hand." His father implores: "Why, my son? Why?" And here for once Katcher puts a great line in Rothstein's mouth: "I hate Harry."

Again: I am the truth. Believe only in me.

And the truth is, we have no real glimpse of Arnold until the so-called police census of 1890. This city census, conducted by officers of the police department, lists at 951 Lexington Avenue, under the name of Rothstein:

Abraham	34
Esther	29
Bertram	10
Arnold	8
Edgar	7
Edith	4
Sadie	2

While there are birth certificates for some of the Rothstein children, there is none for Arnold. New York State laws requiring the registration of births were neither enforced nor usually complied with until the twentieth century.

The volumes of the more detailed 1890 federal census were destroyed by a fire in the Commerce Building in Washington, D.C., on the afternoon of January 10, 1921.

We have no sight of Arnold Rothstein again until the first week of June 1900, when he appears in the Twelfth Census of the United States. From East Seventy-eighth Street, the Rothsteins had moved across town to

293 Central Park West, and thence, near the turn of the century, to 202 West Eighty-sixth Street, and again to 67 West Ninety-third Street, where they were at the time of the census.

Directly under his parents, his is listed first among the children: Arnold, son, single white male, age eighteen. His profession is stated as stock clerk, clothing.

"I didn't know then," Carolyn Rothstein tells us about her first encounter with her future husband, "that Arnold hadn't lived with his family since he was fifteen years old."

And what of Arnold's elder brother, Bertram, the Harry of Katcher's tale, who is not to be found? If Arnold really hated him, he had something to smile about. Bertram Rothstein had died September 6, 1896, at the age of sixteen. The circumstances of his death are still unknown.

No.

It is interesting to note the presence in the household at this time of Jules Goodman.

Norman L. Goodman (1828–1916) had emigrated with his brother, Simon, and his sister, Rachael, from the Russian Pale to the Oregon Territory in 1849. In those covered-wagon days before statehood, the territory was a pioneers' wilderness. Slavery was outlawed there, and so were black folk. Norman Goodman became a naturalized citizen in sparsely populated Marion County in 1853. By 1859, the Goodmans had moved south to San Francisco, where they lived with the Rothschild family. It was in that year that Essie's eldest sister, Jennette (1839–1930), had married Norman. In 1860 a son, Joseph, was born. Jacob Rothschild and the Goodmans made their livings as merchants and were tied by business as well as by blood. The San Francisco firms of J. S. Rothschild & Co. and N. Goodman & Co. were associated.

Norman returned to Oregon with Jennette and their young son in 1862, as Norman conducted his business between there and San Francisco. There were more children: Rosa, Esther, Maurice, Lillie, and Abraham. Their last child, Jules Eckert Goodman, was born on November 2, 1876, in Gervais, Marion County, Oregon.

When the federal census taker came to the Goodman family door in Portland in the spring of 1900, seventy-one-year-old Norman—or Newman or Neuman; it varied—when asked to state his occupation, trade, or profession, declared: "Capitalist."

That same June week, in New York City, a census taker recorded twenty-two-year-old Jules Eckert Goodman living with his aunt Esther Rothstein and her family at 67 West Ninety-third Street. Jules was a writer who wanted to become involved in the theater. He did well in New York. His previews and reviews of the city's stage dramas were published back home in the *Oregon Daily Journal* of Portland beginning in 1904. Within a few years, his own plays found audiences on Broadway, and more than a dozen of them were made into moving pictures. The first of his plays was *The Man Who Stood Still,* in 1908. He was still working in the late 1950s, when he wrote for the New York *Daily News*. He died at his home in Peekskill, New York, in the summer of 1962.

We know that Goodman began his life in New York at the home of the Rothsteins, but we do not know how long he lived with them. By 1904, he was living apart from them, at 20 West 104th Street, and by 1910, he was living with his Montana-born wife, Mai, and their young son, Jules Eckert Jr.

The collection of Goodman's papers in the Harvard Theatre Collection contains no personal documents or writings other than drafts of known plays. We can only wonder what Jules Goodman, who lived with Arnold Rothstein when Rothstein was eighteen, could have told us about him; can only wonder at the reminiscence he could have written.

Abe the Just's prosperity was such by the turn of the century that his household included two servants from Ireland and one from Hungary. His cotton-goods outfit on Greene Street, where Arnold worked as a clerk, was doing well. In 1902, the firm of Rothstein Bros. & Ryttenberg moved to 131 Bleecker Street, between Mercer Street and the stretch of West Broadway that later became LaGuardia Place. At this time, Arnold remained working on Greene Street, but at a new storefront a few doors down. It is at this business address, at 94 Greene Street, that Arnold Rothstein is first listed in the New York City directory of 1902. He was in the shirt racket, but a typographical error fortuitously specifies preoccupation rather than occupation: "skirts."

From the year of Arnold Rothstein's birth through the year of his twenty-first birthday, his family had moved at least thirteen times. The Rothsteins then moved again, to 174 West Seventy-ninth Street. Arnold continued to work down on Greene Street for two years more, but he remained with his family, on West Seventy-ninth Street, until at least 1907, when he was twenty-five. After that, he was gone.

Strange Pull

M ORDECAI MANUEL NOAH OBSERVES in 1819, in his *Travels in En-*
*gland, France, Spain, and the Barbary States in the Years 1813–14 and
15,* that there was no record in New York of a Jew committing murder. Re-
flecting on this "high standard of ethical conduct" more than a hundred
and twenty-five years after, Hyman Grinstein writes, in *The Rise of the
Jewish Community of New York, 1654–1860:* "Later in this period Jews and
Christians alike bear witness to the fact that, while a Jew occasionally per-
petrated a crime against property, the City of New York never knew of a
capital crime committed by a Jew. At a time when the Five Points and the
Bowery recorded a murder almost every day, immigrant Jews who lived
near these areas were innocent of such crime against persons."

When was it that this changed? Who was the first Jew to commit murder in New York City? When and where is that drop of blood on the map
of time and place, that irrevocable moment of true and final assimilation?

Popular legend has made much of the figure of Monk Eastman. He is
often assigned the role of the first Jewish gangster and has been facti-
tiously associated with the Five Points. His real name was Edward Oster-
mann. (German, *ost,* "east," *Mann,* "man." The black slang "eastman,"
denoting a pimp, gigolo, or man who otherwise lives off women, entered
white slang at the turn of the century. In white slang, as in black, it was a
term of louche braggadocio.) Monk Eastman was the youngest of six sons,
the runt of the litter, born in Brooklyn in 1879 to Paulina and Moses Os-
termann, who had emigrated from Hesse-Darm in the German state of
Prussia. Monk emigrated from Brooklyn to New York City in the last
years of the nineteenth century, when the old Five Points ceased to exist as
the neighborhood it once was.

Eastman was more a ward thug than a gangster. He did the bidding of
the political bosses—election enforcements, collections, shake-downs, er-
rands of everyday perdition—and in return was allowed to do some bid-

ding of his own. When he was out of hand, Tammany Hall had nothing to do with him. This happened after the so-called Battle of Rivington Street in the summer of 1903, when Eastman was among the hundred or so who, in the words of the *New York Herald,* "fought through two miles of streets for five hours in defiance of the police." The next time that Eastman was arrested, for firing shots at a Pinkerton man in the spring of 1904, Tammany Hall sent no lawyer to help him, and he was sentenced to ten years at Sing Sing. Paroled in June 1909, he developed an opium habit and was in and out of jail for opium dealing and other charges in the years 1912 to 1917, when he enlisted in the army and fought in France with the 106th Infantry of the Twenty-seventh Division. He returned in April 1919. Late the following year, at dawn of the day after Christmas, Eastman was shot to death on the southwest corner of Fourth Avenue and Fourteenth Street, near the Blue Bird Café speakeasy, by a crooked Prohibition agent with whom he had been drinking.

Dwelling amid the low echelons of ward corruption, until his banishment, Monk Eastman was a brute and a malefactor, but he was not a killer. The same cannot be said of Italian American contemporaries of Eastman such as Franco Paolo Antonio Vaccarelli (1877–1936), who in those days went by the name of Paul Kelly, and his acolyte Louis Poggi. Born on November 31, 1885, the son of Italian immigrants named Guilio and Maria, young Poggi was also known as Louie the Lump.

New York journalists expended much descriptive resources on these two gentlemen. Joseph Pulitzer's *Evening World* of November 28, 1905, describes Vaccarelli as a "sawed-off Italian crook, with a nose like a can opener and arms like a Barbary ape." He is the "Mephisto" of the Bowery, the "boss-herder of all the east side bad lands lying west of that great common divisor, the Bowery." He is the "chief of thugs," the "little Italian Falstaff" who ruled his ragged "army, masquerading under the name of the Paul Kelly Association," from a "batcave" of a saloon called Little Naples, at 57–59 Great Jones Street, near the Bowery. Vaccarelli's brother, who tended bar at Little Naples, is "a little, shriveled sardine of a man, with a gimlet head and yellowish skin." To the kindlier *New York Sun* of December 2, 1906, Vaccarelli is "a slim, weak-looking chap."

In the *World* of October 5, 1908, Louie the Lump is "a slender boy of nineteen"—in reality, twenty-two—"pale, black-haired, with dark, flashing eyes. He is soft-voiced, almost dainty in appearance and attire."

This was written on the eve of Louie's trial for the murder, in Coney Island on May 21, 1908, of Monk Eastman's successor, Max "Kid Twist" Zweibach, under whom the remnants of the Monk Eastman gang had become known as the Kid Twist gang. Amid a crowd on Oceanic Walk that night, Louie had blasted six bullets into the Kid's head and body and also, with a single shot to the back of the head, dispatched Twist's bodyguard, Sam Tietch, who performed as a Coney Island wrestler under the name of Vach "Cyclone" Lewis. Furthermore, Louie had found these men in the company of his own former girlfriend, Mrs. Carroll Terry, a twenty-three-year-old Coney Island music hall singer from Canada. She took a bullet from Louie in her left shoulder that night. Louie fled, was found and captured in May, and pleaded guilty in October. "He is slender, alert, and intelligent, and his record is clean," observes the *Times* of October 6, 1908. He was sentenced on the following day and served thirteen months at the Elmira Reformatory.

The Kid Twist whom Louie the Lump killed is not to be confused with the later Kid Twist, Abe Reles (1907–1941), who worked for Louis "Lepke" Buchalter in the so-called Murder Inc. operation of the 1930s. Nor should Louie the Lump, the Jew-Killer, be confused with Jimmy "Baby Face" McLarnin, the welterweight champion known as the Jew-*Beater*. Born in Ireland in 1907, McLarnin, who ran in New York with Mayor Jimmy Walker, Babe Ruth, and Legs Diamond, is, bless him, still alive as I write this.

Max "Kid Twist" Zweibach was said to be a killer. Abe "Kid Twist" Reles was a killer. By his time, the time of Louis "Lepke" Buchalter (1897–1944), Jacob "Gurrah" Shapiro (1900–1947), and others, kosher butchering had taken on a whole new meaning. We deal here with the rising mist, the coming forth from shadows, in which the tablet of the law became whetting stone for knives, counting slate for *schmeck un' gelt*.

Arrested again for a shooting at Baxter and Franklin streets on February 12, 1912, Louie the Lump was freed after the witnesses to the shooting suddenly retracted their statements. He was next arrested a few weeks later, on March 7, for violating the new Sullivan Act. Passed by the legislature of New York City in 1911, the Sullivan Act introduced gun permits and made it illegal to carry an unlicensed handgun in New York City. Louie jumped bail and failed to appear for his appointed court date, on April 1. On the next day, the *World* commented that Louie, "one of the celebrities of gangland," refused to "be deprived of the ancient gang custom of 'carrying a gat.'" Describing him as "mild-mannered and suave when not fighting," the paper quoted Louie on the new legislation: "This pistol law is a joke. Everybody must protect themselves, and as I have a mother to look out after, I'm going to see that I stay on earth. But these cops—whew—a fine lot, I don't think."

Louie was surrendered, "bright and smiling," by his attorney, Robert M. Moore, on April 3. Once the court agreed to have the forfeited bail money returned to the Empire State Surety Company, Louie, paroled to his lawyer's custody, vanished again.

Big Jack Poggi, Louie the Lump's brother, ran a joint in Chinatown known as Poggi's. Five alleys in Chatham Square led there. One entry was through a dairy store, another through the back door of a barbershop. Poggi's was said to be a place where "anything goes."

An act of Congress strictly prohibiting the importation of opium had gone into effect on April 1, 1909. The illegal trade in opium had been growing ever since. Louie the Lump was a known associate of Charley Boston, a Chinese gentleman whose headquarters on Seventh Avenue served as a clearinghouse for opium traffickers. On April 29, 1912, the *World* ran an intriguing story:

> After a four weeks' search for Louis Poggi, an East Side band leader who jumped his bail in a most original manner at the beginning of the month, the detective bureau yesterday admitted that it found itself up against a stone wall in the form of a "system." The police said this was an underground organization so perfect and flawless in its formation, and backed by such powerful financial and political interests, that it is able in many cases to defy the best efforts of the police, and to flaunt its criminal dealings in the face of the courts, when those courts cannot be commanded. Why this "system" should protect Poggi is what the police would like to tell some day in court.

The system, so the police have been able to ascertain, has for its source and fountain head a group of men whose names are not even known to the rank and file of the workers. Their names if revealed would be a typical instance of an alliance of business and politics. The organization deals chiefly in the smuggling of opium, in large lots, into this country and its distribution by means of its corps of criminal agents, first to big dealers, next to smaller dealers, and at last to the men who sell cards on which is smeared enough opium for two or three "pills" for the individual "dope fiend."

How powerful is this system is shown by the ease with which it aided Poggi to escape from a long jail sentence.

The story continued:

When the police are asked why men high in certain financial and political councils have formed such an elaborate "underworld" organization, they show a few figures which reveal the enormous profit in the illicit dispensing of opium.

For every $1,000 spent in purchasing opium, smuggling it into the country and dispensing it, those at the top of the pyramid collect $6,000 or more as profit. About $500,000 worth is smuggled into the country annually, it is estimated. The net profit on this to the "big men" is about $3,000,000.

There are several points where the opium is brought into the country. One is at Malone, N.Y., near Plattsburg; another at a desolate point on the north Vermont line; a third is at Grand Island, in the Niagara River, near Buffalo; and a fourth is in Wisconsin.

Opium is not brought into the country more than ten or a dozen times a year. Then it comes in $50,000 to $80,000 lots. It is heavy and compact, and can readily be divided into a few express bundles. A can weighing a pound costs about $35, and is only about two inches across and four inches in height.

The men at the top set in motion their secret process of communication and get in touch with their dispensers. These men provide an entire city or community.

The smuggled opium is handled by one particular common carrier or express company, one of the biggest and best known in the United States. New York is usually the point to which it is shipped and from which it is distributed. But when unusual activity is noticeable by the Custom House officers the packages containing the opium are diverted to Newark or Philadelphia.

In New York the packages generally come addressed to some insignificant Chinese in Chinatown who happens to be stopping for a day or two at the address marked on the package.

According to the story, the police considered Louie the Lump as "a man who will stop at nothing if his price is paid."

In the fall of 1913, there was a shooting at Poggi's down in Chinatown. The joint was duly raided, on the early morning of October 1, 1913, but Big Jack was not found.

It seemed to be true of Louie the Lump and of his brother as well. You did not find him. He found you.

An interesting item appears in *The New York Times* of July 29, 1915. The heading reads: LOUIS POGGI SURRENDERS. And beneath that: "Gangster Who Jumped Bail in 1912 to Get Lighter Sentence." The item reported that Louis Poggi "was arrested yesterday in Times Square by Detective Russo of the District Attorney's office." It further reported that "Poggi said following his arrest that when his trial was on, a crusade against gangsters was in progress, and he believed he would get a heavy sentence if his case went to trial then. He had been all over the country, he said, since his disappearance."

President Woodrow Wilson had signed the Harrison Narcotic Act into law on December 17, 1914. The Harrison Act, outlawing the sale, possession, or use of heroin, gave the illegal drug trade new and greater opportunities for profit.

From the *New York Sun,* 1917, perhaps my favorite headline:

LOUIS THE LUMP COMES BACK

The story reports that "Louis Poggi, alias 'Louis the Lump,' the East Side gangster," appeared "in the Federal Court to-day, where he was held by United States commissioner Hitchcock in $5,000 bail for alleged traffic in heroin." He had been "arrested late Saturday night at Chatham Square by members of the police narcotics squad under Lieut. Sherb" after selling, "it is alleged, one-eighth of an ounce of heroin to a 'stool pigeon.'"

Our last glimpse of Louie the Lump is in June 1923. On the twelfth of that month, it is reported that Poggi has been arrested for murder, after thirty-five-year-old Charles Cassazza, described here as "a rival saloon-keeper" (in May 1908 we find a "Guglielmo Cassazza" described as "his friend"), was found with a bullet through his forehead the previous morning in the Royal Café, a saloon that Louie owned at 8 Baxter Street, two doors down from where Harris Rothstein had once lived, in the Five Points of seventy and more years before.

The *Times* of June 13 combines mention of Poggi's arraignment with details of an unrelated murder:

> Irving Sandler of 3 Lewis Street was held without bail for examination tomorrow when arraigned before Magistrate Frederick B. House in the Homicide Court yesterday in connection with the stabbing and killing of Hugh Gallagher of 216 Monroe Street last Sunday night in a store in Madison Street.
>
> Detective Nammeck alleged in an affidavit that Sandler killed Gallagher because Gallagher insisted that Sandler sing a Jewish song.
>
> Gallagher's body was found in an ash heap beside the store shortly after dawn on Monday. The prisoner pleaded not guilty.
>
> Louis Poggi, alias "Louis the Lump," and Louis Repuzzi were arraigned before the Magistrate on suspicion of being connected with the shooting and killing of Charles Cassazza before dawn Monday morning in Poggi's Café Royal at 8 Baxter Street. Poggi said he found Cassazza's body in the place when he opened the store for business and Repuzzi declared he knew nothing of the shooting. They were held without bail for examination on Friday.
>
> The record of this case then falls silent.

Louie the Lump died in Brooklyn, of tuberculosis, on February 27, 1942. He was fifty-six years old and had been working as a truck driver for a plumbing supplies company.

According to his Bertillon measurements, Louie the Lump was five feet three inches tall. Paolo Vaccarelli, whom the *New York Sun* of October 3, 1903, described as "only a 5-footer," may have been even shorter. The average height of a soldier in Caesar's legions was five feet four inches.

For some reason, newspapers of the day were fixed on the size of Italians. When a man was found shot to death in Vaccarelli's joint on Great Jones Street on November 22, 1905—the second shooting there in two nights—the *Sun* began its report the next day with "An undersized man; probably an Italian; was murdered some time last night . . ."

The "undersized man" murdered at Vaccarelli's dive was John J. Harrington. He was a "repeater" who had voted many times in the recent election and who threatened to betray his employers to the state superintendent of elections.

In this election of November 1905, William Randolph Hearst, publisher of the *New York Journal,* had run for mayor against the Tammany Hall incumbent, George Brinton McClellan, on the third-party ticket of his own Municipal Ownership League. Hearst's poll watchers had been threatened; one of them had his face cut and a finger chewed off. Tammany Hall had sent an army of repeaters to the polls. In the days following the election, while the ballots were being tallied, Hearst voiced his suspicions of fraud. When the Tammany mayor was officially reelected, on December 27, it would be by a plurality of less than thirty-five hundred. This was not the time for a repeater to speak of ratting out anybody.

As it would be said of Louis Poggi after him, Vaccarelli was under the aegis of sheltering forces. POLICE HELD BACK BY STRANGE PULL OF PAUL KELLY, declared a headline of the *Evening World* on November 28, 1905. And like Louis Poggi after him, Vaccarelli seemed to come and go as he pleased. It was plainly announced on November 26, 1905, that he "shortly would surrender to Captain Hodgins of the Mercer Street station, and would rely on powerful Tammany politicians to pull him through this latest trouble just as they had done so often before." And so it was.

The associate district attorney to whom Vaccarelli told his story was Benjamin N. Cardozo, the Sephardic Jew whose father, Judge Albert Cardozo, had barely escaped impeachment in the days of the Boss Tweed scandals.

"Mr. Cardozo believes that he told the truth," it was reported after Vaccarelli spoke to him.

Cardozo was later appointed to the Supreme Court to succeed Oliver Wendell Holmes. And Vaccarelli himself went on to greater things. He operated the Noonday Social Club, "a house of evil resort" at 201 West Forty-first Street, near his Stag Auto Garage at 236 West Forty-first. Then there was the Independent Inglander Dramatic and Pleasure Club, a high-class gambling joint at 588 Seventh Avenue, near Times Square. In the summer of 1909, he became a labor organizer and strike leader for the scow-trimmers' union, which then was the only New York local affiliated with the International Longshoremen's Association. By the summer of 1917, he was the president of that local and the general longshoremen's organizer of the port of New York. In 1919, Secretary of Labor William B. Wilson appointed him a member of the special Federal Committee of Conciliation. His associate commissioners were John F. Hylan, the mayor of New York, and James L. Hughes, the deputy federal commissioner of immigration. (Hylan, a Tammany mayor, would remain in office until his bosses replaced him with Jimmy Walker in 1925.) The Stag Auto Garage became the Packard Transportation and Repairing Company, of which he was president and treasurer.

"In a spacious, well stocked library, he will be deep in the heart of an address of Abraham Lincoln or immersed in the philosophy of Benjamin Franklin, or, it may be, delighting his eyes with bound reproductions of famous paintings or this or that modern treatise on art. There is underlying in his nature that inherent fondness for art which is one of the passions of the Italian people." Thus the *Evening Telegram* of Sunday, November 23, 1919. Here we also find the line " 'I never had a gun in my possession,' declares Commissioner Vaccarelli."

He conducted his affairs in a suite of offices in the Times Building. When he died, on April 3, 1936, his obituary in the *Times* was headed "F.P.A. Vaccarelli, Union Leader, Dies."

Monk Eastman was the discarded prototype, taken into service by

Tammany, then discarded. In raising up Paolo Vaccarelli, the *Evening World* of November 28, 1905, makes a rhapsody of such broken maquettes:

> Monk Eastman and Nine-Eyed Donigan wear the State's livery. Humpty Jackson, that gifted gun-fighter, who carries his hardware in his hat, is at Sing Sing, too. Six-Fingered Murphy has been using all six of them to crack rock on the Island, and Yaky Yake Brady, with a cough which unbuttons his vest, is an invalid in Jersey. Pockmarked Paddy Brock, Big Mike Donovan, Jimmino Brennan died in gang fights one time or another. An iconoclast with a gas pipe cracked the skull of that Bowery idol "Eat-'Em-Up" Jack McManus last summer. Barring only such ambitious small fry and fingerlings as "Nigger Mike" Salter and "Razor" Riley, Paul Kelly is the gang leader who has endured, immune from the forces which finally drove his active contemporaries into stripes or the graveyard.

Paolo Vaccarelli was born five years before Arnold Rothstein. Monk Eastman, three years before him. Louis Poggi, six years after him. Arnold Rothstein was there when Monk Eastman came and went. He was there when Louis Poggi and Paolo Vaccarelli were there.

The Fourth, Sixth, Fourteenth, and Fifteenth wards were the East Side's heart. The Sixth Ward was the neighborhood that had been the Five Points. The Fourth Ward was bounded by Spruce Street and Peck Slip to the south, Catharine Street to the north, Park Row to the west, the East River to the east. The Fourteenth Ward was bounded by Canal Street to the south, Houston Street to the north, Broadway to the west, and the Bowery to the east. The Fifteenth Ward, bounded to the west by Sixth Avenue, followed the line of the Bowery from Houston Street to Fourteenth Street. It was in the Fifteenth Ward that Vaccarelli's joint, Little Naples, was located. The Rothsteins' Greene Street, Mercer Street, and Bleecker Street shops were also located in the Fifteenth Ward. To the east, along the river, were the Seventh, Tenth, Eleventh, and Thirteenth wards. This was the East Side and all that became known as Chinatown (so first called in New York between 1887 and 1892), Little Italy (so first called before 1906), and, depending on one's vantage, Jewtown (so first called before 1890), the Ghetto (so first called, by an Irish-born reformer, before 1906), or the Lower East Side (so first called between 1920 and 1929).

"No fort," said Cicero, "is so strong that it cannot be taken with money."

"Money is the first thing to be sought," said Horace, "good reputation after wealth."

"You cannot serve both God and money," said Matthew. But what if . . .

W. W. Drummond was appointed to the Supreme Court of the Territory of Utah in 1854 and took the oath of office on July 31, 1855. Having left behind his wife and family in Illinois without any means of support, Drummond had brought with him to Utah a whore he had picked up in the streets of Washington and, introducing her as Mrs. Drummond, seated her beside him on the judicial bench. He hated Mormons, and he did all that he could against them. He was a gambler, and he avowed plainly and openly that he had come to Utah to make money. Jules Remy, whose *Voyage au Pays des Mormons* was published in Paris in 1860, was there in Great Salt Lake City when Drummond proclaimed in the presence of Chief Justice John F. Kinney:

"Money is my God."

In fact, Drummond had then turned to Remy and said, "And you may put that down in your journal if you like."

Arnold Rothstein was most probably a habitué of the East Side ward haunts well before he turned eighteen, which was little more than two weeks after the century turned. We know for a fact that he was there almost daily from 1900 through 1904, ostensibly working on Greene Street.

In 1904, he is in the menial employ of his father. For the next three years, 1905–1907, he is living with his parents with no visible independent means of support. In 1910, he is well-off, well-known, and mysteriously well-placed.

That phrase: "strange pull." Poggi, Vaccarelli, Rothstein. They had the same God, and the same maker, or benefactor, if you will. His name was Big Tim Sullivan. And he did not care what you were: a kike, a wop, a mick like him. As long as you delivered. And if you did, you would be delivered in turn. To wherever you were big enough to go. It was Big Tim's way. And nobody fucked with Big Tim's way.

B IG TIM SULLIVAN WAS a hell of a man. He was born down there, on the East Side, in the old Sixth Ward, in 1863. And now he ruled it, all of it. If you went below Fourteenth Street in New York City, you were in Big Tim's territory.

Timothy Daniel Sullivan had run as a boy with a gang called the Whyos, whose name came from a variant of the interjection *whew,* as in Thackeray's *Vanity Fair:* "He knew the old gentleman's character well, and a more unscrupulous old—whyou—he did not conclude the sentence." The Whyos were an Irish crew that had grown out of the Chichesters in the years after the Civil War. Their time had passed by 1888, when two of their leaders were hanged in the Tombs city prison at Franklin and Centre streets. But Big Tim's time had just begun. A few years before the hangings, Tim had been recruited by the County Democracy to run for the Assembly from the Second District, on the East Side. The County Democracy was then at war for power with Tammany Hall, which had not yet fully recovered from the fall of Boss Tweed. The Whyos supported Tim in the election by the usual means. At the age of twenty-three, Tim was in Albany. His friend Tom Foley, a Tammany man, suggested that Tim might do better for himself if he gave up the County Democracy. Without looking back, Tim delivered his district to Tammany.

Boss Tweed had been succeeded by Honest John Kelly, who had somewhat reorganized Tammany after the pattern of the hierarchy of the Church of Rome. In 1886, Richard Croker, formerly of County Cork, and formally of the Fourth Avenue Tunnel Gang, succeeded Honest John.

Croker took a liking to Sullivan. This gave Sullivan good opportunity to conspire against him.

As Sullivan and others saw it, Croker had grown soft and complacent. He spent more and more time abroad, leaving the business of vice untended. The advocate Major Asa Bird Gardiner (1839–1919) was a great defender of murderers and thieves, and he served Tammany and its lords of vice well as the district attorney of New York County. Gardiner's "To Hell with Reform" speech during the New York City election season of 1897 celebrated a new day for corruption. At the victory festivities for the new mayor, Robert A. Van Wyck, in 1898, crowds chanted Gardiner's call to arms. Van Wyck allowed his Tammany bosses to oversee each of his appointments to office. In 1900, Theodore Roosevelt, in one of his last official acts as governor of New York, removed Asa Bird Gardiner as district attorney and preferred charges against him. Then, in early 1901, the state legislature expelled William S. Devery, a good Tammany man, from office as chief of police, by abrogating the office itself. Croker, who was in Europe at the time, was neglectful. It was Big Tim who saw to it that Mayor Van Wyck appointed Devery to the position of deputy police commissioner.

When Paddy Divver, an old Croker crony, was up for reelection as district leader on the East Side later in 1901, Tim ran Tom Foley against him; and with the help of Sullivan's ward thugs, such as young Monk Eastman, Foley took the district for Sullivan. Croker was deposed by Sullivan and his followers in early 1902. The East Side was Sullivan's.

Croker renounced politics. He spent his spoils and the rest of his years in England and Ireland, traveling here and there, racing horses, and living well. He died in Glencairn in 1922, at the age of eighty-one.

Big Tim extolled the value of unshaven men. "When they vote with their whiskers on, you take 'em to a barber and scrape off the chin fringe. Then you vote 'em again with side lilacs and moustache. Then to the barber again, off come the sides, and you vote 'em a third time with just a moustache. If that ain't enough, and the box can stand a few more ballots, clean off the moustache and vote 'em plain-face. That makes every one of 'em good for four votes."

But as John J. Harrington discovered in Paolo Vaccarelli's joint in the election season of 1905, repeating was not a joking matter. Of course, Big Tim kept his starched white shirts clean. There was no blood on him.

When Vaccarelli wanted to start a shake-down racket in the scow-trimmers' union a few years later—to help protect "underpaid and overworked brother Italians who were too poor and too inarticulate to make any demands for fair treatment"—he needed authorization from Big Tim.

And, as Vaccarelli liked to tell it, Big Tim said, "Go ahead and do anything you can. I won't stand in your way."

This was how it worked. Big Tim had known Vaccarelli since the days when Vaccarelli was a boy going by the name of Kelly. He had been granted the name of Kelly by court order in 1905. Five years later, in 1910, when Paul Kelly once again became Paolo Vaccarelli, it was "out of respect" for his aging parents, that he might bring pride to them through the probity and success of his rededicated life. He was now a philanthropist, a friend and champion of the workingman who toiled humbly on the garbage barges. As these scow-trimmers were proud of their Italian heritage, so too was he.

After Sullivan's death, Vaccarelli would move into Big Tim's manor in Westchester Village. "Vaccarelli," the *Evening Telegram* would write, "bought it for love of the memory of 'Big Tim,' the one man in the world who, before the great turning point, saw and appreciated what good there was in him and inspired him to effect the change that came into his life." Yes, Vaccarelli said, Big Tim, like himself, was a "man of the poor." In Vaccarelli's obituary, *The New York Times* would say that he "acquired considerable power on the lower East Side through his friendship with Big Tim Sullivan." The turning point. Strange pull indeed.

Little Vaccarelli had served Big Tim, and little Vaccarelli had been served. As for Louis Poggi with his opium and his heroin, well, money was money.

Though he ruled every vice racket, Big Tim was not a man of common vices. As was known to every East Side home where a rosary hung, Big Tim had sworn as a boy that he would never drink or smoke, and he had not once strayed from that resolution.

Every year, in February, to commemorate the birthday of Big Tim's beloved mother, he stood in front of the clubhouse at 259 Bowery giving out thousands of pairs of stout brogues to those who needed them, and for all who came to him he had words of shoring kindness. He told of the long-ago winter's day when he was a ragged and shoeless schoolboy. The weather was so bad that the sainted schoolmarm had kept him after class until she could find shoes for him, so that he might go home to tend to his mother without catching pneumonia. Tim had never forgotten that act of

Christian charity, and later, when he prospered, he saw to it that no man or boy went without shoes. Sometimes the newspapers bungled their telling of the story, and his mother's birthday became the day that the teacher had given him shoes.

And no one on the East Side went hungry on Christmas in the days of Big Tim. There were thousands of turkey dinners, with cranberry sauce, mince pie, coffee, and a pipe and tobacco for every gent who was down on his luck.

He lived apart from his wife, Helen, but she remained his "beloved wife," and there was no divorce, for the church forbade it.

Big Tim had a smile for everybody.

During the last years of his life, Big Tim slowly lost his mind. He vanished on August 31, 1913. Later his body was found in the morgue, where it had lain unidentified and unclaimed for days. Big Tim, in his delirium, had been run over by a train in the middle of the night, in the Westchester switching yards. It could not have been suicide.

"No, they say, Tim was too good a Catholic to kill himself. It must have been an accident, the outcome of the last of many runaways, of many attempts to get from his gentle imprisonment to a train that would take him to the city."

William McAdoo (1853–1930) served as the police commissioner of New York City in 1904 and 1905, a time when the police force was largely controlled by Tammany Hall. Toward the end of his term in office, he wrote: "A combination of interests which thrive on the non-enforcement of law or make large profits by allying themselves in a business way with criminal and vicious groups, can bring a more concentrated and personal pressure to bear for the removal of a Police Commissioner than an army of law-abiding, honest citizens." To be sure, "an honest Police Commissioner must expect a perpetual conspiracy against his continuance in office or the success of his administration."

These words are from McAdoo's book, *Guarding a Great City,* which was published in May 1906. McAdoo, who himself was an immigrant from County Donegal, observed the Jews and Italians of the East Side. He saw "an ill-concealed distrust of the Italians by the Jews. The Jewish population is not apt, unless under great pressure, to resort to force or to commit crimes of violence, and they have a natural horror of the baser sort of Italians who go around with deadly weapons." McAdoo reiterates: "The East Side Jew rarely commits a crime of violence, such as assault or murder."

Jews had been a part of Tammany Hall since the days of Mordecai Manuel Noah, back when the Jewish vote meant nothing. Judge Cardozo had been a key man in the Tweed ring. Max Rothberg, Abe Finkelstein, and the alderman Max Levine were a part of Sullivan's crew. These men were especially close to Big Tim's cousin, the Tammany leader Florence Jenevieve Sullivan, who was known as Big Florrie. Big Florrie lost his mind before Big Tim lost his, ending up in a straitjacket in the Bellevue psychopathic ward in early September 1907.

Big Tim's minion Monk Eastman fell from grace in 1903. Arnold Rothstein, who was twenty-one that year, was a different sort of Jew-boy entirely. Eastman had no class. He looked like a man roused from one of those dago garbage scows. He had a face like a rotten jack-o'-lantern left out in the sun, and he barely knew how to tie a proper bow around his neck.

Rothstein cut a figure. He was presentable. More than that, there was something in his head besides pigeon dust.

He had his eye on the end of the rainbow rather than trained on the cobblestones looking out for the next stray copper penny. He could do with a fountain pen and a column of figures what Louie the Lump could do with a gun, and in just as short a time. He had the stuff to know that fear was a sucker's racket: You used it, or it used you. He was a gambler who knew never to trust in fortune.

Big Tim was a sporting man and a gambling man as well. Under the Horton Law, which held boxing legislation in abeyance from 1896 through 1890, he owned the Lenox Club, where James J. Corbett lost by a foul to Tom Sharkey in the fall of 1898. In the last summer of the Horton Law, after William Brady and Jim Kennedy had obtained Madison Square Garden and scheduled a match between Corbett and Kid McCoy, Sullivan refused to issue them a permit until they made him a stockholder. On the eve of that hot August night when the fight was held, it got out that Kid McCoy had given a bond of ten thousand dollars to Eddie Burke, the bookmaker, that he would not win the match. Word of this occurrence changed the flow of betting money away from McCoy to Corbett, who had lost his heavyweight title in 1897 and who now was so out of shape that the wagering on him had been light. Big Tim knew to go the other way, and he laid down "many thousands" on McCoy, who, true to his bond, was knocked out by Corbett in the ninth round. Big Tim felt that Gentleman Jim had double-crossed him. After paying out to Eddie Burke's commissioners, Big Tim revoked and transferred the license of a saloon at Sixth Avenue and Thirty-third Street that bore Corbett's name. Having put the ex-champ out of business, he reckoned, with a smile, that the score was settled.

Better than most twice his age in the Tammany wigwam, young Arnold Rothstein knew the ways of the noble redskin—that Indian in a war bonnet who looked to the west on every new-struck five-dollar golden coin.

Like Big Tim, Arnold neither drank nor smoked. And, like Big Tim, he had a smile for everybody. It was a rare smile, that. Few men had it. But Big Tim knew it, and understood it, whenever he saw it. And so did Arnold Rothstein.

Yes, he was a good lad, Arnold was.

T HE RAG TRADE WAS good to Abraham Rothstein. He and his brother
still had the place on Bleecker Street. Arnold's brother Edgar was
clerking for them now. Jack, the youngest of them, was steering clear of
the place for now, but he would later be in the old man's employ as well.
Uncle Louis's sons, Arnold's cousins Raymond and Abraham, were down
there, too.

On November 21, 1905, entering her twentieth year, Arnold's sister,
Edith, married a twenty-three-year-old businessman named Sidney
Salinger. The ceremony was performed by a rabbi of the old Sephardic
congregation of Shearith Israel. The marriage did not last. Edith divorced. On August 20, 1916, she would marry again: a twenty-five-year-
old fruit merchant named Henry Lustig. This time she again would be
married by a Sephardic rabbi, Henry S. Morais, but at the synagogue of an
Eastern European congregation, Ohab Zedek, on West Ninety-fifth
Street. When she had married in 1905, she had stated her age to be twenty.
When she remarried, almost eleven years later and three months before she
turned thirty, she stated her age to be twenty-four.

Whatever. Between a father who davened about as though he had been
there with God when the tree of good and evil was a sapling, and a neuras-
thenic sister who stayed away from mirrors and got younger every day,
Arnold must have appeared to his younger brothers as a sort of apostate
Moses: one who led himself out of captivity and left the other Jews behind.
When there came a choice of working for their father or working for their
brother, Edgar and Jack would choose their brother. And Jack would take
after Arnold in other ways as well.

In his fashion, Arnold was in the rag trade, too. Different rags, different mill, but a rag trade nonetheless.

Up in Dalton, Massachusetts, in 1879, three years before he was born,
an old stone-mill paper company named Crane's had gotten a contract

from the United States government to make some special paper, half cotton rag and half linen, with red and blue fibers embedded in two parallel vertical lines. The government wanted a lot of this paper. The company had to acquire a new mill nearby to produce so much paper. What came out of Crane's Government Mill was good stuff. When it was sent in big rolls to Washington, D.C., it was all worth the same. But when the Bureau of Engraving and Printing down there was through with it, all cut up nice and clean into crisp rectangular pieces measuring 7.42 by 3.13 inches, well, some pieces were worth a dollar each and some were worth ten thousand dollars each; and then it was even better stuff.

If you filled your left pocket with certain pieces of this paper, you could buy dinner. If you filled your left pocket with certain other pieces of this paper, you could buy souls. It came into that bureau at pennies on the pound, and it left there as the stuff men slaved away their lives in misery for.

"This certifies that there have been deposited in the Treasury of the United States of America One Thousand Dollars in gold coin payable to the bearer on demand."

In time, they would change these pieces of paper. They would come down to little more than 6 inches by 2.5. They did this the year after Arnold Rothstein was gone, as if to say, Well, he is gone now, we don't need big money anymore. And the rag specs would change too, from 55 to 75 percent cotton and only 25 percent linen, and those red and blue fibers would be shredded and dispersed throughout the paper, which was a hell of a lot easier to do than running them in long parallel lines. And there would be no more thousand-dollar pieces of paper, no more ten-thousand-dollar pieces of paper. And they no longer would be payable in gold, or even in silver. They would be payable in nothing. What you got for them was what you could get for them. The only thing that would not change was that it would still be the stuff men slaved away their lives in misery for.

But all Arnold knew was the old stuff, those bedsheets that were good as gold and a whole lot easier to carry around.

Yes, he was in the rag trade. And by 1909, the year they took the Indian off the penny and put Lincoln there, he was in it good. That was the year he got married.

S HE WENT BY the name of Carolyn Green. She was born on May 6, 1888, the daughter of a Jewish father and a Catholic mother. Her father, Meyer Jerome Greenwald, a butcher by trade, had been born in Germany in May 1852. Her mother, Susan McMahon, in Ireland in December 1866. They had been married in New York on June 19, 1887, by a priest of St. Bernard's Church, on West Fourteenth Street.

Carrie Greenwald was born at 648 Hudson Street, in Greenwich Village, near the Gansevoort Market. Her father's butcher shop was also in the Village, at 34 MacDougal Street. He ran the shop with his brothers Abraham and Isaac. The Gansevoort Market was refurbished and reopened in early 1889 as the West Washington Market. After fire destroyed much of the marketplace in the summer of the following year, the Greenwalds moved uptown, where Meyer opened a new shop on Eighth Avenue near Fifty-fifth Street. By 1894, he had set up business on Ninth Avenue, between Forty-seventh and Forty-eighth streets, close by his home, at 340 West Forty-seventh Street. By 1899, the family moved around the block, to 358 West Forty-eighth Street. There, in the spring of 1890, Meyer and Susie and twelve-year-old Carrie lived with a young servant girl named Annie Price. By 1905, the family moved back around the block to 324 West Forty-seventh Street. By the time the family moved to 301 West Forty-sixth Street, in 1908, nineteen-year-old Carrie had taken up with Arnold Rothstein.

Meyer Greenwald did not impose his religion on his wife or daughter, and Carrie was raised as a Catholic. She dreamed of a life in the theater. One could not be a femme fatale named Greenwald. Thus little Carrie Greenwald, in her aspiring, became little Carolyn Green.

In the spring of 1906, a few weeks before her eighteenth birthday, she appeared, one of many cute girls without names, in the cast of a Shubert brothers musical called *The Social Whirl*. The show opened in April at the

Casino Theatre, at Broadway and Thirty-ninth Street. Twenty-four years later, in 1930, the Casino would be torn down to make way for the expanding garment district.

In her pursuits amid the Broadway milieu that was so close, both geographically and in essence, and yet so far from her father's meat shop, Carrie made the acquaintance of James Grant Forbes (1871–1938), a thirty-four-year-old Canadian who was trying to make his way as a writer in New York. He had written a short story called "The Extra Girl" for *Ainslee's* magazine. Forbes had turned the story into a vaudeville sketch for a young performer named Rose Stahl and now was writing a play, *The Chorus Lady*, based on the sketch. When Forbes struck a deal in 1906 with the producer Henry B. Harris, he saw to it that there would be a part for Carrie.

On September 1, 1906, Carolyn Green appeared in the opening night cast of *The Chorus Lady* at the Savoy Theatre on West Thirty-fourth Street. The show, part comedy and part melodrama, received a good deal of notice. The dressing room scene in the second act became widely known on Broadway. In it, the ladies wore side-slit Tanagra sheath gowns of the sort that had been the scandalous fashion sensation of Paris the previous spring. The show also brazenly presented a woman smoking. The ingénue, Rose Stahl, for whom the show was written, received most of the acclaim. Carolyn was not mentioned in reviews, except in cast listings.

Five weeks after its opening, *The Chorus Lady* moved from the Savoy Theatre to the Garrick, around the block on West Thirty-fifth Street, and then, a week later, to the new Hackett Theatre at West Forty-second Street. The show went on tour and was revived in New York at the Hudson, on West Forty-fourth Street, in November 1907.

Carolyn, or someone hired to be her, tells us that she was in the domestic touring company of the show, "rushing madly around the country, putting on and taking off make-up, living in impossible hotel rooms, catching trains, and playing eight performances a week"—words befitting a weary and jaded professional rather than the butcher's daughter whose heart would have beat with the excitement of every rushing moment of it. We do know that by November 25, 1907, the night of the show's New York revival at the Hudson, she was replaced by Lavina Mason in her role as Mai Delaney.

The Chorus Lady was made twice into a moving picture: in 1915 by Jesse Lasky and Paramount, and in 1924 by Regal. The former starlet Rose Stahl was in neither of these. Her moment had not lasted. She appeared in only three other shows; then, after the failure of *Moonlight Mary* in 1916, she was gone. Carolyn Green's lesser moment dimmed all the more quickly. The writer James Forbes went on to have another ten plays produced, seven of which were made into moving pictures. But he found Carolyn no part in any of them. The producer Henry B. Harris died at age forty-nine in the sinking of the RMS *Titanic,* on April 15, 1912. His widow, who was born with the name Irene Wallach but called herself René, found safety in one of the ship's lifeboats and later filed the single largest liability claim against the White Star Line: two hundred thousand pounds. Remembered as the first female theatrical producer in New York, she was relatively broke when he died in Manhattan in 1969 at the age of ninety-three.

Carrie also made the acquaintance of Jacob J. Shubert (1879–1963), the younger of the Polish-born brothers who had produced *The Social Whirl* in 1906. It was J. J. Shubert who gave Carolyn Green her last theatrical work, a small part that did not gain her mention in the cast. It was in a three-act musical called *Havana,* staged by the Shuberts at the Casino Theatre in 1909. The show opened on February 11 of that year and ran for several months.

A young lady named Edith Kelly, another of Carrie's acquaintances, also got a part in the show, as a character named Gladys. Edith Kelly would later find fortune as the second wife of the Broadway roué Frank Gould. As Edith Kelly Gould, she performed in *Pins and Needles,* a musical revue that opened in February and closed in March at the Shubert Theatre in 1922. Aside from a part, before her marriage to Gould, in a 1918 moving picture comedy short called *Hey, Doctor!,* her show business career went no further. But in the short-lived *Pins and Needles* revue, she won the attention of the show's producer, Albert De Courville (1887–1960), the British writer, director, and producer who worked both in the theater and, after 1929, in moving pictures. Through her marriage to De Courville, she found greater fortune than she had found in her marriage to Gould. Edith and Carolyn would remain friends for many years.

The *Theatre Magazine* declared *Havana* to be "a success." This is the only known notice that the show received, notwithstanding Carolyn's later description of it as "the sensation of the theatrical year."

Jacob Shubert, like James Forbes, was of no further help to her career. But like her friend Edith Kelly, she would find her fortune through matrimony, holy or otherwise.

According to Carolyn: "I was eighteen and Arnold Rothstein was twenty-four when we met for the first time, and felt a decided attraction for each other, at an after-dinner supper party for eight given by Albert Saunders in the Hotel Cadillac in September, 1908. At that time I was in *The Chorus Lady,* the comedy hit of the season."

In September 1908, Carolyn was twenty. Arnold Rothstein was twenty-six. Carolyn was not in *The Chorus Lady,* whose season was 1906. We are told nothing of this Albert Saunders or his relationship to Arnold or to Carolyn, nor are we told anything of the other guests at this dinner at the fashionable Hotel Cadillac at 157 West Forty-third Street.

"He sat beside me and devoted himself to me while we ate broiled lobster, and everyone except Arnold sipped champagne.

"After the supper he drove me home in a hansom cab. And the next day he called for me at the theatre and took me to supper. After that he was in constant attendance."

If, instead of September 1908, the time is fixed at September 1906—when Carolyn was indeed eighteen, and Arnold was indeed twenty-four, and Carolyn was indeed in *The Chorus Lady,* and she could indeed have been at the Savoy Theatre the next day—her account becomes credible.

"Arnold, at that time, was a slim young man with a white, sensitive face, brown, laughing eyes, and a gentle manner. I cannot emphasize too much this gentleness of manner, which was one of his most alluring characteristics.

"He was always extremely well tailored and presented a most dapper appearance, noticeable even on Broadway, where it was the fashion to be well groomed."

Carolyn does not describe herself. She was a slight and delicate girl, five feet four inches in height, with bright gray eyes and dark brown hair, which at the time she wore long and done up. Her small mouth, with its well-defined philtrum above the Cupid's bow of her upper lip, was smiling and attractive.

Out of work for more than two years, a young lady in New York then, as ever since, could nonetheless easily continue to play the role of the actress. A great many of the young ladies who were privileged to perform lewd acts upon my own personage through the years professed careers in the performing arts, yet no one sought their autographs. Arnold Rothstein, who became an intimate of Florenz Ziegfeld, Irving Berlin, Al Jolson, Fanny Brice, and others, surely could have ensured Carolyn's rise in show business if he had wished to do so. His personal life would be full of showgirls. It was not that he cared for the Broadway stage. He did not. It was because showgirls were pretty, and their dispositions tended to be more easily sweetened by jewels, which he could give, than by devotion, which he could not. Yes, for Arnold Rothstein there would always be showgirls, but he would not have his wife be one of them.

Carolyn's last performance in the show *Havana* was in the spring of 1909. That summer, she traveled north by train with Arnold for the racing season at Saratoga, which began that year on August 2 and ended on August 28. Accompanying them were Herbert Bayard Swope and his girlfriend, Margaret Powell, who later became his wife.

Herbert Bayard Swope (1882–1958) was one of Arnold's closest friends. He was the son of Isaac Schwab, a Jewish immigrant from Germany. Relatively unknown, like Rothstein himself, in the early years of their friendship, Swope was to achieve great acclaim as a journalist. He began working at the *New York World* in 1912, when Charles Lincoln, formerly of the *Herald,* took over as editor of the *World* following the death of its longtime owner, Joseph Pulitzer, the Jewish immigrant Civil War veteran who had begun his career in 1867 as a reporter for the *Westliche Post,* a German-language daily in St. Louis. Swope would work at the *World* until 1928, rising to city editor, then executive editor, a position and title invented by the *World* especially for him. His reportage from Germany during the Great War won him the first Pulitzer Prize awarded for reporting, in 1917. After retiring from the newspaper racket, Swope held positions at several corporations and became chairman of the New York State Racing Commission. He was likely the most famous and celebrated reporter of the early twentieth century. He was also a character: a thrill-seeking gambler who lived high and fast. There is no telling what information and turns of "strange pull" transpired between Rothstein and Swope in the years that Swope held sway at the *New York World*.

On August 12, 1909, Herbert and Margaret rode with Arnold and Carolyn to the home of Fred B. Bradley, the justice of the peace of Saratoga Springs.

"We four then drove to the cottage where we had a happy but simple dinner in celebration of the marriage, and then Arnold and I retired to his bedroom, man and wife.

"No sooner were we alone together than he said to me:

"'Sweet, I had a bad day today, and I'll need your jewelry for a few days.'"

OLD-TIMERS IN Saratoga would later recall that Arnold Rothstein had first appeared there in the racing season of 1904. He had arrived with three or four other men, of whom only one was remembered.

Abe Attell (1883–1970) was at that time considered to be the featherweight champion of the world, a title he had assumed in 1903, after Terry McGovern had forfeited it by failing to make the weight limit of a hundred and twenty-two pounds. Abe, who came from a poor Jewish family in San Francisco, had won his first professional fight in 1900. In his early years in the ring, he did not believe in finesse, nor did he have it: He knocked out twenty-four of his first twenty-eight opponents as fast and as hard as he could. But later, Damon Runyon would call Attell one of the five best fighters of all time, and Nat Fleischer, who founded *The Ring* magazine in 1922, would rank him the third best ever in his class. He held the featherweight title for almost a decade, until 1912, when he lost in twenty rounds, on his birthday, to Johnny Kilbane. Attell was tough but good-natured. He was known as the Little Champ and the Little Hebrew. He would also be known as Arnold Rothstein's garde du corps and as the man who was implicated with Rothstein in the fixing of the World Series in 1919.

"They came to bet on the races and worked on a cooperative agreement as to profits, losses and expenses," wrote Hugh Bradley in his 1940 book, *Such Was Saratoga*. "The venture was not a success. Then, on the afternoon when the communal bankroll was down to $100, luck shifted. All hands were happy. Even when they somehow became separated from the holder of the new two-thousand-dollar bankroll, the others were not duly perturbed. They merely left the track and went with all haste to the hotel where they lived.

"They found that Rothstein had just checked out and boarded a train for New York. Since the laws about unpaid bills were even more strictly enforced then than now, it was several days before they could borrow enough money to bail themselves out of the hotel and follow him."

We should not quite believe this little story. It is the sort of fanciful hearsay that is dear to the vagrant communal memory of a place and used eagerly by chroniclers to liven their books. Who could not skip out on a hotel bill, let alone confederates of Arnold Rothstein? But I feel that the grain of truth here—that Rothstein first came to this resort of high society and high stakes as a cozener whose purse held more of ambition and cunning than of money—serves as a tableau curtain for our pilgrim's progress in Saratoga over the years to come.

The start of the Saratoga racing season on August 1, 1918, would bring celebrants to festivities at the grand opening of the Brook, a stately old mansion on Church Street that had been converted into a gambling casino by Arnold Rothstein and two partners. Gambling houses had thrived in Saratoga Springs since the first racing track opened there in the summer of 1863. The Club House, which was opened by John Morrissey in 1871, had become under Richard Canfield (1855–1914) one of the most elegant establishments in the world. There never had been, and never again would there be, a gambling house as splendid as the Club House that Canfield operated in the Saratoga summers from 1894 to 1907. Canfield had closed the Club House when the pall of state reform threatened to poison the sweet, sylvan Adirondack air. There had been less baronial gambling houses since then, but they were out in the countryside, near Saratoga Lake. The Brook was near the town center of Saratoga Springs, close to the majestic Grand Union Hotel.

Rothstein's partners were Nat Evans, a close fellow gambler from New York, and Henry Tobin, a bookmaker. Rothstein and Evans shared the majority interest of 56 percent. Tobin held 28 percent. The remaining 16 percent of the profits went to Saratoga political campaign funds. It was Rothstein who calculated the net profits from a gross take of which he was the sole auditor. It was Rothstein who tallied and deducted from the gross all unpaid markers, real and imagined, and all operating costs, real and imagined, down to every real or imagined light bulb and three-penny stamp and every scrap of paper and droplet of ink, real or imagined, spent on tallying them. It was Rothstein who knew that 16 percent of a variably quantifiable sum was, ipso facto, also variably quantifiable. It was Rothstein who knew that a Dalton ten-key adding machine betrayed only he who betrayed himself.

The Brook also served as the summer destination for a sort of Fresh Air Fund that Rothstein operated for a small group of inner-city youths who apprenticed themselves to him. They were all immigrant lads: the eldest, Francesco Castiglia (1891–1973), was from Calabria; Salvatore Lucania (1897–1962), from Sicily; and the youngest of them, little Maier Suchowljansky (1902–1983), from the Russian Pale. In the full blossom of their manhood, these young men—Frank Costello, Charles Luciano, and Meyer Lansky—would be the true inheritors of Rothstein's legacy, taking his ways, principles, and vision to their fullest end. It would take the three of them to carry on as one of him; but together they would evict God from his own garden of earthly Eden, that they might feast.

"It was under the umbrella of Arnold Rothstein," writes Lansky's biographer Robert Lacey, "that aspiring young wiseguys like Meyer Lansky and Lucky Luciano first came to Saratoga.

"In Saratoga, as everywhere else, Rothstein worked through loose and flexible partnerships. He had to have at least one local partner who could arrange the fix with the local politicians. Then Rothstein needed specialists to take care of the dining room and entertainment, along with the individual gambling games and tables in his casino. It was through running franchises inside Rothstein's Saratoga casinos that Meyer Lansky and Lucky Luciano graduated from crap games to greater things."

Rothstein's tutorial role was personal as well as professional. "He taught me how to dress," Luciano would recall, "how not to wear loud things but to have good taste; he taught me how to use knives and forks, and things like that at the dinner table, about holdin' a door open for a girl, or helpin' her sit down by holdin' the chair. If Arnold had lived a little longer, he could've made me pretty elegant; he was the best etiquette teacher a guy could have—real smooth.

"I did lots of favors for Rothstein, too. I used to back him in poker games. We both made money. But he could spend it so fast just livin' that it made even my head spin, and I was a pretty good spender myself."

Luciano sought Rothstein's advice on the eve of a major social event in

September 1923. The younger man was concerned with presenting himself in precisely the right and proper image.

"So I got hold of Arnold Rothstein and the next morning he picked me up and took me down to John Wannamaker's department store. Actually, I felt a little guilty, and I told Arnold that maybe I owed it to Ben Gimbel to go to his old man's store, but he said to me, 'No, Charlie, John Wannamaker's men's department has the stuff you need. I'm going to turn you into another Francis X. Bushman.'"

At the department store, Luciano began to buy two or three of whatever struck his fancy. He wanted to order custom-tailored suits.

"No," Rothstein told him. "I want you to wear something conservative and elegant, made by a gentile tailor."

Rothstein gave him hundreds of neckties from the house of Charles Charvet in Paris. Arnold also bought silk by the bolt for his own custom-tailored Sulka shirts, and he often made a gift of such shirts to his protégés. "That's how I got the rep for wearin' silk shirts and underwear and pajamas," Luciano said, who credited Rothstein with giving him "a whole new image." Under Rothstein's influence, Luciano cast a somber and dignified figure. "I always wore gray suits and coats, and once in a while I'd throw in a blue serge."

Frank Costello, by far the most intriguing and powerful of the triumvirate, was especially drawn to Rothstein, who was one of the few men he respected. It has been said that Arnold Rothstein and Joseph Kennedy were the only two men he admired. In his biography of Costello, Robert Katz writes:

"Rothstein was one of Frank Costello's close associates in those days. He was a thin, sallow-faced man who started out as a gambler and became the financier of the underworld. Rothstein worshipped money. It was his personal god. He would do anything for money and had his finger in loansharking, bootlegging, phony securities, gambling, drugs, fencing stolen Liberty Bonds, and anything else that promised a pay off.

"He was New York's biggest racketeer in the twenties and put together the largest gambling empire in the nation," says Katz, who goes on to further describe Rothstein as "a financial genius of sorts who ran his empire pretty much out of his hat. Yet he kept track of every dime ever owed him.

If he loaned a man money, he would insist that a life insurance policy be taken out for the amount advanced. This way, if death prevented the pay off, he would collect anyway.

"He was a compulsive gambler who hated to gamble. He played cards methodically, showing no passion. Often he played in games where the turn of a card meant winning or losing $250,000."

Katz goes on to state that both Frank Costello and his brother Eddie were on Rothstein's payroll at various times and that Frank and Arnold frequently borrowed from each other. Costello knew that no one ever got the better of Rothstein in a business deal.

"There is no question that the younger, less sophisticated Costello admired Rothstein's shrewdness and learned from him many things not taught in Harvard's School of Business."

Costello's words to a newspaperman, many years after Rothstein's death, are quoted: "All I know, I stole. If I saw you hold a cigarette a certain way, and I liked it, I would steal it from you."

There was a forty grand IOU from Costello among Rothstein's papers at the time of his death.

Lansky remembered meeting Rothstein at the Bar Mitzvah celebration of the son of a mutual acquaintance in Brooklyn. "He invited me to dinner at the Park Central Hotel, and we sat talking for six hours. It was a big surprise to me. Rothstein told me quite frankly that he had picked me because I was ambitious and hungry."

To list the other young Jews to whom Rothstein was a rabbi would be like transcribing the criminal index of twentieth-century Jewish enterprise. Among this generation were Louis "Lepke" Buchalter (1897–1944), Arthur "Dutch Schultz" Flegenheimer (1902–1935), Philip "Dandy Phil" Kastel (1886–1962), Jacob "Gurrah" Shapiro (1900–1947), Irving "Waxey Gordon" Wexler (1888–1952), Abner "Longy" Zwillman (1899–1959), and many more. The list of mackerel-snappers who learned from and served him is longer.

America was a country of ethnic and racial strife and of petty prejudice that liked to see herself as a "melting pot." It was Israel Zangwill (1864–1926), a son of Russian immigrants, who gave her that phrase, in a 1909 stage-play:

"There she lies, the great Melting Pot—listen! Can't you hear the roaring and the bubbling?" exults the character of David in the fourth and final act of *The Melting Pot*. "Here shall they all unite to build the Republic of Man and the Kingdom of God."

In this country, where the phrase "equal opportunity" gained currency only as a stupid late-twentieth-century legislative term, anticipating a human actuality that never came, Arnold Rothstein was the first true and great equal opportunity employer. It was he who brought together the Christian and the Jew. It was he who took a neglected nine-year-old child, recalled by the name of Red Ritter, off the streets and into his home to be sheltered and fed. It was he, in a lily white world, whose money was behind *Shuffle Along,* the groundbreaking black musical stage success of 1921; he whose personal assistant, Thomas A. Farley, born in Virginia in 1875, was a gentleman of color, a gentleman whose tuition to Columbia University was paid by Rothstein, a gentleman who was well remembered in Rothstein's will, and a gentleman who later established himself in the New York real estate business.

Rothstein was a man who practiced rather than preached, paid no lip service but simply paid. If his power is to be judged as having been criminal, then what harsher judgment have we reserved for the far deadlier, more ruinous, and malfeasant corporate and political powers that increasingly oppress and rob us with the blandest of smiles and the most vacuous of blandishments?

WHEN ARNOLD AND CAROLYN RETURNED to New York in the late summer of 1909, they moved into the Ansonia, a luxurious seventeen-story residential hotel at Broadway and Seventy-third Street.

It was a grand structure, the Ansonia. Designed by Emile Paul DuBoy of Graves and DuBoy, and completed in 1904 after five years' work, it now dominated the skyline of the growing Upper West Side. The Ansonia had Turkish baths, the world's largest indoor swimming pool, basement shops, and several restaurants decorated in Louis XIV style. A rooftop farm provided tenants with the freshest food. From Flo Ziegfeld to Igor Stravinsky, Enrico Caruso to Babe Ruth: They all stayed at the Ansonia.

Carolyn later looked back with complaint. The room "was, in no sense of the word, a suite," she informs us. "It was in this room at the Ansonia," Carolyn says, "that the lonesomeness, which was to be the keynote of my married life, began. From the moment of our return my husband contrived to leave me by myself."

A few months later, in early 1910, they moved to a three-story brownstone at 108 West Forty-sixth Street, down the block from where Carolyn's parents were living. (Carolyn does not mention this parental proximity in her book.) They also kept the room at the Ansonia until 1913. Arnold listed his business as "real estate" in the city directory. In the 1913 directory, he listed himself as the secretary and Carolyn as the president of the firm, with an office downtown at room 901 of 44 Cedar Street. By 1915, he would be listed as a "broker," and by 1918, the year he opened the Brook in Saratoga, he would be listed only as the secretary of the Carolyn Holding Co., of which Carolyn was listed as the president, with an office at the Cedar Street address.

With the benison of Big Tim Sullivan, Arnold had been involved in bookmaking, shylocking, and gambling enterprises since at least the turn of the century, when he still had been working at the shop on Greene Street and Big Tim had been overthrowing Richard Croker at Tammany

Hall. Sullivan controlled the informal Tammany "gambling commission" that met weekly to grant or renew "licenses" and assess the "tax" to be levied on each operator according to the volume of his profits. It was under Sullivan that Rothstein was green-lighted. Now Arnold set about refurbishing the first floor of the brownstone into a casino. It was at this time that thirty-five-year-old Thomas Farley became Arnold's personal attendant, a position he would hold until there was no more Arnold to attend.

"This house," says Carolyn, "was on the south side of the street, next to a garage which formerly had been a stable. The way I knew it had been a stable was this. One night I was sitting alone in the dining room when I heard a peculiar noise, a gnawing sound. I asked Thomas, our Negro manservant, what it was, and he said:

" 'Rats, Mrs. Rothstein. Rats always hang around a stable.' We had exterminators of all kinds, ferrets and what not, constantly busy in that house, but it never was freed of the rats."

Sometimes a grain of unfamiliar fear entered with the draft of life beneath the closed door of a man's soul and lodged there, where he could not reach it to extract it; and it accrued all the fear that had been put to rest and forgotten through the years, until it choked the breath of his being. Big Tim had not been quite the same after they had put that straitwaistcoat on Big Florrie and left him howling with his arms pinned to his sides. It was as if he sensed a cloak rack with one of those things awaiting him in every chamber of his daily and nightly movements.

"I used to sit up in the bedroom and listen to the roulette wheel to learn whether the house was winning or losing. This was simple because if the house won, all that was necessary was for the croupier to rake in chips, but if the house lost he had to take time to count out chips for the winners. Thus, when the house was winning the wheel spun with short stops, but if the house was losing the wheel spun with long stops."

This makes no sense. What if the house lost a dozen fifty-dollar bets and won a single thousand-dollar bet on a turn of the wheel, or some other configuration of multiple disbursements and solitary or fewer but greater imbursement such as that?

"I was willing to listen to the rats and the roulette wheel because I loved Arnold."

No greater love hath she than that she lay down and waited to be fed.

As Big Tim Sullivan came to converse increasingly with madness, and to withdraw from the reign of his power to that of his inner demons, the human vermin of his system began to come forth brazenly to pursue forbidden crumbs of spoil in the absence of authority. The most offensive of these vermin were the lowest of them: those in suits of blue wool and buttons of copper.

Herman "Beansy" Rosenthal was a twenty-nine-year-old Jewish immigrant from Russia who ran a gambling joint, known as the Hesper Club, in his home at 104 West Forty-fifth Street, around the block from Rothstein's place. Rosenthal had opened the joint with a loan of two grand from Big Tim Sullivan. Beansy was not known for what lay between his ears, and he subsequently made the mistake of also taking another fifteen hundred from Charles Becker, a large and intimidating New York City police lieutenant whose specific job under Commissioner Rhinelander Waldo was to oversee the suppression of vice. In a year when his salary was under seventeen hundred dollars, Lieutenant Becker deposited almost fifty-nine thousand dollars in his personal savings account.

In return for his fifteen hundred, Lieutenant Becker wanted 25 percent of Rosenthal's take. It was not a loan that he had made, Becker informed him, it was an investment. To protect his interest, he would post a man named Jacob "Bald Jack Rose" Rosenzweig within the Hesper Club, and Rosenthal was to pay Becker's share to Rose.

By this time, the spring of 1912, Big Tim Sullivan was virtually *non compos mentis,* and Tammany was in disarray. There was nowhere for Rosenthal to turn. When one of Becker's criminal associates was indicted for murder, Becker insisted that every gambling operator must contribute five hundred dollars to a "defense fund" that would ensure his acquittal. This was too much for Herman Rosenthal to take. He turned to Rothstein and sought his advice. Rothstein told him that he could not fight City Hall, that he should bear up and pay, and that was that.

But Beansy refused. With a belly full of booze and Dutch courage, Beansy spilled the beans to a reporter: Rothstein's friend Herbert Bayard Swope. Rosenthal's drunken and incriminating words appeared in the *New York World* of Sunday, July 14, 1912. He was being harassed, he said, by the very cop who had imposed himself on him as a partner. He named Becker and implied that he was ready to tell everything he knew.

When Rosenthal saw the newspaper that Sunday, he turned again to Rothstein. He had meant only to scare Becker, to get him off his back, he said. He insisted that he could never be made to say what he did not want to say. Rothstein offered him five hundred dollars to get out of town. Rosenthal refused to take either his advice or his money.

When Becker saw the newspaper that Sunday, he turned to Bald Jack Rose and told him what to do. One of Becker's collection men, William Alberts (1882–1912), better known as Big Jack Zelig, was in the Tombs at the time. Following Becker's order, Rose arranged Zelig's release and gave him two thousand dollars. He told Zelig that Rosenthal must not see another sunrise. Four men were hired as a killing crew: Jacob "Whitey Lewis" Seidenschnier, Louis "Lefty Louie" Rosenberg, Harry "Gyp the Blood" Horowitz, and Francesco "Dago Frank" Cirofici.

Beansy had returned to Rothstein and told him that he had decided to take him up on his offer. Rothstein told him that he had waited too long.

"You're not worth five hundred dollars to anyone anymore, Beansy."

Late on Monday night, Beansy was in the bar of the Hotel Metropole, a popular gathering place for gamblers, at 149 West Forty-third Street near Broadway. He was told that there was somebody outside who wished to talk to him. It was four minutes before two o'clock in the dark summer morning of July 16. He stepped out under the incandescent bulbs of the Metropole canopy. The four killers emerged simultaneously and suddenly from an automobile and opened fire. A cabaret singer, identified as Charles Gallagher, happened to be passing by. He noted the license number of the automobile as it sped away.

Within two weeks, Lieutenant Becker, Bald Jack Rose, and the four members of the killing crew were under arrest. Becker's pleas for help from Tammany Hall went unanswered. When he was ratted out by the killers, Jack Zelig, a man who was more terrified of death—his own, that is—than most, agreed to testify for the state. On October 5, 1912, the morning before the trial was to begin, Zelig was murdered while boarding the Thirteenth Street trolley.

Bald Jack Rose had also agreed to turn state's evidence; and even without Zelig's testimony, the four killers were convicted and were executed in the electric chair at Sing Sing on April 13, 1914. Becker was convicted as well but was granted a new trial by the court of appeals. His original conviction was upheld on May 22, 1914: the first reconviction in the city's history. There were more appeals, more attempts to bargain, but on the morning of July 30, 1915, Becker went to the electric chair at Sing Sing. His last words were "Into thy hands, O Lord, I commend my spirit."

If one were of dark mind, it might be seen that Rothstein had played Rosenthal well, using him, with Swope's witting or unwitting help, to get rid of a business competitor—Rosenthal himself—and at the same time, and far more important, a cop who had been a considerable source of trouble. In doing so, he would have served not only his own ends, but the journalistic career of his dear friend Swope as well. Big Tim Sullivan, who had died during Becker's trial, surely would have enjoyed the coup. Bald Jack Rose later worked for Rothstein.

On April 14, 1909, the Mitchell Music Publishing Co. of New York copyrighted a song under the names James Dempsey and George Mitchell. The words were credited to Dempsey, the music to Mitchell. The song was called "The Ace in the Hole."

This town is full of guys
Who think they're awful wise
Just because they know a thing or two.

You see them every day
Walkin' up and down Broadway,
Telling of the wonders they can do.

There's con men and there's boosters,
There's card-men and crap-shooters;
They congregate around the Metropole.

They wear fancy ties and collars,
But where do they get their dollars?
They all have got an ace down in the hole.

CAROLYN DESCRIBED Sid Stajer as "always closest of any man to my husband." It was Stajer who transferred a six-year-old chestnut gelding named Virile to Rothstein on November 16, 1916. It marked the beginning of Rothstein's years as an owner of Thoroughbred racehorses.

Short, stout Sidney Stajer is a mysterious figure. Where Rothstein is, Stajer often is not far from there. Twelve years his junior, Sidney was a very young man when Rothstein took him under his wing. His parents, Louis and Mary Grosz Stajer, were from Hungary. Sidney, their fifth child, was born at 286 Second Avenue, near East Seventeenth Street, on March 12, 1894.

It is not known to us how the twenty-two-year-old son of immigrant workers had come to possess a Thoroughbred that had won, placed, or shown in the majority of his times out that year.

HERE I PAUSE. I was lying in bed yesterday, half-asleep, when I heard a voice coming from my telephone answering machine. The voice was saying that one of my best friends was dead.

This friend of mine had died often. But he had always come back, smiling his beautiful smile, his blue eyes so full of life. This time he will not be back. My saints have always come from hell, and now, with his passing, there are no more saints. The world is different. Yesterday, as he lay dying, the sky here in New York was dark and full of rain. Today it is the color of those eyes of his.

All that remained of his lungs was one piece like a small black stone that the doctors' X-rays could not penetrate. The rest of his lungs had been cut out and thrown into a hospital dump bin along with a good many of his ribs a long time ago; and he had lived for most of his seventy-five years taking his breath with that small black stone.

If you asked him how he was doing or what he was up to, he would say: "I breathe in, I breathe out." He would get angry at people who said, "Have a nice day." Everyone wants to take, he used to say, and no one wants to give. I truly believe that if someone had ever said to him, "Give a nice day," he would have thrown his arms around that person. "I breathe in, I breathe out." He knew that this was the main event, not only for him, but for everybody. I stole the line from him. It gets rid of a lot of idle talk.

He gave so much with that blessed breath: not only to his friends, but to the whole world. Now the world is different, and we will have to breathe without him. Breath, inspiration, it is the same; and that small black stone was a source of divinity. I imagined him living to a hundred because I wanted him to live to a hundred. After all, he had gone so long and come so far with his small black stone unclaimed by death, it seemed that maybe death had forgotten him.

About a year ago, last spring, he wrote to me:

*I dont know whats going on. It feels like Ive forgotten how to write
like i forget everything else. Everything has changed, cant breathe, cant
stay awake, cant move much. Sometimes I sit and cry. My hearts broken by this whole thing. Ive worked very hard to learn how to write a
simple line and have it mean something, and now I cant put what Ive
learned to use. Obviously Im asking life to be fair. Pretty funny, eh?
But theres an element in my life now that I have not experienced in the
past . . . being ashamed of my government . . . my country. I have certainly disagreed with some of the clowns we elect, but what is happen-
ing now is disgraceful. That really adds to the heart break. I too have
thought of moving to Europe, but I cant now, its too late. I cant
breathe, cant walk much, plus my family is here. See what you did El
Woppo, you got me all excited. Anyway, I love you my friend and am
grateful for your life and all the beauty and insight that you have
added to our ability to understand this human experience. A river
derci.*

Now it seems that he was saying good-bye. But there were more
words after that. The last time he wrote to me, he asked if I ever wondered why we bothered to go on. I wrote back to him that we must not
give satisfaction to those who want to see us dead. But I did not hear from
him again.

It's good to know that he died in his sleep, with the classical music he
loved so much drifting through the room, his dog on the bed, his last wife
and friend and children there. According to the doctors, he died of something called chronic obstructive pulmonary disease. Words that mean
nothing. It is as if the small black stone, like he himself, was tired.

He was a great man, a beautiful man, a wise man. He lived life. He en-
dured life. He renewed the lives of many. He was a source of light and
love and strength. The years bring death after death, but his is a loss not
only to those who knew him, but to the world as well. He was one of the
few great writers that the United States could ever call her own. Yet he was
more respected, honored, and admired in Europe than in his native land.
Some hours ago, a reporter from Paris asked me why this was. "America,"
I told her, "has never respected her own resources. As a nation, America

was a short-lived child-brat: She was born late, made a great deal of childish noise, then died young. America has been dead now for several years." I told her that my friend had outlived America, that America was dead before he was. "It meant a lot to him," I told her, "that Europe embraced his books. He knew that European culture is not yet quite completely measured by shelf life." The culture of Europe went back almost three thousand years to Homer's rosy-fingered dawn. America, in her bassinet of benighted privilege, was barely older than television, and it showed.

He would be glad to know that I am working. He knew what that sign said above the entrance gate to Auschwitz: ARBEIT MACHT FREI. "Work makes you free."

He once ended a letter to me with the old line "Write if you find work." It hits me only now that there are at least three ways to take that line.

I pause here because I can pause here. Yes, I write to you from the congested intersection of illusory time and illusory place: the alarm-ringing tick-tock of the present that is designed not so much to follow the cycles of nature, but rather to facilitate the cycles of bill paying, rising, and sleeping to serve our masters, and being "on time," an expression that, revealingly, does not appear until the nineteenth century. A friend tells me of a Wall Street colleague who leases an ostentatious Rolex wristwatch. He has chosen to make a show of pretended success and importance, and he has chosen a golden-and-diamond-studded symbol of his subservience, to the illusion of time, the lackey's wrist shackle to the punctual bidding of others, as the means of his show.

Such is the intersection where I write. But I also write to you from a continuum, in which none of this congestion matters. Whatever I write is all of a single flowing. I have long ago given up the "tricks" of my trade. I know them well: the enticing beginning that will draw you in, the crescendo and the diminuendo of artful passages designed to seduce you by the dance of words, the calculated techniques that bring *jouissance,* the words that will endear you and the words that will excite you and the few words here and there that will evince feelings of sophistication and self-satisfaction.

But I no longer wish to be a purveyor of lies or cheap entertainment. The world is full of them. We rush out with urgency to see a moving picture, then we forget it, for it becomes almost instantaneously passé and we must rush to see another, and on and on. There are different dance halls, different dances.

To write artificially, to seek to manipulate you, to offer you candy in a world full of candy: This, as I now see it, would be to treat you with arrogant condescension. It would be more honorable to simply cut your purse than to try to take your money with false words. Besides, you are one of a devoted few who have accepted me for what I am. Every book that I write sells the same number of copies: thirty thousand. This is what the publishers' accountants tell me, anyway. It is never thirty thousand and one. It is never twenty-nine thousand nine hundred and ninety-nine. It is always thirty thousand. I should have thought that one of you might have said something to somebody by now, one way or the other.

In other words—and, yes, this should not be done: ending one sentence with a word and then using the same word in the next—we are in this together. Here I am with my big bad life, and there you are with yours. And this is the only way that we have of being together. And I've come to like you. And, in a way, to know you. You wouldn't be here if you were so easily manipulated. I mean, don't get me wrong: When I was young, I'd rob a hot stove. That was before I could make money with words. And words meant a lot to me back then. They were almost sacred. Then I learned that, for the most part, it was just a racket like anything else. Publishers, even before they became appendages of dying corporate conglomerates, did not care about words or books. But fuck that—I'm not getting into that again. What I mean to say is that I don't know what I mean to say, and that is why I'm saying it. All that I meant to say is that words, writing, meant a lot to me when I was young, and now that I am old, they mean even more.

When I set out to write this book, I was intrigued by the figure of Arnold Rothstein. I still am. But as I researched more deeply, I came to see that the picture of him that history gave us was wrong. Was I to offer a different picture? Was I to take a man's life and make of it an exercise in interpretation? Was I to claim to have arrived at the "truth"? Was I to fabricate a "riveting portrait" by hiding one aspect of him and presenting another, without ever knowing—who could?—which aspects of him held weight and meaning for him, in his life, as he lived it? This would be to compound the misknowing that already was.

I remembered how the poet Charles Olson had praised certain works that gave facts but no fanciful thesis to color or miscolor them. One of these works was *The Melville Log* by Jay Leyda (1910–1988). It was a two-volume "documentary life of Herman Melville," published in 1951: "a simple chronology of events" based on "contemporary evidence," which is to say, facts. Olson praised it as "*an act of mind* precisely because it: (1) presents the known facts; (2) recognizes that these are only the known facts, that others obviously existed which have disappeared or have not been recovered; and (3) leaves those facts as facts, and does not claim to analyze Melville's use of them."

Many books about Melville have appeared since *The Melville Log,* but it is this bare documentary labor that remains the most revealing and, yes, in its way, the most enjoyable and satisfying source on Melville's life, work, and times. I decided then that my true purpose, above all others, was to unearth the facts, the true facts, of Arnold Rothstein's life.

Why Rothstein's life? Why Melville's? Why anyone's? After all, we are dead soon enough and forget all we knew anyway, and none of it will serve us after that last breath.

But I will tell you why: Because Arnold Rothstein is a shadow figure beyond good and evil. If we are going to go anywhere, that is where we should go. And if that shadow is ultimately unknowable, as it must be, I was resolved that it should not go ultimately misknown, or wrongly known, as it has been. Let others tell you the shade and length of Christ's hair without offering a single bare fact establishing his existence.

It has been almost twenty years since I have read any book, or more than a few pages of any book, that I have written. Once I consider it to be written, I move on. The experience of the book, for me, lies in the writing of it. When I begin, I do not know the end, and I cannot look ahead to the last pages to discover my words and feelings, because those pages do not yet exist. And I cannot look back on what already exists because he who looks back, falls. But I emerge from the writing of every book having learned new things, and maybe even with new feelings and new sight.

God, I've written a paragraph that ends four typewritten pages after it begins. From "When I set out" to "new sight." They have told me that no one reads long paragraphs anymore. (Editors are the only people who have anxieties about size where they want it to be shorter. It's like "100% Guarantee! Decrease the Size of Your Paragraph.") This is the one thing they have told me that I have come to believe. So now I will go back and indent here and there, to cut it up into portions for you. To tell you the truth, I wouldn't even read it the way it looks now. And I want you to read it.

I once wrote a sentence that was over two pages long. It was a great sentence. I can't remember what the sentence was, but it was perfectly grammatical, even classically so, although I did have to draw up equations to clarify the variables of subjects, objects, and pronouns as they swam from one estuary to another.

An editor called me—I'm indenting again as I go along now—and said, "This sentence is over two pages long."

"Good," I told her.

"Do you think that maybe we could—"

"No," I told her.

You see, I want you to read what I write. I don't want you to read what I write after it's been processed. You can get that in the next aisle.

I'm sure that it is the death of my friend that has brought me to pause here. As I say, writing is writing. We should not segregate it into individual parcels any more than we should segregate it from the rest of our lives. In pausing, it occurred to me that my friend was born the year that Arnold Rothstein died. He drew his first breath the summer before Arnold Rothstein drew his last. Like almost everything else, this means nothing.

But something else also occurred to me. It occurred to me that everything I knew and loved seems to be drifting away: a whole way of living, loving, and being. It occurred to me that anyone who wastes one single breath is a fool. Life is all that we have, and we must live it, for real: like leopards, like beautiful creatures, like stars that pass through the nighttime sky over the wildest, darkest, deepest sea.

Fucking Sailors
in Chinatown

———o❦❧o———

ARNOLD ROTHSTEIN'S FINANCES seem to have taken a leap during this period. We will recall, from our fond glance at the life and times of Louie the Lump, that President Woodrow Wilson signed the Harrison Narcotic Act into law on December 17, 1914. The act, which went into effect on March 1, 1915, outlawed the sale, possession, and use of heroin and opened a world of opportunity to men of vision. A heading six weeks later, in *The New York Times* of April 15, 1915:

Illicit Peddling of Heroin and Cocaine Practically at an End, Police Say.

Sidney Stajer has been described with dismissive glibness as a "drug addict" and a "large-scale drug dealer." No one mentions his distinguished service during the First World War, which began in 1914, the year of the Harrison Act. "The war to end all wars," they called it, from an October 1914 booklet by H. G. Wells, *The War That Will End War*. Sid Stajer entered the United States Army on April 4, 1918, shipped out after six weeks' training in trench warfare at Camp Upton, New York, and returned to civilian life with a victory medal on May 10, 1919, six months after the war's end. He wore his honorable service lapel button with pride.

As Charles Olson said, we should present "the known facts" and leave "those facts as facts." But to do so, as in the case of Sidney Stajer, often presents us with an intractable ambiguity, an unsettling uncertainty, which we dislike. We want those brought before us to be clearly defined either as good or as bad. But he was a human being. When we, as human beings, look at our own lives, what can we find that is spelled out in clear and orderly black and white? Yet while we remain mysteries even to ourselves, we seek concise and clear understanding of the souls of others. This absurd paradox colors all of history, in which we seek to construct an impossible algebra of heart and mind. None of us is so pure as to be wholly good or wholly evil, and the gray between the two, which is where we dwell, is vast and unmappable.

Arnold Rothstein was the principal financier of the international heroin trade. Traffickers were subject to arrest. He was not. United States Assistant Attorney John M. Blake questioned Rothstein about his ties to known drug traders. A month after Rothstein's death, Blake stated:

"The best explanation Rothstein could give us was that he loaned money to different people, but he never kept tabs as to the manner in which they invested such loans as long as he was repaid with a profit."

Rothstein's young associate Lucky Luciano was first arrested in the spring of 1916, when he was busted for peddling dope at a poolroom on Fourteenth Street.

Ten years later, in the biggest narcotics case since the passage of the Harrison Act, Charles Webber and an ex-cop named William Vachuda were accused of importing twelve hundred and fifty pounds of heroin into the country. Rothstein acted as the bail guarantor for both Webber and Vachuda.

On July 13, 1928, federal narcotics agents arrested Sidney Stajer along with Abraham Stein, another Rothstein associate, and George Williams at the Hotel Prisament at Broadway and Seventy-fourth Street. Rothstein appeared at the hotel on the night of the arrest and later posted bail for all three men, who on March 11, 1929, four months after Arnold Rothstein's demise, were indicted by a federal grand jury on charges of conspiring to import narcotics.

At this time, heroin sold in the streets of New York for about forty dollars an ounce, compared with a price of more than three thousand dollars today. By 1930, street dealers were using children to deliver dope to customers. Dominic Folgiro, who operated a tailor shop at 173 Hester Street on the Lower East Side, employed a six-year-old girl to run heroin to his customers.

Papers found in Arnold Rothstein's safe after his death led federal narcotics agents to the biggest bust of the era: an estimated two million dollars' worth of heroin—today's equivalent of more than twenty-one and a half million dollars—discovered in trunks being loaded aboard the

Twentieth-Century Limited at Grand Central Station, bound for Buffalo, on the night of December 7, 1928.

The passenger to whom the trunks belonged was a small man in his fifties named Joseph Unger, who was seized in his Pullman sleeping car as the *Limited* was red-balled entering Buffalo. According to United States District Attorney Charles H. Tuttle, the arrest of Unger was the most important arrest in the history of the federal narcotics force. Joseph Unger had been Rothstein's man.

Eleven days later, on December 18, a ton of heroin, valued at over four million dollars—a ton would be valued at more than a hundred million dollars today—was seized at Pier 2 in Jersey City, after arriving from Le Havre in five crates aboard the steamship *Rochambeau*. The shipment was in the name of one "Joseph Klein," an alias of Joseph Unger, who was presently being held in the Tombs.

Two days later, Unger was brought to trial hastily at the Federal District Court on charges from the December 7 seizure. On Christmas Eve, to the chagrin of the authorities, Unger pleaded guilty. There would be no examination of the defendant. Nothing would be revealed.

A curious report in *The New York Times* that Christmas Eve spoke vaguely of "overtures to the Government last night which led to a compromise on the change in the indictment and prepared for his guilty plea.

"Under the compromise Unger may receive a maximum sentence of fifteen years, whereas a conviction of the charges contained in the indictment would have made possible a maximum of twenty-seven years." Furthermore: "If he should change the attitude which has caused him to tell United States Attorney Tuttle and others that they were on the side of the law and he would be dishonorable to betray his friends to them, the sentence might be as little as five years."

Three days later, on December 27, forty-one-year-old James R. Kerrigan, the chief federal narcotics agent who had been overseeing the case, died under mysterious circumstances. "His death," reported *The New York Times*, "was attributed by M. R. Livingston, Acting Narcotic Agent in Charge, to injuries sustained Sept. 28 in a raid on an opium den in Newark's Chinatown. Kerrigan, he said, fell eight feet into an areaway. Instead of resting, he then battered his way into the building with a sledge hammer. Thereafter he complained frequently of sudden pains." A doctor at Misericordia Hospital on East Eighty-sixth Street spoke of a condition "as if he had been kicked in the abdomen." Both Agent Livingston and the physician "asserted that there was no foundation for a rumor to the effect that Kerrigan had been poisoned by drug dealers." The *Times* described Kerrigan as "a drug war martyr."

The judge presiding over the Unger case was United States District Court justice Francis A. Winslow. On April 15, 1929, Congressman Fiorello La Guardia had introduced in the Seventy-first Congress a resolution to investigate Judge Winslow. The resolution was referred to the Judiciary Committee. Subsequently, on December 20, 1929—the day that Unger was hurriedly brought to trial before him—the Judiciary Committee submitted a report recommending the investigation cease owing to Judge Winslow's resignation. But there was no resignation. Winslow's judicial seat would not be vacated until 1936, two years after La Guardia became mayor of New York.

Following his guilty plea, Joseph Unger refused to talk. About anything. He said, "The government double-crossed me, and I cannot do anything to help in any investigation." Asked how he was double-crossed, he said that the government had tried to bring his sister into court to testify against him. "My sister is a good woman," he said, "and has a sick child. She has nothing to do with my affairs." Unger's sentencing was scheduled for January 4, 1929. There were conferences between Joseph Unger and his lawyers, Henry Stern and J. Arthur Adler, a former assistant federal prosecutor, then conferences between the lawyers and United States Assistant Attorney John M. Blake. When Friday, January 4, arrived, sentencing was deferred until the forenoon of the following Monday, January 7. Joseph Unger's sentencing was subject to further postponement. On May 2, he was sentenced at last by Judge Winslow to eleven and a half years in the Atlanta Federal Prison. Unger's lawyer Henry Stern, pleading for leniency, had told the court that his client was "a mere messenger boy." After the sentencing, nothing was heard of, or from, Joseph Unger ever again.

The consensus among old-timers was that heroin was better in New York in the days before the Italians took control from the Jews. In a fine book by David Courtwright, Herman Joseph, and Don Des Jarlais, *Addicts Who Survived: An Oral History of Narcotic Use in America, 1923–1965,* an elderly black man called Mel said:

"When I first started dealing I had Chinese and Jewish connections, later I had Italian connections. It was a beautiful thing when the Chinese and the Jews had it. But when the Italians had it—bah!—they messed it all up. They started thinking people were just a bunch of animals—just give them anything."

An old Jewish gentleman named Al recalled of the drug trade on the Lower East Side: "See, years ago, the Jews had power, so it was very cheap." Al said: "When the Italians took over, when they became the real bosses of the junk business, they started raising the prices up." Furthermore: "The Italians stepped on the H much more than the Jews, and they charged more money."

Jack, who was German Irish, born in Jersey City in 1909, said that "the Italians infiltrated" when "Arnold Rothstein got killed." He remembered that "them Jews were tough bastards, believe me, I'm telling you, they were. And them Italians, they stayed in their place as long as he ruled the roost, as long as he was there they didn't butt in. But, once he was gone that's when they started to infiltrate." There is a footnote here that says: "Jack's story is corroborated by the 1964 Senate testimony of federal narcotic supervisor Charles G. Ward." This testimony before the Senate subcommittee is quoted: "The Jewish racketeers of New York almost exclusively controlled narcotics, but back in the 1920's, the leader at that time was Arnold Rothstein. He was murdered and the advent of the Italian racketeers taking over began."

Charlie, born to Italian immigrants in Greenwich Village in 1908, remembered: "The wops started to get in it, and they started to knock off the Jews, they started to clip them. This was '26, '28, around there, and the wops took over. They'd find Jews in the East River if they kept selling it."

Another of Rothstein's crew was Jack "Legs" Diamond (1897–1931), the son of a worker in a Philadelphia coffee-roasting plant who also was a Democratic committeeman. In addition to his part in the trafficking trade that Unger operated under Rothstein's aegis, Diamond was on Rothstein's payroll as a bodyguard in 1928, until a few months before Rothstein's death.

Diamond was a colorful character. He had a drawn and pallid look and appeared older than he was, from the wear upon his body of the many bullets that had tarried awhile or established residence in him in the course of several failed attempts to take his life. But he showed no concern. After the fourth such attempt, he was warned by his chauffeur that gunmen were out seeking to kill him yet again. "What the hell do I care?" he told him.

The word "sociopath" was introduced in *The American Journal of Psychiatry* in 1930. It was none too soon, because Jack would not be around much longer. In a front-page story in *The New York Times* of December 19, 1931, Meyer Berger paints a lovely picture:

ALBANY, Dec. 18—Jack (Legs) Diamond, human ammunition dump for the underworld, was killed in a cheap rooming house at 67 Dove Street here this morning, a few minutes after he had dropped off in a drunken sleep, following celebration of his acquittal in Troy last night on a charge of kidnapping.

Three soft-nosed, .38 calibre bullets fired from a pistol held against the back of his head did the job. The gunmen left him lying on the bed with his arms at his side, his white face twisted in a dying leer.

The night of the acquittal is re-created:

Mrs. Diamond fairly leaped over the rail to fly to her husband's arms. She kissed him, his sister-in-law kissed him and little Johnny Diamond, his nephew, embraced "Uncle Jack" and added his kisses. Accompanied by his relatives, his attorneys and two or three of his friends, Diamond left the court. He was in high spirits because he had "beaten the rap again."

Storey, who had been hired as chauffeur for the duration of the trial, led the way to his cab. The Diamonds piled in and the rest of the party followed in other cars to an establishment at 513 Broadway in Albany where they celebrated the acquittal.

Little Johnny Diamond fell asleep in one of the chairs and the celebration was ebbing at 1 A.M. The jubilant gangster was getting glassy-eyed, drinking his own health and success, and showed signs of getting restless.

He tells everybody to stick around. Then he tells the chauffeur to take him to the rooming house where his sweetheart, the former chorus girl Marion "Kiki" Roberts, has been staying for the past two weeks. He goes upstairs.

A half hour passed, an hour, and he did not come down. Lawyers and friends began to desert the Broadway establishment, one by one, until only Mrs. Diamond, the sleeping nephew and Mrs. Eddie Diamond remained. The hours dragged on, but they waited.

About 4:30 A.M. Diamond staggered into the street.

"Take me home," he ordered Storey, and the chauffeur obeyed.

The deed is done. Jack is dead. With trembling hands, his hysterical wife wipes the blood from his lifeless "sunken cheeks" and "leering lips." She is a "big, red-haired woman, somewhat hard-featured." The police arrive at the scene. "I didn't do it," she cries. Detectives search the room.

Diamond's trousers were on the back of a chair. On the floor lay his brown chinchilla coat and his brown fedora, next to them a new traveling bag.

In the tawdry dresser they found a plain signet ring with the initial "D," a rosary and some dog-eared religious tracts.

There is an undated postcard: "God bless you. From a mother with a large family."

Sidney Stajer, "always closest of any man" to Rothstein, died more quietly, unnoticed by the press. He was forty-six years old, living in Woodside, Queens, with a wife named Wilda. He had been living there at the time of his last known arrest, in 1937, in connection with a series of post office safe burglaries that had taken place throughout the country. On December 11, 1940, Sidney Stajer succumbed to coronary arteriosclerosis at Bellevue Hospital in Manhattan. On his death certificate, Wilda stated his profession to have been "Sales Promotion."

There is no evidence that Arnold Rothstein himself ever used drugs, except as a commodity with which to make money. There is one account to the contrary:

He Always Had Cash.

A former policeman who knew the lower east side during Rothstein's occasional forays there says that Arnold became conspicuous because he was the one lad who always had cash in his pocket. That became a lasting characteristic; he always had cash within finger's reach.

This old policeman also says that Arnold loitered about the "hop joints"—what the Sunday supplements of the day called "opium dens"—when the smoking of opium was quite common.

Found in a "Hop Joint."

A pipe load cost a quarter, and the police bothered about the business only desultorily, as they did about stuss games and disorderly houses—as they do now about speakeasies.

On one of the occasional, desultory raids, however, this officer remembers finding Rothstein in an opium den.

This same policeman, moreover, says he remembers, after being transferred to an uptown precinct, during the reign of William Travers Jerome over the District Attorney's office, of seeing Arnold in very questionable company there.

He recalls that Rothstein was spending many hours in the companionship of established opium peddlers, and in the house of Quong Wa, at 43rd St. and 6th Ave., where "Coxey" Hogan cooked the pills.

This is enticing, but I do not trust the source, which is the third of the ten-part series of articles on Rothstein that appeared in the *New York Telegram* in early November 1929. The writer of this series, Joseph Lilly, has already shown himself to be suspect in his article on Rothstein's youth. Here he attracts more suspicion. Who is the nameless "old policeman"? Why does the copper, who is not accused of wrongdoing, have no identity, while the Chink, who is accused, is named? Is it because the name of even, say, a John Kelly could be checked in police records from the "reign" (1901–1909) of the good upright reformer William Travers Jerome, while a Quong Wa would be indiscernible amid a sea of look-alike Chinese with sound-alike names? The location of Forty-third Street and Sixth Avenue is certainly vague: a vicinity of many leased rooms. But Quong Wa is not at all a common Chinese name, and there seems to be no other mention of it elsewhere in connection with criminal activities. And who is this "Coxey" Hogan, a name tossed forward as if all should know it?

Above all, what renders this singular account of Rothstein's youthful opium smoking most questionable to me is that I cannot believe that anyone who has smoked good opium would ever turn away from it. As regards any other drug, I would not say this.

In the year before Stajer transferred Virile to Rothstein, the colt had run nineteen races, won four of them, placed in two of them, and shown in another four of them. The colt had been racing since 1912, when he belonged to J. E. Davis. The horse later ran for Harry Payne Whitney, a racing man of great repute. Sidney Stajer acquired Virile from Greentree Stable in 1916. In 1917, after Virile was transferred to Rothstein, the horse, now seven years old, had only nine starts, won none, placed twice, and showed once. Virile's purse money for the year was a mere two hundred dollars, a fraction of his previous year's winnings. After 1917, Virile ran no more. The last record of ownership shows the name of one J. Fuentez. Stajer is the colt's owner of record from 1916 until the name of Fuentez appears in 1917. Rothstein's name is not encountered as Virile's owner in the chart books. But Virile marked the beginning of Rothstein's years in the Thoroughbred-racing owners' circle, among wealthy Southern gentlemen and New York aristocrats such as August Belmont Jr., who had opened the Belmont Park racetrack in 1905, in honor of his father, who had died in 1890. The elder Belmont's love of horses and racing had been second only to his love of money. Like his son after him, he was able to weave his loves into a distinguished avocation.

Rothstein's presence at the New York tracks had been long established, but as a bookmaker and a bettor. At Belmont Park, as at the Jamaica race park, which was built in 1903 with Tammany Hall money, bookmakers sat on high stools under the grandstand, their changing odds posted in chalk on slate. Gambling was illegal, but the law, and the track owners, looked the other way. This arrangement operated well until 1910, when reform forces imposed a law that held racetrack owners responsible for any organized gambling activities being conducted at their tracks. In effect they could be indicted and prosecuted as gambling-house keepers. New York tracks closed in 1911 and 1912. By 1913, when the tracks once again opened, it had occurred to bookmakers that there were no laws against personal, man-to-man wagering. So in 1913, the bookmakers simply became men who made a great many personal, man-to-man bets. They came out from under the grandstand to the lawn, displaying the odds that were printed in the racing program and indicating changes verbally instead of with chalk and board. Bets were made with or without being noted on slips of paper. These days were known as "the oral days," a sort of golden era in racetrack gambling. The oral days came to an end in 1940, when mechanical mutuel systems transformed racetrack gambling into a tax-producing government racket.

Anthony Zito wrote about racing for the *New York World* under Rothstein's friend Herbert Bayard Swope. As a journalist he went by the name of Tony Betts. Like Swope, he was a gambler as well as a reporter. Zito remembered Rothstein well.

"When I first met him he was a middle-sized, baldish, rather handsome man, who might have been mistaken for an investment banker. He was addressed, like big executives, by his initials, which later became a sort of protocol in the underworld.

"In a way he was an investment banker, except that most of his dealings lacked the wispy air-brush of legality."

Zito also well recalled a hot summer day that would never be forgotten:

Perhaps the most memorable date in the history of the Oral Days was July 4, 1921. The scene: Aqueduct Race Track. Temperature: 94° in the shade. Post Time: 4:28 P.M. A minute and a fraction later Rothstein had won $800,000 on a horse named Sidereal, more money than anyone in America ever before had won on a horse.

But he was not satisfied. Sidereal did not pluck out his obsession. Rothstein had a mania to win $1,000,000 on one horse. Sidereal, 30 to 1 at the opening, had been backed down to 5 to 1, and was rubbed out by many books in the rush just before post time.

Al Capone had an obsession akin to Rothstein's. It was to bet $1,000,000 on a horse. And he missed, too. He was able to get off only $980,000 in wire-rooms throughout the country. The horse, an odds-on favorite, lost, but Capone pulled out on other horses the same day, for a small profit.

Sidereal had failed to win in three previous starts. Owned and trained by Max Hirsch of Texas, who also worked with Rothstein's horses, the two-year-old chestnut colt, by Star Shoot out of Old Squaw, had been named by Herbert Bayard Swope.

Rothstein worked with Park Avenue men as beards in the clubhouse, and with Broadway characters, such as Morris the Boob on The Lawn, and he probably bet away from the track, too. Nonprofessional horse players got closing odds, but the professionals could obtain average odds.

Maybe Sidereal had fast, secret workouts at Belmont uncaught by the clockers. It was suspected Rothstein had help in the race, but whatever set him off on this betting spree, he failed to tell anyone. Even Swope was dealt out and lost money on the favorite.

Bear in mind that the eight hundred thousand dollars that Rothstein won that day by betting on Sidereal is equivalent to eight and a quarter million dollars in today's money.

Rothstein planned a betting coup as patiently as a chief-of-staff maps out a campaign for large-scale invasion, but it didn't always follow the blueprint. Rothstein fixed a four-horse race, at Saratoga, that went wrong. The horses were priced at 6 to 5, 2 to 1, 7 to 2, and 20 to 1. Rothstein arranged to get the two in the middle out of the way and he bet on the 6 to 5 shot. The way gamblers figure, he was working with 55 percent the best of it.

Asked about the 20 to 1 shot, Rothstein smirked, "Forget about it. I don't like the fellow who trains that horse." The 20 to 1 shot, of course, won and the hidden percentage cost Rothstein $100,000.

The big payoff was that the trainer Rothstein didn't like could have been bought for a hundred-dollar bill.

At that time the horse spongers were active at Belmont Park and Rothstein had an interest in a book. He was approached with a proposition to take care of a 4 to 5 shot. He paid the professional fee and told his book to take in all the bets it could get on the favorite. "But don't be clumsy," he warned him. "Don't go from 4 to 5 up to even-money. Be gentle and make the first rise in price 9 to 10. Ease the suckers into the trap."

A sponge had been inserted in the horse's nostril so it couldn't breathe freely and was a sure thing to be out of the money. The horse won by five lengths, clipping Rothstein for $70,000. Word got around that the sponger had the right stable but the wrong stall.

There were also large sums of money won and lost on trips to and from the races, and not only with a deck of cards. John Scarne tells that the gambler and conman Alvin Clarence Thomas (1892–1974), who came to New York from the South, once took a group of fellow gamblers, including Rothstein, for a good sum. Every day one season, aboard the train from Grand Central Station to the Jamaica track, the men would bet on the number of white horses they would pass in the fields along the way. One day, Titanic Thompson had a hunch. "It looks like a good day for white horses," he said, putting his money on a number that was eight higher than the standing high guess. "He won that one in a walk because he had made a deal with a livery stable and had arranged to have eight white horses planted at a crossroads which the train would pass." Scarne adds, "Not everybody will go to that much trouble to win, but it pays to keep the possibility in mind."

Rothstein organized his Thoroughbreds into Redstone Stable in the fall of 1919. "Red" from *roth,* "stone" from *Stein.* It was merely the literal translation of his family name. The stable was announced in the March 21, 1920, issue of the *New York World.*

Something distinctly novel in the way of racing colors will introduce Arnold Rothstein as an owner of thoroughbreds when the racing season opens at the Jamaica track on May 15. They are described as follows:

Maroon with gold horse front and back, maroon cap.

These colors were designed by Algernon Daingerfield, Assistant Secretary of The Jockey Club, and because of their novelty and effectiveness are sure to attract much interest when seen for the first time.

Arnold Rothstein has long been interested in racing, but this is the first time he has ever branched out as an owner, and in his characteristic way he has done nothing by halves.

His horses will run under the name of Redstone Stable, and Willie Booth, the one-time steeplechase jockey, who raced a small string with remarkable success under his own name last season, has been engaged as trainer.

As a matter of fact, the Booth horses make up the nucleus of the Redstone Stable. Rothstein has purchased Neddam, Gladiator, and Georgio among others, all three of which are likely to be prominent in some of the three-year-old stakes this year.

Sixteen horses now make up the string, and they involve an investment of close to $200,000. Others may be added from time to time, as Rothstein is ambitious to own one of the strongest stables in the country.

Most of the sixteen are two-year-olds, which have been selected with the greatest care, because of their bloodlines. A number of them were bred at August Belmont's Nursery Stud, and were purchased as weanlings by Jimmy Fitzsimmons. One of these is by Fair Play•Felicity, and has been aptly named Sporting Blood.

Observers had high expectations for Neddam, one of the Booth horses. Neddam, a three-year-old colt that had been bred by John Madden, the founder of the Hamilton Place farm in Kentucky—Neddam was Madden spelled backward—had been given his first start on June 6, 1919, in the race in which Gladiator and another two-year-old, Man o' War, made their debuts. Neddam, of course, had lost to Man o' War but had gone on to win five out of eight races as a two-year-old, and there were some who ranked him second only to Man o' War. But it was to be the bay colt Sporting Blood who would become Rothstein's darling.

Rothstein entered Sporting Blood in the August 20, 1921, Travers Stakes, in Saratoga. It was a race that, before its running, almost everyone had already given to Harry Payne Whitney's filly Prudery, who was a three-to-ten favorite, expected to win in a carefree canter.

Late in the evening before the race, Rothstein had learned from someone within the Whitney stable that Prudery was not in her best condition. *The New York Times* would later say that she "was indisposed, as race horses of her sex sometimes are." With the information from the Whitney stable, and the odds being what they were, Rothstein perceived that a killing might be made. Even greater opportunity presented itself on the morning of the race, when Sam Hildreth entered Grey Lag, one of his fastest horses, in the race. Hildreth's champion three-year-old was surely capable of overtaking Prudery even at her best.

Now it was a three-horse race, with the betting concentrated on Prudery and Grey Lag, allowing the odds on Sporting Blood to drift to three to one and higher. Rothstein wired New York and instructed that a hundred and fifty thousand dollars in bets on Sporting Blood be spread among bookmakers throughout the country. Very near to the last moment, Sam Hildreth withdrew Grey Lag from the race. It was speculated that Hildreth did not wish to see his horse lose to Prudery; and in what time there remained to still place bets, the money went with Prudery. It was a two-horse race again, and Prudery could not lose.

The time of the mile-and-a-quarter race was two minutes and five seconds. Sporting Blood won by a good two lengths, easily and unwinded. Rothstein won almost half a million dollars. He also won the Travers Stakes, the twelve-thousand-five-hundred-dollar purse, and the glory. Perhaps his Saratoga gambling house, the Brook, had a profitable evening as well.

Sam Hildreth never spoke publicly of why he withdrew his horse at the last moment from the Travers Stakes that summer.

Rothstein had acquired Sporting Blood and fifteen other Thoroughbreds for a total of twenty thousand dollars. Four days after the Travers

Stakes, he sold Sporting Blood to Bud Fisher, the cartoonist who had grown rich from his *Mutt and Jeff* comic strip, for an undisclosed price said to be in the neighborhood of sixty thousand dollars.

A few weeks later, on September 17, Sporting Blood won the Latonia Championship, from which Grey Lag emerged as an also-ran.

Rothstein did well with Gladiator as well. The three-year-old won the Olympic Stakes at Jamaica on May 26, 1921. It was a selling stakes, but when Gladiator won, Rothstein refused to sell. The horse went on to win the Toboggan Handicap at Belmont on Memorial Day, then the Little Neck Highweight Handicap, also at Belmont, on June 14. Georgio, another Rothstein horse, also won a race that day at Belmont.

August Belmont Jr. detested Rothstein, who gave the lie to Belmont's grand and stately charade. His real name was Schönberg, and the very presence of this wise-smiling Arnold Rothstein was as unwanted as that name. Belmont would not confront Rothstein directly but rebuked Rothstein's trainer, Max Hirsch, for the unsavory light that Rothstein cast on the Thoroughbred-racing establishment. Hirsch stood up to Belmont. At one point, Belmont, who was also chairman of the Jockey Club, asked that Rothstein keep away from Belmont Park. Rothstein threatened to see to it that the racetrack would be shut down, no matter what it cost him. In time, intermediaries worked out a compromise between the two men. The compromise permitted Rothstein to have his full way at Belmont Park on the Sabbath and on holidays.

Some time later, Belmont encountered Rothstein near the paddock on a weekday afternoon. "What are you doing here today?" he inquired.

"It's a holiday."

"A holiday?"

"Why, yes, you ought to know, Mr. Belmont. It's Rosh Hashanah."

When he sold Sporting Blood to Bud Fisher, he let it be known to the racing community that the rest of his horses were for sale as well. By the end of October 1921, Redstone Stable was no more.

I T HAD BEEN in the fall of 1919, while organizing Redstone Stable, that Arnold Rothstein was supposed to have fixed the World Series. Of all the transgressions of which he has been accused, this, the most celebrated of them, was perhaps the only one of which he was innocent.

Of course, given the opportunity to fix the World Series, he almost surely would have done so. But given the way the fixing of the 1919 series unfolded, there was no need for him to do a thing, except to profit from the mistakes of others.

These others, knowing that certain of the favored Chicago White Sox ballplayers were ripe for fixing, and assuming that Rothstein would be eager to finance the venture, had set the World Series fix in motion and then approached Rothstein about what they were sure would be his eager involvement. Two gamblers, the retired Major League pitcher Sleepy Bill Burns (1880–1953), from Texas, and the retired lightweight boxer Billy Maharg, from Belfast, had arranged the fix with two Chicago White Sox players, pitcher Eddie Cicotte (1884–1969) and first baseman Arnold "Chick" Gandil (1888–1970).

In Cicotte's room at the Hotel Sinton in Cincinnati on September 30, 1919, the night before the opening game of the series, Abe Attell had met with Burns, Maharg, Cicotte, Gandil, and six other Chicago White Sox ballplayers. Like Burns and Maharg, Attell was a former professional athlete now involved in gambling. Maharg had fought the Welsh lightweight champion Freddie Walsh in 1906, Attell had fought Walsh in 1908. Attell worked for Rothstein and knew his boss well enough to believe that he would not overlook an investment as lucrative as this. He had assured Burns and Maharg that Rothstein would put up the hundred thousand dollars that the players wanted. But the mistake had been to proceed without him at the outset.

Now that the one set of fools had already purchased the other set of fools—granted, they had been bought on the installment plan, the old hire-purchase plan by which Arnold's grandfather had gotten his first Singer sewing machine, a few dollars down; but bought nonetheless and all the same—he could partake of the fix without pitching in a dime to make it happen. They had blown the chance to have his backing the moment that Attell revealed to him that everything was in place, that all they needed now *was* his backing. To hell with them. Let them all come out of it empty-handed, the fixers and their fixed ballplayers alike. They deserved one another. He would make his. They had seen to that. He told them that he did not believe such a fix was possible, then he acted on what they had given him.

At Redland Field in Cincinnati on October 1, 1919, the Cincinnati Reds beat the Chicago White Sox by a score of nine to one. Eight days later at Comiskey Park in Chicago, the series ended in victory for Cincinnati.

Rumors that the series had been fixed were in the air, but it was not until September 1920 that grand jury hearings in Chicago led to open public scandal. The ballplayers testified that none of them had been paid in full. Shoeless Joe Jackson (1889–1951), from Pickens County, South Carolina, complained that his teammate, pitcher Lefty Williams (1893–1959), had lied to him. In his testimony of September 30, 1920, Jackson said:

"When Claude Williams unfolded the plan to give the series to the Cincinnati Reds, I demanded twenty thousand dollars for my share. We had several conferences and squabbles over the amount, but I finally consented to take the five thousand dollars.

"Williams told me that we were all getting the same. Had I known that some of the others were getting ten thousand, I would have held out for twenty thousand."

Later, outside the grand jury room, Jackson summarized his testimony: "I got in there and said, I got five thousand dollars and they promised me twenty. Lefty Williams handed it to me in a dirty envelope."

Accompanied by Alfred S. Austrian, the attorney for the Chicago White Sox, Arnold Rothstein appeared voluntarily before the Cook County grand jury on October 26, 1920. He summarily blamed Attell, then returned to New York. He was officially exonerated of any blame.

After Rothstein's death, Attell would claim until the end of his life that Rothstein had been the culprit behind the fix.

The Illinois State Attorney's Office announced that there would soon be a full investigation involving Burns, Maharg, and Attell. Though seven of the Chicago ballplayers were indicted in November 1920, no indictments were brought against Burns, Maharg, and Attell.

Burns was to be a witness for the prosecution when the ballplayers were brought to trial. Abe Attell had assured authorities in New York that he was not the same Abe Attell who was sought for questioning by the grand jury in Chicago. After Rothstein's appearance, neither he nor Attell was bothered again by the Chicago authorities.

The trial of the ballplayers began the following summer, on July 18, 1921. Five days later, on July 23, it was revealed by the state attorney's office that the signed confessions of Cicotte, Jackson, and Williams were missing. On August 2, after less than three hours' deliberation, the jury returned a verdict of not guilty. On the next day, the eight ballplayers involved in the scandal (including pinch hitter Fred McMullin, who had not been indicted) were banned from the game for life by baseball's first commissioner, Judge Kenesaw Mountain Landis (1866–1944). The office of an independent commissioner had been created, and Landis had been chosen to fill it, in November 1920, because of the scandal. Landis, who held his position as commissioner of baseball until 1944, owed his long-lived sinecure to the very men whose livelihoods he ruined.

Just as Sporting Blood later showed that he could have beaten the favored Grey Lag fairly at the 1921 Travers Stakes, so it is likely that the Cincinnati Reds very well may have beaten the odds-on favorite Chicago White Sox even without the botched fix, as has been strongly argued in William A. Cook's play-by-play study, The 1919 World Series (2001).

As usual, the "inside dope" of outsiders was a one-way ticket to stupidity. Rothstein's reputation as the fixer of the 1919 World Series grew with the passing of years. In his novel The Great Gatsby, published in the spring of 1925, F. Scott Fitzgerald (1896–1940) introduced as Jay Gatsby's business associate "a small flat-nosed Jew" named Meyer Wolfsheim, described by Gatsby as "the man who fixed the World's [sic] Series back in 1919."

Fitzgerald was a bad writer who has somehow gained the reputation of a good one. Meyer Wolfsheim is a poorly drawn caricature in whose mouth Fitzgerald puts words such as "business gonnegtion." Although Fitzgerald's fictional narrator, Nick Carraway, is supposed to be a bond salesman, Fitzgerald's knowledge of the financial world, and the world of financial fraud, is poor. It seems to derive largely from digests of the Fuller-McGee case, which was making headlines in New York at the time Fitzgerald was writing his novel and, more so, while he was revising the galleys of it, in the fall and winter of 1924–1925, living at the Hôtel des Princes in Rome. Years later, in a 1937 letter to the writer Corey Ford, Fitzgerald would claim that he actually met Rothstein, that he drew "on my own meeting with Arnold Rothstein" to lend form to the character of Meyer Wolfsheim.

Edith Wharton (1862–1937) had made from schoolyard mud her own Jew, Simon Rosedale, a nouveau riche who seeks desperately to enter society in her 1905 novel, *The House of Mirth*. On the publication of *The Great Gatsby,* she wrote to Fitzgerald, congratulating him for having written "the perfect Jew."

Henry Ford (1863–1947), founder of the Ford Motor Company, deployed a force of investigators known as the Sociological Department to oversee his many workers. The Sociological Department's mission was to establish and maintain throughout the company standards of behavior that Henry Ford deemed to be proper. As one Ford adviser said, "The Sociological Department was necessary, in order to teach the men how to live a clean and wholesome life." Beginning in early 1919, Ford also published his own newspaper, the *Dearborn Independent,* in which he expressed his views. The *Independent* of September 3, 1921, carried a long article by Ford titled "Jewish Gamblers Corrupt American Baseball."

"American baseball can be saved," he wrote,

> if a clean sweep is made of the Jewish influence which has just dragged it through a period of bitter shame and demoralization.
>
> Whether baseball as a first-class sport is killed and will survive only as a cheap-jack entertainment; or whether baseball possesses sufficient intrinsic character to rise in righteous wrath and cast out the danger that menaces it, will remain a matter of various opinion.

But there is one certainty, namely, that the last and most dangerous blow dealt baseball was curiously notable for its Jewish character.

Yet only lesser Jews were indicted. Inevitably the names of other Jews appeared in the press accounts, and people wondered who they were. A Jewish judge presided. Jewish lawyers were prominent on both sides of the cases. Numerous strange things occurred.

Ford invokes Rothstein by name:

Then there is Arnold Rothstein, a Jew, who describes himself as being in the real estate business, but who is known to be a wealthy gambler, owner of a notorious gambling house at Saratoga, a race track owner, and is reputed to be financially interested in the New York National League Club.

Rothstein was usually referred to during the baseball scandal as "the man higher up." It is stated that in some manner unknown he received the secret testimony given before the grand jury and offered it to a New York newspaper. However, the fact is this: the grand jury testimony disappeared from the prosecuting attorney's safe-keeping. It is stated that, when Rothstein found out it did not incriminate him, he then offered it for publicity purposes. The price which it is said to have cost is also stated. It is further stated that the New York paper to whom the secret stolen testimony was offered, in turn offered its use for a larger sum to a Chicago newspaper, and that the Chicago newspaper, to protect itself, called up Robert Crowe, the new prosecutor, who advised that, in printing it, the newspaper would incur an unpleasant risk. Other Chicago editors were warned, and the testimony was not printed. Even the New York newspaper thought better of it, and did not print it.

In this connection, Rothstein threatened suit against Ban Johnson, of the National Commission, the big-bodied, big-minded, honest director and protector of straight baseball—but the suit, like others of the kind, has not been brought.

Rothstein is known on Broadway as "a slick Jew." That he is powerful with the authorities has been often demonstrated. His operations on the turf have led to suggestions that he be ruled off.

Alfred S. Austrian, herinbefore mentioned, was the legal adviser of Rothstein during the baseball scandal.

Alfred S. Austrian is elsewhere identified by Ford as "a Jewish lawyer, of Chicago."

Hugh S. Fullerton, the able sport writer of the New York *Evening Mail,* writing on July 28, 1921, made a plea that "a person guilty of crooked work on a race track should be expelled not only from the race track but from ball parks, tennis courts, football fields and every place where sport is promoted. These sport spoilers must be barred from every sport."

And in the same paper, referring specifically to Rothstein, Mr. Fullerton writes:

There is in New York a gambler named Rothstein who is much feared and much accused. His name has been used in connection with almost every big thieving, crooked deal on the race track, and he is openly named in this baseball scandal. There has been no legal proof advanced against him beyond the fact that he is the only man in the entire crowd who had money enough to handle such a deal. At least $200,000 was used in actual cash, and no one concerned could command that much money excepting Rothstein, who is either the vilest crook or the most abused man in America.

Rothstein sits in the box with the owner of the New York Giants. He has the entrée to the exclusive clubhouses on race tracks; he is prominent at fights.

Then, after naming Abe Attell and Bennie Kauff, who also enjoy exceptional privileges around the New York club, Mr. Fullerton makes his plea for the exclusion of "sport spoilers" from every ground where sport is promoted.

Ford continues in the *Independent* of the following Saturday:

Every non-Jewish baseball manager in the United States lives between two fears, and they are both describable in the Biblical term "the fear of the Jews." The first fear concerns what the Jews are doing to baseball; the second fear concerns what the Jew would do to the manager if he complained about it. Hence, in spite of the fact that the rowdyism that has afflicted baseball, especially in the East, is all of Jewish origin—the razzing of umpires, hurling of bottles, ceaseless shouting of profane insults; in spite of the fact that the loyalty of players had to be constantly guarded because of the tendency of individual Jewish gamblers to snuggle up to individual players; in spite of the evidence that even the gate receipts have been tampered with—the managers and secretaries of baseball clubs have been obliged to keep their mouths closed. Through fear they have not dared say what they know. As one manager said, "Good God, man, they'd boycott my park if I told you!"

This is in free America, and in the "cleanest game"! It is time for baseball to begin to look round.

Incidentally, the fans have been looking round. The fans *know*. If managers only knew how much the fans have observed, they might feel more certain of support in the event of a move toward a cleanup.

All that a Jew needs to make him eligible to baseball or any other sport on the same terms with other people, is to develop a sportsman's spirit. The Jew has crowded into all the lucrative sports, but only on the commercial side of them, seldom if ever in sympathy with the sport as a real sportsman. The Jews referred to as gamblers in these articles are not really gamblers: they take no chances; they are not sportsmen enough to gamble; they are "sure thing" men. The "Gentile boobs" who walk into their traps are the people who provide the money. Even in the field of money, the Jew is not a sport—he is a gangster, ringing a gang of his ilk around his victims with as much system as a storekeeper supplies clerks and delivery boys.

Ford concludes:

If baseball is to be saved, and there are those who seriously doubt it ever can be restored, the remedy is plain. The disease is caused by the Jewish characteristic which spoils everything by ruthless commercial exploitation. The disease may be too far gone for any cure. There are those who, like the *Chicago Tribune,* deny that professional baseball ever was a sport, and who are glad that Jewish exploiters, like scavengers, have come along to reduce it to garbage. But there is no doubt anywhere, among either friends or critics of baseball, that the root cause of the present condition is due to Jewish influence.

In the spring of the following year, Ford brought the financial resources of the Dearborn Publishing Company into service for the widespread dissemination of *The Protocols of the Elders of Zion,* the late-nineteenth-century Russian forgery that Hitler would embrace as truth a few years later in *Mein Kampf.*

Baldur von Schirach (1907–1974), the Hitler Youth leader, would later recall that "if Henry Ford said that the Jews were to blame, why, naturally we believed him." For more on Henry Ford, the reader is referred to *The International Jew* (1920), which collects Ford's articles from the *Dearborn Independent,* and Neil Baldwin's *Henry Ford and the Jews: The Mass Production of Hate* (2001), from which I have lifted the von Schirach quotation.

A "BUCKET SHOP" was a brokerage house that dealt in small, or even single-share, stock orders and charged a slight premium over the listed stock prices. For would-be investors of modest means, who could not afford to place orders of the size handled by the big brokerage firms, bucket shops were the only game in town. But most bucket shops played on the ignorance of would-be investors. Money was taken, but the orders were not executed. As every stockbroker knows, ignorance is a quality shared by many large investors as well as small, and bucket shops that put up a good front also attracted the good-size accounts of a few prosperous but unwary speculators to whom the bucket shops offered rates that were preferential to those of the big brokerage houses. In time, the crooked shop was manipulated or looted into bankruptcy, or simply vanished overnight, leaving empty offices behind.

No one knows for sure why they were called bucket shops, though the phrase certainly seemed perfect. Some believed that the term reflected the shops' legitimate but unconventional origin in the shadows of the Chicago Board of Trade, where one could not deal in grain options of less than five thousand bushels. To accommodate those who wished to speculate in lesser amounts, an unauthorized business commenced in an alley under the regular Board of Trade rooms. This alleyway market was called the Open Board of Trade. An elevator carried the members of the Board of Trade to their rooms, and occasionally a member, if trade was slack, would call out, "I'll send down and get a bucketful pretty soon," referring to the speculators in the Open Board of Trade below. Hence the term "bucket shop" came to be applied to all irregular grain speculation systems, and then to all irregular commodity and stock exchanges and brokerage operations. As early as 1880, *Bradstreet's* of New York noted that the recent "failure of the 'Produce Exchanges,' or bucket shops" had "caused little excitement."

An 1881 article in the *New York Evening Post* posited a different derivation: "A 'bucket-shop' in New York is a low 'gin-mill,' or 'distillery,' where small quantities of spirits are dispensed in pitchers and pails (buckets). When the shops for dealing in one-share or five-share lots of stocks were opened, these dispensaries of smaller lots than could be got from regular dealers were at once named 'bucket-shops.'" But when was a pail or bucket of spirits ever "small"?

By 1886, *The Statist,* a London financial journal, declared the bucket shop to be "an American institution." The worst class of them were "thimble and pea sharpers under a more polite name."

By the early twentieth century, the bucket shop racket was simply one in which a sham stockbroker gambled against his customers on the prices of stock exchange securities without ever really acquiring those securities. Like the proprietor of a gambling house, the bucket shop operator relied on the fact that most bets were losing bets. Of course, no bucket shop operator referred to his racket as such. And no sucker knew that he had lost his money to a bucket shop and not a legitimate brokerage firm until it was too late. Fortunes were made in bucket shops, and the tide of suckers was endless.

It was the great Fuller-McGee scandal that brought an end to the golden era of the bucket shops. Edward Markle Fuller and William Frank McGee operated a bucket shop under the name of E. M. Fuller & Co. Fuller and McGee's bucket shop racket had failed three times on the Consolidated Stock Exchange for more than four million dollars. (The Consolidated, at Stone Street and Exchange Place, was a disreputable nineteenth-century excrescence of the New York Stock Exchange. It was shut down in 1925 by New York State attorney general Albert Ottinger under the Martin Act, the state's first "blue sky" law, as measures against securities fraud then were known, after hustlers who, as it was said, would sell shares of God's blue sky if they could.) Fuller and McGee were tried three times but never convicted. Their lawyer, who was also one of Arnold Rothstein's lawyers, was William J. Fallon.

In the spring of 1923, William Randolph Hearst assigned his *New York American* reporter Nat Ferber (1889–1945) to discover "who was protecting the bucket-shops." From New York County district attorney Joab Banton, Ferber received permission to examine the records that were under federal guard at Fuller and McGee's vacated office on the third floor of 30 Church Street. Going through the disarray of files, he came upon a sheaf of canceled checks. One of them, in the amount of ten thousand dollars, had been made out to and cashed by Thomas Foley, the Tammany Hall boss. There were also checks made out to Arnold Rothstein.

Hearst was very happy. Ferber's exposé in the *American* brought about the jailing of William H. Silkwood, president of the Consolidated Stock Exchange. Seventy-three-year-old Tammany boss Tom Foley himself took the stand. He said that he had lent Bill McGee fifteen thousand dollars. He was asked why he had not taken a note from McGee for that amount.

"What the hell good is a note? If you pull out, all right. If not, put it down as a bad bet."

Big Tom said he had also arranged a loan of one hundred and forty-seven thousand five hundred dollars to Fuller and McGee from Charles A. Stoneham, principal owner of the New York Giants.

"How did you happen to intercede for these almost bankrupt men?"

"I didn't know the partners very well," Foley said. "I am a fool, and I've been a damned fool all my life. But I was asked for help by McGee's wife. I have known her since girlhood."

"But didn't you know this was a bucket shop?"

"I don't know the difference between bucket shop, the Curb, or the Big Exchange. I only knew McGee's wife, Nellie Sheehan, and that she needed help."

Such was Big Tom Foley. He went through millions in life, taking it in, with men such as Rothstein, and giving it out, in bars, in the street, in back rooms. He was born in 1852, he would die in 1925, and it was the old Second District all the way.

Ferber also discovered that Bill Fallon had brought about a hung jury in the third Fuller-McGee trial by bribing one of the jurors to hold out for acquittal. Fallon. The great mouthpiece. Who threw all of his exclusives to Herbert Bayard Swope of the *World*.

On July 2, 1923, a federal grand jury handed up four sealed indictments, which were not opened until July 11. The principals named in them were Edward Markle Fuller, William Frank McGee, William J. Fallon, and Charles W. Rendigs, the juror Fallon had bribed. Rendigs cut a deal to turn state's evidence and entered a plea of guilty. Fuller and McGee also became rats penitent. But Fallon argued his own case well and was acquitted. Then, in May 1924, Rendigs decided to tell everything that he knew about Fallon. The lawyer became a fugitive as new charges of conspiracy to obstruct justice were brought against him. He was found and remanded to the Tombs. That summer, Fallon again defended himself in court; and that summer, Fallon again was acquitted.

Fallon's liver hardened. Doctors told him to quit. During a binge in the summer of 1926, a jealous woman threw acid in his face. Doctors fixed his face but not his liver. Gastric hemorrhage and heart seizure took him on the morning of April 29, 1927. He was forty-one years old.

Fuller and McGee, who bucketed the money of others, lost most of it gambling. Arnold Rothstein, who cared more for their money than he did for them, was the one who took it.

In the twelve-month period from November 10, 1920, to November 9, 1921, E. M. Fuller & Co. paid out checks to Rothstein amounting to more than one hundred and eighty-seven thousand dollars. The *New York American,* May 24, 1923:

> One of the latest persons to come right into the limelight of the great politico-bucketshop scandal made bare by the Fuller & McGee scandal is Arnold Rothstein, one of the most notorious gamblers New York has ever known.
>
> Arnold Rothstein is now in the insurance business at No. 30 West Fifty-seventh street. He boasts that, due to his political influence, he has landed many big accounts, among them the personal business of certain Tammany politicians.
>
> It is said that through Rothstein the individual members of the Fuller firm have bought themselves annuities, but this has never been proved.
>
> One of Rothstein's biggest customers is Charles A. Stoneham, Foley's friend. The insurance on the Polo Grounds, home of the New York Giants, was written by Rothstein.

He showed up at the hearing room at 217 Broadway on July 27, 1923, with Sidney Stajer. He was asked if there had been conversation between him and Fallon in August 1922 regarding difficulties that Fuller and McGee were having.

"I don't recall going to Fallon at any time to talk over the Fuller case."

"Your answer is that you don't remember?"

"My answer is that I don't care to discuss it."

"On what ground?"

"On the ground that it would incriminate or degrade me, whatever that means."

"You say it would incriminate or degrade you to answer the question?"

"Yes, to save a lot of time."

He was asked if he knew Emil Fuchs. Judge Fuchs was a former city magistrate and the future owner of the Boston Braves ball club. Rothstein said that, yes, Fuchs was one of his attorneys.

"Did you ever hear him say he could tell a lot about the Fuller assets?"

"I never heard him mention the name Fuller."

"Did you agree to pay Fuller and McGee any money for Fuller and McGee?"

"Certainly not. I don't think so. I don't know what you mean. I've loaned them money. I don't know what they did with it."

"Have you loaned money to Fallon and McGee?" The question referred to Fallon's law partner, Gene McGee.

"What's that got to do with this case?"

He was directed to answer.

"It's none of your business, but I have loaned them money."

"How much and at what time?"

"I am not going to tell you because it has no bearing on this case."

"Did you ever loan them money on the account of Fuller?"

"Yes."

"Is that as strong as you'll put it?"

"Yes."

He was asked if he could offer any information regarding several hundred thousand dollars that he was alleged to have won in bets from Fuller.

"The law," he said, "makes betting a misdemeanor."

He returned to court on October 8, 1923. Fuller had said that he had lost twenty-two thousand five hundred dollars to Rothstein betting on the

1919 World Series, and a lawyer for Fuller and McGee's creditors had successfully argued that Rothstein would be liable to the creditors for that amount if it could be shown that he had been a party to the fixing of the series.

"Absolutely, I would be liable. I know that. This baseball thing has been a sore spot in my career. I faced the Cook County Grand Jury in Chicago, and got vindication."

"Do you know a man in Boston named William J. Kelly?"

"What's that got to do with this case?"

"He's an attorney, isn't he?"

"I know him as something different. I think he's a blackmailer to tell you the facts."

"Did you engage W. J. Kelly to represent you in the Grand Jury proceedings over the World Series of 1919?"

"You ought to be ashamed to ask that."

The interrogator tried to press more deeply.

"Do you know Abe Attell?"

"Yes, I know him."

"As a matter of fact, you were represented at the hearing by William J. Fallon and Kelly?"

"I have no attorney."

"Don't you know that the White Sox players made the charge they'd been double-crossed, and didn't get the money after they had thrown the first game?"

"I never promised them any money. I don't even talk to ball-players."

"Do you know a lawyer in Chicago named Leo Spitz?"

"Yes, very well."

"Did you have Spitz and a man named Sammy Pass here about the extradition of Abe Attell?"

"I don't remember."

"Are you prepared to testify you didn't ask Sammy Pass to come here to testify in the proceedings against Attell?"

"Yes, did he?"

"Didn't you pay Pass one thousand dollars to come here?"

"No."

"Did you make him a loan?"

"Yes, if it's any of your business. I loaned him one thousand dollars, and he paid me back five hundred. He'll return the other five hundred. He's a nice little boy."

"Did he ever say he didn't consider that a loan?"

"No, he's a nice boy and wouldn't say such a thing."

"Do you know Charles W. Rendigs?"

"I believe I do."

"He's the man indicted in the Fallon case in connection with bribery. Didn't you have a conversation with Rendigs while he was a juror in the Fuller trial?"

"Oh, behave. I refuse to answer."

"Did you have a conversation with Fuller about Rendigs at the third trial?"

"No."

There were more questions about Rendigs, the repeat juror-for-hire. Rothstein became more fed up.

"The next thing," he said, "you'll be blaming the Japanese earthquake on me. There must be something the matter with those cough drops you're eating."

Three weeks later, October 29, 1923:

"When you win a bet, it's a matter of income, isn't it?"

"I wouldn't know. I'm not up on the law."

"Well, if you won a bet would you call it income or outgo?"

"I'd call it lucky."

A month later, November 28, 1923:

"This is the last time I'm coming down here," Rothstein told the examiner. "If you want to get your name in the papers, why don't you go to an advertising agency and pay for it."

"You think you can get away with something in this court as in other places."

"You've been getting away with more than I have all my life."

On February 6, 1924, Rothstein allowed that, in April 1922, Fuller had come to him to ask for six thousand dollars and offered him as security a chattel mortgage on his new Pierce-Arrow motorcar.

"I put my hand in my pocket and gave him the six thousand in one-thousand-dollar bills."

Was this not a lot of money to be carrying about?

"Well, I have it. It's a good thing to have, too."

Rothstein had sold the Pierce-Arrow for five thousand dollars to a Rector Street lawyer on July 11, 1922, two weeks after the bankruptcy of E. M. Fuller & Co.

On April 22, 1924, the federal government of the United States complained that Arnold Rothstein had paid only thirty-five dollars and fifteen cents in income tax for the year 1921.

It must have been those fifteen pennies.

Inez Norton's Gams

THERE WAS so much paperwork, and so much of it senseless, for to Arnold Rothstein paperwork by nature was subterfuge. On July 27, 1923, he said that he could not recall the names of the officers of A. L. Libman, Inc., of which he was the president, unstated and unseen.

His name in fact rarely appeared on legal documents. Pan-Continental Film Distributors, Inc., had been incorporated on August 1, 1919. But Arnold Rothstein's name was not to be found in the papers of incorporation that were filed and recorded that day at the New York County Clerk's Office. Listed among the film company's seven directors were Agnes Rose May of Woodhaven, Long Island, and Agnes C. Head of East Orange, New Jersey. The Juniper Holding Company, Inc., was incorporated on the afternoon of June 30, 1921. We find the names Stern, Halpin, Mittleman, but not Rothstein. The insurance firm of A. L. Libman, Inc., was incorporated on the afternoon of October 10, 1921. Here we find A. L. Libman, Agnes Rose May, now of Jamaica, Long Island, Agnes C. Head, now of Newark, New Jersey, and Teresa A. Schickerling of New York. May, Head, and Schickerling are the names that appear as well in the incorporation papers of the Warranty Brokerage Corporation, on July 20, 1922. The namesake of Arnold Rothstein & Company, Inc., July 25, 1922, appears nowhere else on the record; instead we once again find the ladies May, Head, and Schickerling. The Rothstein Brokerage Co., Inc., January 22, 1924, lists Edna Bednowitz and Sam and Isaac Reiss. There is no Rothstein to be found in the incorporation of the Redstone Building Material & Supply Co., December 22, 1924. In the Rothmere Mortgage Corporation, November 11, 1925, we again find Bednowitz and the brothers Reiss, as we do in the Hooper Realty Corporation, November 23, 1925.

Rothstein's name and signature appear only infrequently on secondary corporate documents: along with those of A. L. Libman on a certificate of payment of one half of the capital stock of the Warranty Brokerage Corporation, dated August 17, 1922, where Edgar Rothstein is listed as secretary; along with those of his brother Jack on a certificate of payment of one half of the capital stock of Arnold Rothstein & Company, Inc., dated August 19, 1922.

Before changes to the corporate tax laws in the 1970s, each corporation held by an individual party or parties was taxed separately rather than as part of a commonly held group. This meant that the lowest possible corporate tax rate could be achieved and maintained through the creation of new corporations as needed, so that no single corporation's net taxable income ever exceeded the lowest marginal tax rate.

The sources, destinations, and amounts of money that passed through these corporations, and many others that Rothstein held, is unknowable. Scrutiny of the papers of incorporation often yields not even his name. As far as the record went, he was an unseen ghost at the heart of a spectral corporate empire. No trace exists of moving picture endeavors on the part of Pan-Continental Film Distributors, Inc. Did it operate as a glorified casting couch? Was it a channel for the heroin trade? Was it a Broadway bucket shop, fleecing suckers who were eager to purchase worthless shares at a high price? Whatever the case, its impenetrability, its inscrutability, were as intended. As a rule, not even the directors of these corporations knew the true business of these corporations.

The Volstead Act, which went into effect on January 16, 1920, like the Harrison Narcotic Act five years earlier, presented the opportunity for new and immense fortunes to be made. From this time, until the end of his life, Rothstein was the investment banker for the country's biggest bootlegging operations. Irving "Waxy Gordon" Wexler, who controlled almost all smuggling activities along the New York and New Jersey shoreline, worked for Rothstein. He made some two million dollars a year from Prohibition. There is no telling what Rothstein made.

O<small>N THE HOT SUMMER DAY</small> of August 10, 1920, thirty-seven-year-old
Mamie Smith opened her mouth and sang into the recording horn.

I'm gonna do like a Chinaman,
Go out and get some hop;
Get myself a gun
And shoot myself a cop.

THE NEW YORK TIMES, June 7, 1919: "A Grand Jury returned two indictments yesterday against Arnold Rothstein, well known in certain sporting circles, charging him with assault in the first and second degrees by shooting Detectives John J. Walsh and John McLaughlin of Inspector Dominick Henry's staff on Jan. 19, when they attempted to break into rooms of an apartment at 301 West Fifty-seventh Street. Walsh and McLaughlin, who had been trailing and arresting gamblers, said they suspected that gambling was in progress in the apartment rooms and when denied admission they forced the door, but were driven back by pistol shots."

The New York Times, July 25, 1919: "In dismissing the indictments Judge McIntyre criticized the presentation of the case to the Grand Jury by the District Attorney's office as a waste of time and of public money. He said not a word of evidence was produced showing that the defendant committed an assault on anybody."

IT WAS ARNOLD ROTHSTEIN's last day. Arnold Rothstein understood
this. What he did not understand was all that had come before this day.
The late autumn sun descended beyond the western river, casting shadows
on him. His eyes did not see, but he felt the shadows upon his skin. These
shadows were great purchase. Whose purse had bought them, whose will
and gun delivered them?

W HAT DO YOU BELIEVE Arnold Rothstein would have made of Damon Runyon (1880–1946), the reformed drunk from Manhattan, Kansas, who worked for Hearst's *New York American?* In writing of Arnold Rothstein, on November 9, 1928, three days after Rothstein's death, Runyon says that he "encountered" the man he is writing about. Runyon later covered the trial of Rothstein's accused and acquitted killer in a series of articles that ran in the *American* from November 19 to December 3, 1929.

The writings of Damon Runyon, who moved to the city in 1910, are central to the romance of Jazz Age New York. Runyon was not a purveyor of truth. His short stories about Manhattan—New York, not Kansas—are above all entertainments. The articles that he wrote on deadline about Rothstein for the *American* became a short story called "The Brain Goes Home," which was published in the May 1931 issue of *Cosmopolitan* and was included that year in his collection *Guys and Dolls.* Arnold Rothstein became Nathan Detroit. *Guys and Dolls* was a very successful book, and Runyon became a wealthy man during what most other people knew as the Depression. However, he was no longer around for what would have been his big payday, when *Guys and Dolls* premiered as a Broadway musical in the fall of 1950.

Played by Russian-born Sam Levene, Nathan Detroit now brought laughter through stage buffoonery and song.

Rothstein was an intimate of the most powerful producers on Broadway, and his money helped to finance many shows. In January of 1910, he had organized a successful ongoing crap game in the property room of Oscar Hammerstein's Victoria Theatre on West Forty-second Street. Al Jolson, who performed there at the time, began his act by telling the audience who was winning and who was losing. When he left the stage, he returned to the game.

One of the many bandleaders with whom Jolson worked in the 1920s was Ray Miller, whose big band included at times C-melody saxophonist Fred Trumbauer, cornet player Muggsy Spanier, trombonist Miff Mole, and other jazz legends. Among Miller's hits were "The Sheik (of Araby)" and "I'm Just Wild about Harry" in 1922, the latter from the black revue *Shuffle Along,* which Rothstein bankrolled. The biggest of his hits was "I'll See You in My Dreams," in 1925. Like Jolson, Miller left Columbia Records for Brunswick in early 1924. When Miller cashed seventy-six thousand dollars' worth of bad paper in Chicago, Rothstein settled with the banks for him and became the main beneficiary of his career in exchange.

There were few people in show business at the time who would not later have their Rothstein stories to tell.

Fanny Brice was married to Nicky Arnstein, who was associated with Rothstein in a scheme involving five million dollars' worth of stolen Liberty Bonds. Arnstein went to prison. Ever the goatherd, never the goat, Rothstein did not. When Fanny bought a five-story town house on West Seventy-sixth Street, Rothstein helped to arrange matters. He went so far as insisting to tend to the furnishing of the home. He simply insisted on it. The furniture arrived, and with it a bill for fifty thousand dollars. Fanny called an appraiser, and he told her that the furniture was worth between ten and thirteen thousand dollars. Fanny then knew that this had been Rothstein's way of collecting interest on the bail bond that he had posted for her husband.

Billy Rose remembered opening up a speakeasy called the Backstage Club early in his career. A few days after the place opened, Rose was visited by a man he described as Rothstein's bodyguard. "The cops like me," he told Rose, advising that a partnership would be mutually advantageous. Rose replied that it was a small place; there was really no need for a partner. The joint was raided that night, and Rose lost all his liquor. The man returned the next day. "Meet me at my lawyer's and we'll draw up the papers," Rose told him. "Who needs lawyers?" the man told him. "We both know how to add."

Rothstein was there before Times Square. The wedge of land bounded by Broadway and Seventh Avenue, Forty-fifth and Forty-seventh streets, had been Long Acre Square when he was a young man. The cornerstone of *New York Times* publisher Adolph S. Ochs's new Times Building was laid at Broadway and Forty-second Street in January 1904, and in April of that year Long Acre Square became Times Square, an area that extended the old square south to Forty-second Street and the Times Building. The Interborough Rapid Transit Company brought its subway line to Forty-second Street in October 1904.

Fifty years before, Forty-second Street had been nothing: a foul dirt road of livery stables and a foul marsh pond on the northwestern outskirts of the city. Charles Wilmot, alderman of the Thirteenth District in 1858, had been a boy in that remote and rural neighborhood during the 1832 summer of cholera. As his granddaughter Josephine told the story, young Charles Wilmot "was fishing one day at Forty-second Street and Broadway" when "his family physician rode along in a buggy. He asked my grandfather if he could get any leeches in the pond, as all of the imported ones had been used for the cholera patients. So Grandfather sent his dog into the pond and out he came with many leeches clinging to him. The doctor offered to buy them by the hundred, so when enough were caught Grandfather delivered them to the hospital downtown.

"As he went into the hospital he saw stacked up by the door rows of roughly made coffins, and he became so frightened that he made up his mind to send someone else with the next catch. He found an idiot boy who resided in the neighborhood and he delivered them for a commission.

"My grandfather made quite a lot of pocket money at that time."

A part of the new IRT subway was a shuttle service linking Times Square to Grand Central Station, some long blocks to the east. If you get on that Times Square shuttle platform today, bound for Grand Central, and you walk to the dismal northern end of that platform, you'll see a sealed door and above it an old and dark and decaying sign that says KNICKER-BOCKER. Behind that sealed door is a flight of stairs that once led to the lobby of the grand Hotel Knickerbocker, the tiara of Times Square, which opened in the autumn of 1906 at the southeast corner of Forty-second Street and Broadway. It would be something all right, to pass through that entrance and ascend those stairs to 1906 and Times Square in its youth. But there is nothing up there now, above the ground, worth seeing.

The subway cost a nickel then, like a cup of coffee in a fancy china cup.

It stayed at a nickel for a long time, too: more than forty years, until it went to a dime in the summer of 1948.

But Arnold Rothstein was not one for the theater (rhymes with "he-ate-'er"). His wife said that he had almost never attended stage plays or shows and believed that he had never seen a moving picture, not even *The Jazz Singer,* the great Broadway sensation of 1927.

So what might he have thought of *Guys and Dolls,* of the buffo song and dance of Nathan Detroit, formerly Arnold Rothstein, as in the headline of the *New York American* of November 6, 1929: WHO SHOT ROTHSTEIN?

Why have there been no musical comedies about major heroin traffickers?

There should be. There really should.

O-o-oh! My name is Sidney Stajer
And I'd like to place a wager
That this cop that they call Becker
Will be dead as Kelsey's pecker
When the son of Abe the Just
Writes his name upon the dust
Of the o-o-old pushke-box back home!

M Y WIFE CALLS ME up in the middle of the night from the land of the dead. She asks me: "What do you call those little things that Jews put outside their doors?"

"Little things that Jews put outside their doors?"

"Yeah," she says. "You know, those little things that Jews put outside their doors."

"Those little things that Jews put outside their doors. I don't know," I told her. "Little Jew things. You call them little Jew things."

Later she calls again to tell me that she married a Chinaman in Las Vegas.

"And they're called mezuzahs," she says. "Those little things that Jews put outside their doors. They're called mezuzahs."

A RNOLD ROTHSTEIN AND HIS WIFE, Carolyn, lived apart: he at 20 West Seventy-second Street, between Central Park West and Columbus Avenue, at the fifteen-story Fairfield Hotel, which he owned; she directly across town at the grand apartment overlooking Central Park at 912 Fifth Avenue, the last place where they had lived together. Their parting came in the summer of 1927.

The marriage seems to have been cold from the very start. I have found no personal mention of her by Arnold, no evidence of shared occasions, no pleasant photographs of the sort that even unhappy couples keep to lend illusion to their lives. By Carolyn Rothstein's own account, the marriage ended almost the moment it began. Her account also tells of his entreaties to her not to leave him. Her account does not tell us that she did leave him for extended periods, as she desired, and at his expense. A petition to the surrogate's court of February 5, 1929, is revealing. In it Carolyn Rothstein states:

> That during petitioner's entire married life, she was supported and maintained by her said husband and she had no independent income or means whatsoever. For more than ten years before his death, decedent paid not less than sixty thousand ($60,000.00) dollars per year for living expenses. The rental of the apartment in which they lived at 912 Fifth Avenue, New York City, was seven thousand ($7,000.00) dollars per year. The household retinue consisted of a cook, house-maid, butler and decedent had his personal valet and your petitioner her personal maid. Decedent operated a Rolls-Royce and a Hispano, two of the most expensive makes of automobiles, and employed a chauffeur and mechanic to attend them. Decedent and/or petitioner had charge accounts in every one of the leading apparel and fur shops in New York, and in innumerable other shops, as well as in the leading shops and es-

tablishments in London and Paris. In fact, petitioner was privileged to purchase any and all wearing apparel she desired, irrespective of its cost, and all these bills were paid by decedent. For Christmas 1927, decedent purchased for petitioner a fur coat from Jaeckel's, costing four thousand one hundred and fifty ($4,150.00) dollars. Petitioner's average annual expenditures for clothing and other personal expenses was fifteen thousand ($15,000.00) dollars. Petitioner's annual vacations for these past ten years consisted of trips to Europe which usually cost about ten thousand ($10,000.00) dollars per trip and which sum decedent paid. It was his practice to deposit cash in the Colonial Bank of New York, in which bank petitioner had an account, and petitioner would draw whatever moneys she needed on said trips from said account. Since August 1927, up to the time of decedent's demise, petitioner has been in receipt of a fixed allowance for her own personal needs and expenses of twenty-four thousand ($24,000.00) dollars per year, which sum she received from decedent in monthly installments of two thousand dollars each, and on several occasions since said last-mentioned date, decedent gave petitioner additional moneys to take care of certain unexpected expenditures.

Arnold Rothstein never desired to leave Manhattan, especially after he sold his share in the Brook in Saratoga in 1925. In fact, Chicago seems to be the farthest that Arnold Rothstein ever went. His home was Broadway. Heroin traveled, he didn't.

But as he grew wealthy, Carolyn became a devotee of luxury liners and fine European hotels and châteaux. Records from the Department of State show that she went to England aboard the *Aquitania* in the summer of 1914. After the Great War, she went to Europe aboard *La Savoie* in 1919, again aboard the *Aquitania* in 1920, aboard the *George Washington* in 1922, aboard the *Leviathan* in 1923. These are the only voyages for which documents survive: She herself says that her first passage to Europe was in 1913. A passport photograph from 1919 shows her smiling haughtily, her dark hair bobbed, strings of pearls around her neck. Her head is round. Though she had no occupation, she stated her occupation as "actress" or "motion pictures."

Her account tells of Arnold's infidelities. It does not tell of her own unfaithfulness. There is no mention of the young merchant Robert Behar of London. After her petition to the surrogate's court, which was made twelve weeks after her husband's death, Carolyn returned to London to be with Behar. That spring, on June 3, 1929, at the Register Office of the District of Holborn, London, they were married. Bobby Behar was twenty-eight years of age. Carolyn was forty-one, but she gave her age as thirty-six. She stated her address as the Savoy Hotel, in the Strand. There was a space designated "Rank or Profession of Father." She described her father, the old butcher Meyer Greenwald, as "Retired Gentleman."

She did not return to New York until January 4, 1933. She returned alone, calling herself Carolyn Rothstein Behar. A new attorney, Alexander A. Mayper, was retained to pursue her interests in the estate of her late husband. Mayper was an associate of the firm of McManus, Ernst & Ernst, which also represented the interests of Arnold's brother-in-law, Henry Lustig, the second husband of his sister, Edith. In January 1941, Alexander Mayper was the administrator of the estate, having taken over upon the resignation as administrators of Arnold's brother Jack and the attorney John J. Glynn.

In 1942, claims against the estate were still incoming. The estate had been paying attorneys and taxes for more than thirteen years. Long documents addressed intricate matters: "The Rothmere Mortgage Corporation was indebted to Arnold Rothstein personally, and, therefore, to his estate in the sum of $400,000, leaving the Rothmere Mortgage Corporation without any net assets . . ." And so on. Alexander A. Mayper, still the administrator, was now a partner in the firm of Mayper, Lazarus & Otten, which served as "Attorneys for Petitioner, Alexander A. Mayper, as Administrator, c.t.a., d.b.n., of Estate of Arnold Rothstein, deceased."

A court document signed and sworn by Mayper on September 3, 1942, enumerates recent disbursements from the estate, including payment to Mayper, Lazarus & Otten "for legal services in litigated matters.

"This leaves a balance to the credit of the estate of $339.13."

The last document in these voluminous probate files dates to October 10, 1946. It regards a creditor's outstanding claim of "$14.22 with interest, less the Treasurer's fee."

By then they all were gone.

Arnold's brother Edgar took a heart attack and died at Bellevue Hospital on January 18, 1934. He was fifty years old.

Arnold's mother, Esther, died of a stroke at Mount Sinai Hospital on the morning of June 7, 1936. She was seventy-six.

Arnold's sister, Edith Lustig, killed herself—"asphyxia by illuminating gas"—at her home at 180 East Seventy-ninth Street on September 3, 1936, some weeks shy of her fiftieth birthday.

Arnold's father, Abe the Just himself, went on to check for dust in heaven on November 20, 1939, four days shy of his eighty-third birthday. He died at Beth Israel Hospital, where he had been for the past seven months. He had outlived his sister and brother: Julia had died on December 19, 1909; Louis on January 4, 1919. He had outlived his wife. He had outlived all his children, save Jack.

Jack had a bit of his brother in him. In 1927, Jacob Solomon Rothstein became Jack Rothstone. He also gave himself a Dartmouth background at the same time. As the Dartmouth-educated merchant Jack Rothstone, he married one of the most well-to-do young spinsters in the city: Virginia Fay Lewisohn, granddaughter of industrialist Randolph Guggenheimer. They were wed by the justice of the peace of Greenwich, Connecticut, on December 3, 1927. Jack was thirty-six. Fay was pushing thirty, but she told everybody she was twenty-five. On October 11, 1934, Fay was granted a Reno divorce on the ground of cruelty. She restored her name to Lewisohn from Rothstone.

Jack then moved on to Bernice Levy, the Dalton School daughter of Borough President Samuel Levy. They eloped to Elkton, Maryland, where they were married on Bernice's twenty-first birthday, March 12, 1936. Jack was forty-five. It looked good. The newlyweds took up residence at the Hotel St. Moritz. Bernice gave birth to a son, Martin Rothstone, on April 16, 1937.

The son would later be described in legal documents as "an imbecile." Bernice and Jack drew away from the child, who was cared for by Bernice's parents. When Samuel Levy died in 1953, he left a fortune in trust to Martin. In 1957, after the death of Levy's widow, Sadie, a great court battle broke out over the control of Martin's wealth.

All of a sudden, everybody loved Martin and wanted only the best for him. Bernice fought against her own brother, who was a lawyer. A hired caretaker fought against everyone. The battle went on for more than twenty years and continued after Martin died, intestate, at South Oaks Hospital, in Amityville, New York, on April 7, 1978. Through the documents of this long court battle, Martin seems to wither and be lost in a brutal storm of greed, trampled underfoot by the cloven hooves of the respectable. Here, unfolding over decades in a Manhattan court, is a "banality of evil" that is so appalling—no less so, in terms of what it tells us of the "human" soul, than the trial at this time in Jerusalem of Adolf Eichmann, which forth that phrase from Hannah Arendt—that it makes of Arnold Rothstein's ways a seeming missioned saintliness. The advocate for Bernice was Carl J. Austrian, who had been one of Rothstein's flustered inquisitioners in the Fuller-McGee hearings.

If any good can be said here of Jack, it is that he remained a distant figure through most of these degradations. Bernice had divorced him in 1946. She then became Bernice De Castro, then Bernice Kimmel, then Bernice Mercado. She died in Florida in 1982.

Jack died there, too. The words in the window of the Miami Seamen's Institute had said:

Snow White Linen
BEDS 50¢
M. W. Bradley
Superintendent & Pastor

That was his address in the late 1950s. He remained in Florida, a drifting outcast in the Jewish burial grounds. He ended his days at the Hialeah Convalescent Home, on April 7, 1972. He was eighty-one years old. I was down there, in Dade County, at the time, selling blood for peanut butter and hunting hemotoxics in palmetto scrubs for Dr. Haast. If only I had known. If only I had cared.

Jack was probably the last man alive who knew Arnold Rothstein well. And there he was. It was the month I first heard "Tumbling Dice" come over that beat-up car radio. I bet he had a tale to tell, all full of them fine old-man lies. One thing he couldn't tell me, though, was what happened to his brother's money.

The book *Now I'll Tell* was copyrighted on its publication date, May 3, 1934. The seven thousand eight hundred and eighty-nine feet of moving picture film attached to it, the only moving picture that Edwin J. Burke (1889–1944) ever directed, was copyrighted by the Fox Film Corporation four days later, on May 7. After returning from England the previous year, Carolyn had taken up residence again on Central Park West. Douglas Gilbert, a staff writer for the *New York World-Telegram,* interviewed her there when the book was published.

"Today Mrs. Rothstein wears her legal widow's weeds with a decorum nurtured in an association she can only speak of batedly. A sad, wise lady, prematurely silver, she broods still as an imprisoned bird."

Her "smallish" but "exquisitely furnished" apartment is described. "Pieces of jade adorn the mantelpiece, relics of Rothstein that she cherishes for their intrinsic beauty." Carolyn herself is "strangely untarnished by the sordid panorama of lying, cheating, stealing and killing to which she has been a forced, disinterested witness."

Of her husband, she tells the reporter: "He banked with some of our largest financial institutions. Did they ever say to him, 'I'm sorry, Mr. Rothstein, but you are a person of unsavory reputation, and we do not care to have anything to do with you'? They never did. I'll tell you what they did do. They would telephone him that a loan they had made to someone of the underworld was still unpaid—and would Arnold please use his influence to collect it?"

Again, it seems, there was no picture to be found of the couple. The newspaper printed the eerie photograph of Carolyn from the dust jacket of *Now I'll Tell* and a photograph of Arnold with his mistress Inez Norton, smiling gaily as they lie together on the beach.

Carolyn's neighbor in the building, it was noted, was Willard Huntington Wright (1888–1939), who wrote the Philo Vance murder mysteries under the name of S. S. Van Dine.

I am told by the Library of Congress that Carolyn renewed the copyright of *Now I'll Tell* on February 28, 1962. She was then in her seventy-fourth year. It is there that she vanishes.

Nobody knows how he met Bobbie Winthrop. Some of the biggest of the Broadway vamps would feed their sugar daddies and suitors to him. He lavished them with gifts and favors, and they led their fat-cat suckers to his lair.

One of his best enticers was the Virginia-born stage star Peggy Hopkins Joyce (1893–1957). She came first, and the phrase "gold-digger" came later to describe her. She was one of the best-looking pieces of head that ever lived, and she played it for every dime it was worth. She married six times, always for money. Showgirls with suckers brought other showgirls with other suckers. Rothstein knew how to treat them, both the huntress and her prey.

But Peggy Hopkins Joyce didn't enter Rothstein's circle until 1915 or so. It must have been someone else who introduced him to Bobbie. Maybe it was Bobbie who brought her own sweet self around. They were almost certainly together by 1913, when she was twenty-two or twenty-three and he was a young thirty-one. And they stayed together. If there was love in his life, Bobbie Winthrop was it.

Bobbie appeared under her rightful name, Barbara, in two moving pictures, *The Crucible* in 1914 and *Secret Strings* in 1918. She was said to have been a Ziegfeld girl. They all were. We do not know if the name of Winthrop was acquired through imagination or marriage. Her father's name was James Kenney. Her mother, whose maiden name was Mary Johnson, was from Ireland. Barbara seems to have been born in New York in 1890. She was a good-time blonde. She was probably everything that Carolyn was not.

So why did Arnold Rothstein marry Carolyn, and why did he keep her little sorry ass around? No: you tell me.

Maybe she had the best of him, and he had the best of her. I don't know. All I say is, let's keep our nose out of other people's hearts, especially as we don't do too good with figuring out our own. The figure of Bobbie Winthrop somehow calls to me but evades pursuit or even vision. I don't even see her as a blonde, but as a brunette.

She drank herself to death. No, I shouldn't say that. It sounds like a negative thing. When these assholes drop dead jogging to work in the morning, we don't say they jogged themselves to death. I don't even know what "alcoholic polyneuritis" means. More familiar words, "lobar pneumonia," are there, too. Whatever happened, her body was found by Rothstein at her place, the Hotel Langdon, at Fifth Avenue and Fifty-sixth Street, on September 5, 1927. She was thirty-seven years old. On her death certificate, her occupation is stated as "Writer." What did she write? And where did it go?

It appears that a woman named Anna Hartman took care of her burial at Woodlawn, making room for her in the small plot she owned. A legal document from 1946 shows that Anna herself was no longer to be buried in this plot. Instead, a slab at the foot of Bobbie Winthrop's grave marks the final resting place of James Jay Brennan (1882–1961), who was the stage partner of Bert Savoy (1888–1923), the female impersonator from whom Mae West said she learned how to walk like a broad. Brennan himself had been a female impersonator but had switched to a straight-gent role in his partnership with Savoy. Rumor had it that Savoy was struck dead by lightning on the Long Beach shore after a loud blast of thunder prompted him to comment: "Ain't Miss God cuttin' up somethin' awful?"

Cemetery records revealed the name of the law firm that had administered for Mrs. Anna Hartman in the use and care of the grave. I traced the law firm to Floral Park, Queens. I wrote but received no reply. I double-checked the listing. It was correct. After the names of the four law partners, in parentheses, it said: "Italian Restaurant."

Why didn't Arnold Rothstein take care of her burial arrangements? He should have. That little bitch Carolyn wasn't even around. It was her season for being abroad. (That's one word, not two.) This makes his character very problematic to me.

If only I knew as much about his mother as I do about his father. If only I could see Carolyn move across the room, or the way she fingered her pearls. If only I could hear Bobbie's voice. Then I could begin to understand. And I would pass that understand on to you. For my code of life is a simple one. Help a friend. Be a friend. See to it that no declining female impersonator faces death without burial at someone's feet. It's the way of the scout. It's my way.

W HEN BOBBIE WINTHROP DIED, he bought a new one. Her name
was Inez Norton, which, to me, says a lot. The name to which she
was born is not known. I have been able only to find that her mother's
maiden name was stated to be Emma Gaskin. When asked to provide her
father's name for a legal document, Inez said simply, "James." On that same
occasion, she said that she herself had been born in Jacksonville, Florida.
According to her stated age, she was born in late 1901 or early 1902.

One account has her as a Baptist Sunday school teacher as a girl. She
was said to have fallen in love with army captain Claude Norton when she
was fifteen years old and to have run off and married him. A son, Claude
Norton Jr., was born about 1918. The marriage apparently ended in divorce, and she took the child.

In New York, on April 21, 1926, she was married at the Municipal
Building by the city clerk to Myles E. Reiser of 750 West End Avenue, near
Ninety-seventh Street. He was the twenty-three-year-old son of Ely and
Carrie Reiser. He was born on December 16, 1902, and he died, in New
York, in April 1972. At the time of her second marriage, Inez was living
with her son at 363 Lexington Avenue, near Fortieth Street. Myles worked
in his father's cabinetmaking business, Ely J. Reiser & Co., Inc. After the
marriage, he took a job as manager of the Pierce Dye Works, First Avenue
and Twenty-eighth Street.

In Lake George, New York, on the night of August 8, 1927, Inez Norton Reiser was arrested on a warrant sworn out before county judge
Thatcher by her husband, Myles E. Reiser, charging disorderly conduct in
entering an automobile controlled by him and refusing to leave.

"Mrs. Reiser declared she received a telegram from her husband yesterday indicating that he was in Atlantic City. She also said she was wonder-
ing where her automobile was, as the car her husband had was a New
Jersey car.

"Judge Thatcher adjourned the case and Mrs. Reiser left by train for New York."

It was probably some weeks later, perhaps in September, the month of Bobbie Winthrop's death, that Inez met Arnold Rothstein at Lindy's, the delicatessen restaurant at 1626 Broadway near Fiftieth Street where he regularly held court in his private booth. Lindy's Catering Co. had been opened in 1921 by a young German immigrant, Leo Linderman. Lindy's never closed. Lunch cost less than fifty cents. Dinner was about a buck. The telephones at Lindy's, Circle 3317 and Circle 10490, were as much Rothstein's as they were Lindy's. Many believed that Rothstein had a piece of the joint.

Beautiful, blond Inez is supposed to have found work that season as a chorus girl in the new edition of the *Ziegfeld Follies,* which had opened at the New Amsterdam Theatre on August 16, eight days after her arrest in Lake George and less than three weeks before the death of Bobbie Winthrop.

In the new year, having dropped Reiser's name, Inez Norton was residing at the Fairfield Hotel, which Rothstein owned, on Seventy-second Street near Central Park West. Rothstein called her son, ten-year-old Claude, the Sweet Potato Kid.

During this time, Rothstein's attorneys, under Maurice Cantor, were drafting his will according to his instructions. The Last Will and Testament of Arnold Rothstein, which he signed on March 1, 1928, was a document of seven pages.

It bequeathed fifty thousand dollars each to his brothers Edgar and Jack and fifteen thousand dollars to his attendant, Thomas Farley. After these bequests, the rest of his estate was to be equally divided.

Half was to be placed in an investment trust, the net income of which was to be paid to "Caroline Rothstein, who is now my wife, during her life."

The remaining half of the estate, allotted as follows, was also to be placed in trust. The net income of seventy-five thousand dollars of that trust was to be paid to Sidney Stajer for a period of ten years.

Eighty percent of the net income of the remaining amount was to be divided equally between his brothers, Edgar and Jack, for a period of ten years.

The other 20 percent of the net income of the remaining amount was to be divided equally for a period of ten years between his business associates Samuel Brown and William Wellman.

Sam Brown had served as the accountant and treasurer of Rothstein's many legitimate enterprises. Bill Wellman performed various executive duties and served as a construction manager for Rothstein. He was the acting president of Rothstein's Cedar Point Golf Club.

"It is my intention that provision be made for hospital purposes, and I particularly specify the Beth Israel Hospital as a deserving recipient of charity from my estate. My trustees, however, are hereby given the absolute right to choose and designate means and to whatever persons or institutions they may deem proper in disposing of this bequest for charitable purposes."

Along with his attorney Maurice F. Cantor, Brown and Wellman were also appointed to be the executors and trustees of the will.

Some months later, in October, he instructed that a new will was to be drafted. There were to be only two significant changes to the prior will. Under the new will, after the bequests to Edgar Rothstein, Jack Rothstein, and Thomas Farley, a third, rather than half, of the remaining estate was to be placed in trust to provide income for his wife. The one sixth that remained of this half of his estate was to be placed in trust to provide income for a period of ten years to Inez Norton.

This was the will to which Rothstein's hand would be placed as he lay dying.

The so-called deathbed will, which bears a frail *X* rather than a signature, contains only these two changes: two aspects, really, of single change. But Carolyn Rothstein, whose bequest had been reduced by one sixth, and those members of the Rothstein family who were not named in the will, perceived a conspiracy against them by Rothstein's lawyer and mistress.

Abe the Just rushed to court with a petition on November 12, six days after the death of his son. The petition stated:

"That although the decedent Arnold Rothstein was married to said Caroline Rothstein, a large portion of the decedent's estate is alleged to have been devised in said alleged will to a certain woman named Inez Norton, in no way related to him or his family either by blood or by marriage."

Abraham listed himself, his wife, and his three living children as the "only next of kin and heirs at law" other than the good widow Carolyn. The petition also noted that the decedent "left him no child or children."

Three days later, on November 15, Carolyn signed an affidavit supporting the appointment of Abraham Rothstein as a temporary administrator of the estate, saying that "it is your deponent's belief that his appointment would by no means be to the interest of any of the beneficiaries of the estate, including your deponent, save and except the said Maurice F. Cantor and one Inez Norton, a client of said Cantor's, whose name appears in the said alleged will as a beneficiary, but who was in no wise related to the decedent and who has no claim to decedent bounty, and whose name is not mentioned and does not appear in any prior will of any kind heretofore made by said decedent." Carolyn stated:

"That Abraham E. Rothstein, deponent's father-in-law, is an outstanding member of the Jewish community of this city, with a reputation second to none for honesty, integrity and business ability, and in your deponent's opinion, eminently qualified to fulfill the duties as temporary administrator of this estate."

It was not true that Maurice Cantor was not named in the earlier will exactly as he was in the later will. As for Abraham's terrible indignation that Arnold's next of kin had been neglected for love of a Jezebel, what man making out a will in the prime of his life would pause to consider not surviving his seventy-two-year-old father and sixty-eight-year-old mother? It is true that Arnold's sister, Edith, was not mentioned; but Edith was married to a successful businessman, Henry Lustig. Arnold had helped to make him a success, and he did not much like his brother-in-law, either. Let him take care of Edith.

On November 13, a letter was sent to Inez at the Hotel Fairfield, typed on the stationery of Abraham Rothstein's attorney, I. Gainsburg of 35 Wall Street. It advised her that a formal application for the appointment of Abraham Rothstein as temporary administrator of the estate of Arnold Rothstein would be made at the surrogate's court on the forenoon of the third day thence.

As it turned out, Abraham Rothstein was appointed a temporary administrator of the estate, with Samuel Brown, by Surrogate John P.

O'Brien on November 17. They were replaced on August 1, 1929, by Jack Rothstein and the attorney John J. Glynn, who in turn were replaced more than a decade later by Carolyn's attorney, Alexander A. Mayper.

For a while, only Inez Norton seemed to have made out. And not from any last will and testament. It developed that Rothstein had named her as the beneficiary of a twenty-thousand-dollar life insurance policy that he had taken out on April 28, 1928. But here too there were court actions and legal problems—involving Inez, the Farmers & Traders' Insurance Company of Syracuse, and Abe the Just, who laid claim on the money in the name of the estate—that went on for years and in the end brought her nothing.

Leaving Maurce Cantor to pursue the insurance money, Inez went south to Florida. She returned on February 1, 1930, announcing that she was to appear in a stage play based upon the murder of Arnold Rothstein. Mark Linder's play *Room 349* opened six weeks later, on March 17, at the Boulevard Theatre, Northern Boulevard and Eighty-third Street in Jackson Heights, Queens. The name of Norton's character was Babette Marshall. The show moved to the National Theatre at 208 West Forty-first Street on April 21. At this time, Inez was living at 205 East Fifty-seventh Street. The play received much attention owing to its subject, but none of the attention was good.

"The less said about 'Room 349,' the much heralded opus based on the Rothstein affair and featuring one of its central figures, the better it will be for all concerned," wrote one reviewer. "In the third act one of the characters remarks: 'The show business is shot to hell.' She might have added: 'Q.E.D.'"

Another reviewer, Robert Littell, wrote more about Inez:

Possibly suspecting that their play was, as it turns out to be, pretty feeble stuff, the producers of "Room 349" have planned to lure the great scandal-loving public into the National Theatre by hiring for the leading female part no less a person than Inez Norton, who was in real life Rothstein's sweetheart for over a year, who held his affections, contested his will, and is supposed to have received a considerable settlement from the estate.

So that what Miss Norton receives in return for lending her noto-riety to a creaky dramatization of the events that made her notorious is just so much velvet.

On the stage last night Miss Norton appeared to us as a person-able and very blond young lady, rather demure and self-possessed. Her acting in the scene where she discovers Stromberg (the pseudo-nym used in the play for Rothstein) dying in the next room was ex-ceedingly bad.

J. Brooks Atkinson (1894–1984) was kinder: "Miss Norton, whose en-gagement in this drama practically marks her return to the stage after an absence of six years, plays with blonde ductility—assertive in the moments of fortitude, comely in the interludes of affection."

Room 349 closed after only fifteen Broadway performances. Inez seems to have appeared then in another play, a "Southern drama" called *Dark Hands,* of which nothing is known. She arrived in Hollywood in the summer of 1931, where she had been named in the divorce case of the Los Angeles businessman Irving Weinberg and actress Ruby Blaine. In Holly-wood, Inez went by the name of Arlene Atherton. With her was an actress friend named Alma Mitchell.

Inez was alleged to have attempted suicide in Los Angeles in the early morning of August 19, 1931. She was admitted to a hospital under the name of Inez Mitchell, a conflation of Inez Norton and Alma Mitchell.

On April 3, 1932, she arrived in San Francisco. Two days later, on the evening of April 5, she was sought by a deputy sheriff who had a judgment against her for nonpayment of a hotel bill from two years past. The judg-ment also named her friend Alma Mitchell. Inez failed to appear in court, and a default decree was entered.

Back in Los Angeles, on December 16, 1933, Inez announced that she was leaving Hollywood, disappointed by her failure to break into the moving pictures. She said that she would depart in January for Chicago, where she had a stage engagement.

She wanted to play herself in the Fox version of Carolyn Rothstein's book. But the role went to Alice Faye. Inez, however, was given a small part with four lines in a scene set in Lindy's. On April 10, 1934, while in

Hollywood for *Now I'll Tell,* her fifteen-year-old son, Claude, was placed on probation and made a ward of juvenile court when he appeared before Judge Stanley Sutton on a reckless-driving citation. He was ordered not to drive again until he turned eighteen.

Inez was back in New York by 1935. It was announced that she was to marry Thomas C. Neal Jr., of Chicago. He was twenty-four. She said that she was thirty-two. The young master Neal was a college man. Better yet, he was the only son of the retired president of the City National Bank in Chicago. But the old man came to town on an airplane and called a halt to their plans on September 12, 1935. I hope, for the sake of Inez, that the Arkansas-born banker had to buy her off to protect his smitten moon-calf son.

It is then that Inez Norton vanishes, as does the Sweet Potato Kid.

WHY AM I writing this, and why are you reading it? What are we doing here? We should get the fuck out of here and live. By the time these words have passed to you, I will be found either at Circa Tabac on Watts Street or the Club de l'Aviation on the avenue des Champs-Elysées. Meet me there, good scout. You're buying.

I T WAS DOWN to an inventory of tchotchkes. On March 9, 1939, in a petition by the administrators to sell jewelry from the estate, were listed:

1 Split-second Gold Watch
1 Garnet or ruby wedding ring in case
1 gold bracelet with one diamond
1 lady's miniature gold watch with studded diamond chips
2 gold wedding rings
1 enamel and sterling silver cigarette case
1 amber cigarette case
1 pearl stickpin
1 diamond drop pendant
3 shirt studs, diamond studded, 4 buttons, 1 pair cuff links
1 French "Put and Take"
1 Foxtail chain
1 other chain
1 gold memorandum pad—empty—initialed A.R.
Small lot of jade beads
1 gold-sapphire stone mesh purse
1 Platinum Baroque pearl chain
1 amber cigarette holder
1 enamel cigarette holder
1 gold cigarette case
1 gold vanity case
1 horseshoe stickpin
1 platinum diamond and emerald ring
1 Holy Medal
1 gold wedding ring
1 Hebrew token

1 bird-cage
1 imitation string of pearls
1 small coin
1 pair of platinum cuff links
4 charms
2 Rosary beads

It was noted that these and other items had been appraised by a jeweler in the sum of one thousand four hundred and twenty-five dollars and that "the administrators have received an offer to purchase the aforesaid jewelry from George Modell, a jeweler located at 67 Nassau Street, New York City, for the sum of $1,600.00." It was also noted: "The administrators deem it for the best interests of the estate that this jewelry should be sold at the aforesaid price and accordingly ask authority of the court to do so."

AFTER THE AUTOPSY, Rothstein's body was claimed by his brother Jack. Upon arrival at the Riverside Memorial Chapel on West Seventy-sixth Street at Amsterdam Avenue, the body was placed in a bronze-finished mahogany casket, which was said to have cost five grand, the equivalent of about fifty-four grand in today's devalued currency.

Abraham Rothstein arranged for the funeral services to be conducted, on the morning of November 7, by Rabbi Dr. Leo Jung (1892–1987) of the Jewish Center, one of the most revered and distinguished rabbis of the time. The prayer for the dead was intoned by Cantor P. Jassinowski of the Jewish Center.

On January 20, 1930, the Riverside Memorial Chapel petitioned the surrogate's court to collect five thousand three hundred and ninety-nine dollars in funeral expenses.

His body was laid to rest in Union Field Cemetery, off Cypress Avenue in Ridgewood, Queens. Known today as Union Field Cemetery of Congregation Rodeph Sholom, it is where all the Rothsteins were buried, most of them in plot 860, save for Jack, who lies in Lakeside Memorial Park, Miami.

When I lingered there among the Rothstein gravestones, I saw that most of them bore words of Hebrew death marking and the English word "beloved"—BELOVED SON, BELOVED HUSBAND SON AND BROTHER, BELOVED DAUGHTER, and so on. Henry Lustig, husband of the self-killed Edith, must have been anathema; for Edith is remembered as BELOVED DAUGHTER alone and not WIFE as well.

There is no Hebrew carved into the rock of Arnold Rothstein's grave, nor is he BELOVED. He is simply dead, and all it says is MAY HIS SOUL REST IN PEACE.

When I went to place a stone atop the granite of his grave, I saw that there were two already there. I sometimes wonder, until this very day, who put them there. And I will never know. Something as plain and as simple as that, two stones in the cemetery breeze atop a grave; and it is beyond knowing.

T HOSE STONES SPEAK more to me than the lesser mystery of Arnold
Rothstein's murder. Not lesser in that the mystery of that murder
can ever be solved: it cannot, and it never will be. But lesser in that the
mystery of the stones, set in silent sacred breeze, is more illimitable and
vaster-beckoning by far. One stone for good, and then a stone for evil—
and what of the third, which I myself place there beside them, not really
knowing why?

On Sunday night, November 4, 1928, Arnold Rothstein went from his
West Fifty-seventh Street office to Lindy's. There was a call there, beckon-
ing him to a card game in the room of George "Hump" McManus
(1893–1940), a gambling friend, at the Park Central Hotel, at 200 West
Fifty-sixth Street. Rothstein sent his chauffeur, Eugene Reimer, to go fetch
him more money. One of the automobiles that Rothstein used was a
Hispano-Suiza H6B, one of the premier cars in the world. The Hispano-
Suiza had been designed by a Swiss engineer. And forty-year-old Gene
Reimer, who drove and maintained Rothstein's car, was from Switzerland
as well.

Rothstein went to room 349 of the Park Central Hotel. He is said to
have played cards for high stakes, tens of thousands of dollars, for a while
with McManus and other men. He was not there for long. At about ten
minutes to eleven that night, an elevator operator found him moving slow
on a staircase. "I've been shot," Rothstein.

That's all he would say. He never said who shot him or when, where,
and why he was shot. He did not even say if he knew the answers to any of
these things. The headline on the front page of *The New York Times* the
next morning said: ROTHSTEIN, GAMBLER, MYSTERIOUSLY SHOT; RE-
FUSES TO TALK.

Rothstein was dead the following morning, election day, November 6,
1928. Whatever had happened—and no one appears to have known ex-

actly what did happen; and no one ever would—it shook the secret system of the city to its bones.

No one seemed to know the source of the unsettling waves that shook that system. The murder was not properly investigated. It was not even properly covered up. Evidence was recklessly hidden, discarded, compromised: not so much in conspiracy as in anxiety. Rothstein's body had not even been fingerprinted—the most routine part of an autopsy—so that there were no fingerprints to compare with any that had been left. It was as if no one, lawman or criminal, wanted to be close to this murder in any way. There were disorganized, unconvincing trials of McManus and others: shambles of diversionary formalities. Nothing came of them but more confusion, more disquiet.

There was fear throughout Tammany Hall. The police commissioner, Joseph A. Warren, Mayor Walker's former law partner, was replaced by the benign figure of Grover Whalen, under whom, in the spring of 1930, there was published a forty-one-page police department report, *In the Matter of Charges Preferred against Various Members of the Police Department, in Connection with the Shooting of Arnold Rothstein.*

The impact of Arnold Rothstein's murder, and the mystery, fear, and disquiet surrounding it, led to Governor Franklin D. Roosevelt's commission in 1931 of the jurist Samuel Seabury to fully investigate the government of the city of New York. As Herbert Mitgang recalls in *Once upon a Time in New York,* Mayor Jimmy Walker, sharply dressed in blue, observed before he took the stand: "There are three things a man must do alone. Be born, die, and testify."

The whole matter led to Walker's resignation, on September 1, 1932. The former mayor departed for Paris. New York's Jazz Age was over. It had ended when Rothstein took that bullet in the gut. All since then had been but reverberation.

That bullet: from nowhere, like those stones in silent breeze atop the grave.

Since the moment Rothstein was shot until today, the mystery has grown. Speculation has run and roamed wildly in a desire to identify not only the hand that pulled the trigger, but also the interplay of hidden forces that controlled the hand.

One of the most enticing of recent readings, rooted in the observances of the *New York American* reporter Nat Ferber, is found in David Pietrusza's earnest *Rothstein*. It suggests a possible connection to the disappearance of the Belgian national captain Alfred Loewenstein, "the mystery man of Europe," a character of legendary wealth and dark dealings, who may have met with Rothstein in the summer of 1928 to mastermind a heroin deal of unimaginable dimensions. Loewenstein had said that he would return to New York that fateful November but then had vanished aboard an airplane in Europe on July 4: an airplane from which there was no possible in-flight escape.

But speculation has led nowhere, nor will it lead anywhere hence. The source of the bullet is like the source of the stones. It does not matter.

As in the religions of mystery, there is no answer outside of the mystery itself. It is mystery that must be celebrated, in the holy sense of that word; for it is the mystery, the bullet from nowhere, the theody in the gloom, the silent stone, that is the answer.

I linger here with breath in the quiet before dawn, about to say more, but I won't.

I want to express my thanks to Graydon Carter, Russ Galen, Rob Grover, Bennet Grutman, Heather Halberstadt, Dan Halpern, Bruce Handy, Shannon Malone, Jeff Roth, David Smith, Michelle Talich, Sona Vogel, Dawn Weisent, and a very many others whom I am too careless to here remember. My gratitude to these good people should not in any way be construed as an implication of their complicity.

N.T.